THE ANCIENT WORLD

SECOND EDITION

R. J. COOTES
AND
L. E. SNELLGROVE

LONGMAN

LONGMAN GROUP UK LIMITED,
Longman House, Burnt Mill, Harlow,
Essex CM20 2JE, England
and Associated Companies throughout the world.

Published in the United States of America
by Longman Inc., New York.

First published 1970
Second edition 1991
Third impression 1994

Set in 11/13 point Plantin (Linotron 202)
Printed in Hong Kong
SWT/03

ISBN 0 582 31785 1

The Publisher's policy is to use paper manufactured from
sustainable forests.

British Library Cataloguing in Publication Data

Cootes, R. J. (Richard John)
  The ancient world. — 2nd. ed. —
  Longman secondary histories)
  1. World, ancient period
  I. Title   II. Snellgrove, L. E. (Laurence Ernest)
  930

ISBN 0-582-31785-1

Library of Congress Cataloging in Publication Data

Cootes, R. J. (Richard John)
  The ancient world / R. J. Cootes and L. E. Snellgrove. — 2nd ed.
    p.   cm. — (Longman secondary histories)
  Includes index.
  ISBN 0-582-31785-1
  1. Civilization, Ancient — Juvenile literature.   I. Snellgrove,
Laurence Ernest.   II. Title.   III. Series: Longman secondary
histories (unnumbered)
CB311.C78   1991
930—dc20   90-48270
                                                  CIP

CONTENTS

PREFACE

The main purpose of this book is to interest young readers in the study of history. To this end, great care has been taken to keep the langùage clear and simple. The scope of the book is wide, partly because of the nature of the subject but also to give teachers as many points of departure as possible. Rather than attempt an encyclopaedic coverage we have tried to look closely at selected aspects so that these 'come alive' for the reader. This approach is of course used by teachers in the classroom, because a close look at any 'patch' of history is nearly always more interesting and informative than a skeletal overview.

This *second edition* takes account of significant changes in the teaching of history in recent years. Frequent attempts to relate the narrative to its sources were a feature of the first edition, but now longer passages are quoted in the text, pictorial evidence is made much more explicit, and, above all, extensive documentary work sections have been included. Each of the eight main divisions of the book has at least one collection of documents and questions (Greece and Rome both have two), and the remaining chapters all have a shorter 'Sources and Questions' section which contains at least one substantial piece of documentary evidence and usually picture questions too.

The many documents in this new edition have been selected on grounds of interest, relevance to the text, and, not least, accessibility to the young reader. All have been carefully edited and glossed to remove barriers to understanding. Original source material is not an end in itself. Its function in this book is to sharpen historical awareness and develop the ability to use and evaluate evidence critically.

At best, general textbooks are a springboard for more thorough study. We wish this book to be viewed as such and hope it will prove useful.

R. J. Cootes
L. E. Snellgrove

December 1990

THE BEGINNINGS OF CIVILISATION

DIGGING UP THE PAST

How old is the earth? How old is the human race? These questions have puzzled men and women for centuries. In 1650 Archbishop James Ussher thought he had found the answer to the first question. The world, he claimed, was created by God 4004 years before Christ was born (BC). Another clergyman came to the same conclusion but went one better. The world, according to this man, was created at 9 a.m. on 23 October 4004 BC.

Both men had been using the Old Testament as their guide. Such Bible stories were not meant to be read as scientific textbooks. We now know that our planet is billions of years old. We have found this out by studying its crust. We also know that ape-like humans of one kind or another have lived on earth for at least three million years. Such discoveries have been made by digging down, finding and examining the remains of our ancestors. People who do this are known as archaeologists.

The earth does not give up its secrets easily. Skeletons, clothes, tools, food scraps are first covered with dust. Slowly such remains sink beneath the surface. They become narrow layers of crushed rock or soil. Obviously the lower layers are older than those above them. So we really have to get to the bottom of things to find the truth.

'Nutcracker Man'

Olduvai Gorge, a deep valley in Tanzania, was formed by the gradual flow of a river. The earth was sliced open, revealing layer upon layer of rock, soil or ash. It is easier to get at the earth's secrets in such a place and it has become famous because of the

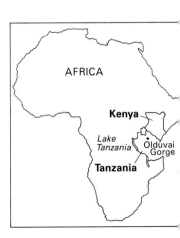

Position of Tanzania

Mary Leakey sitting on the stone which marks the spot where she made her famous find. She is holding a plaster cast of Nutcracker Man's skull

finds of two archaeologists, the husband and wife team of Louis and Mary Leakey. At first they found stone tools but no trace of the people who used them. The breakthrough came one day in 1959 when Mary was working alone in the Gorge.

As she brushed and sifted the soil, she noticed something different, a bony scrap which seemed to be attached to something. More brushing revealed part of a skull; she could see the bone round the ear quite clearly. It was a thrilling moment when she also uncovered two large teeth and an upper jawbone. She had found the skull of a *hominid*, an ape-like ancestor of the human species. What was even more exciting was *where* Mary Leakey had found it. It was set between two layers of volcanic ash whose age was known. This find could be dated.

Mary and Louis soon found that the skull was 2 million years old. This was much older than anything the Leakeys had found before and today there is a stone to mark the place where Mary made her great discovery. Louis named it *Zinjanthropus*, which means East African Man. The Leakey's young son, Philip, called it *Nutcracker Man* because of its big teeth.

Another son of the Leakeys, Richard, grew up to be as famous as his parents. He chose a wild region in northern Kenya by Lake Turkana for his searches. In 1969 he and his assistants discovered and pieced together even older skulls which belonged, not to hominids, but to a truly human species. They were given serial numbers, not names. The most famous is 1470.

Primates

Human beings belong to the animal family known as *primates*. Their nearest relatives are the three large apes (gorilla, chimpanzee and orang-utan) and the smaller gibbons. All these animals are tailless and most prefer to live in trees. They are also mammals, which means they breast-feed their young. Mammals have lived on earth for about 160 million years. Their numbers increased rapidly after their chief enemies, the dinosaurs, died out about 60 million years ago. Some grew into animals we still know: the horse, giraffe, whale, elephant, lion and wolf for example. Others lived in trees and developed into apes.

About 25 million years ago certain types of ape stopped living in trees. They left the safety of the forests to get food, or perhaps because the forests themselves were dying out. They also began to walk upright. Apes tend to walk upright even when living in trees, monkeys do not. Gradually, these walking apes grew less like animals and more like humans.

Walking upright meant that the front limbs with their useful fingers were free to do other things. After many thousands of years of trial and error, humans learned to make and use tools. Other animals have only natural equipment: claws, teeth, paws and hair. Humans were able to scratch the ground with picks, shovels and axes, or skin an animal to make a hairy coat for their own bodies. There are great advantages in this. An artificial coat can be taken off if it becomes warm. A shovel or axe can be replaced if broken. In other words, these developments allowed humans to adapt themselves to changing conditions. This is one reason for their success compared with other animals.

The first toolmakers

The first tools were made of stone, like those found by the Leakeys at Olduvai. About 2 million years ago humans began to collect pebbles and use them to break things. They discovered that if these were of an unsuitable shape, or too smooth, they could be chipped and flaked until they had a sharp or rough edge.

About 100,000 years ago people found out how to make different tools for different jobs. A sort of hand-axe was developed, which might be pointed for boring holes or sharp-edged for cutting. Axes of this kind were first found in northern France. Later they turned up in many parts of Europe, Asia, Africa and India. At first, Stone Age workers wrapped stones in grass or moss to help protect their hands. About 50–30,000 years ago they began to make wooden handles – and so produced a two-piece tool. Other major steps forward were the sewing needle, whose shape is still

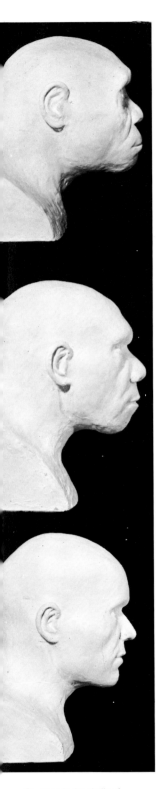

Changes in the skulls of primates over 600,000 years. The bottom one is modern man – called homo sapiens, *which is Latin for 'wise man'*

the same today, and the discovery that fire could be produced by rubbing two sticks together or rubbing a stick round and round in a hole full of wood shavings.

Humans could now hunt with spears, sew things together and dig holes with a heavy stone pickaxe. These achievements may not seem much to us but they gave the humans of those far-off times a great advantage over other animals.

The talking animal

Such inventions were the result of working together. Humans were forced to cooperate in this way because they were physically weak compared with some other animals. Only a gang could hope to trap and kill a woolly rhinoceros or a mammoth (a large elephant with huge tusks). Only a family could protect human babies during the long years when they were small and helpless. Yet because they sheltered in tribes and families humans eventually became more powerful than the animals who threatened them.

Co-operation was helped by talking. Humans have powerful larynxes and strong tongue muscles. For this reason their throat sounds are more varied than those of other animals. So different noises could be made to indicate different actions or things. These gradually grew more complicated until they became a language. This was important for two reasons. First, it meant that humans could understand each other more easily than most animals seem to do. Quite difficult commands and instructions became possible.

A mammoth. It was found preserved in ice

Some stone tools: top to bottom, an early hand axe, a cutting blade and a more advanced hand axe

Second, language made them think. Words not only express thoughts; they help create them. Most thinking is done with words even if they are not spoken. In fact, really advanced thinking is impossible without words. In this way humans gradually overcame their weaknesses. They became thinking, talking animals.

Skull of Nutcracker Man after it had been pieced together by Louis and Mary Leakey. The lower jaw was never found, and it is thought that the sides of this reconstruction may be too long

Sources and questions

1. Here Richard Leakey describes one of his most famous finds at Lake Turkana.

   I was able to return to Lake Turkana for three months in the summer of 1969. The eastern shore of the lake proved to be formed of layer upon layer of sandstone which contained a rich store of fossils .... While I was walking down a dry river bed my eyes fell on something that made me stop in my tracks: it appeared to be a hominid *cranium* [skull] sitting on the sand. We advanced to the spot to find the ancient bony face staring at us. It was an extraordinary moment. The cranium had been embedded in the bank of a stream. Rain and the flow of water along the stream eroded the bank away, and the cranium had probably rolled out during the last heavy rainstorm ... [it] was of the type that my mother had discovered at Olduvai exactly ten years before.

   Source: Richard Leakey, One Life, *Michael Joseph, 1983*

   (a) Richard Leakey was surprised by such a find. Where are such remains more usually found?
   (b) What was the name of the discovery made by his mother?
   (c) Which part of this passage tells us *why* Richard Leakey had chosen this spot to search for remains?
   (d) Why would the connection with his mother's discovery mentioned in the last sentence be a help to Richard Leakey in finding out the age of the skull?

2. Look at the reconstructed skull of Nutcracker Man pictured on this page and compare the shape of the head with the plaster cast of modern man on page 9. What are the main differences?

3. Make a list of modern tools which have similar uses to the tools you have read about in this chapter. Which implements on your list most resemble Stone Age tools?

4. Find out more about the work of the Leakeys in Africa. Why is it easier for archaeologists to work in that continent rather than Europe when trying to find out about early humans?

HUNTERS, ARTISTS AND FARMERS

About a hundred years ago workmen digging a trench in the Ambrona Valley in Spain found a cemetery of large bones. They were at least 500,000 years old and some were larger than the bones of any animal known today. This interested the Marquess de Cerralbo, a Spanish nobleman, and he spent some time working at the site. He found stone tools as well as bones and wrote an account of his discoveries. Two things puzzled him. Had the animals really gone there to die? It seemed unlikely. And why were all their remains smashed and broken? In the whole 'graveyard' there was not a complete skeleton.

The mystery of Ambrona Valley

We call the humans who lived at that time *Homo Erectus*, meaning Walking Man. Walking Man was first found in a large cave at Choukoutien about 25 miles from Peking in China in 1927. Peking Man, as he was then called, walked upright on two legs and knew how to use tools and fire. During the 1930s similar remains were found in Asia, Africa and Europe. It was clear that this kind of human had spread across continents which were at that time connected. In 1961 Clark Howell, a US expert, began a scientific search of the Ambrona Valley, using Cerralbo's description as a guide. What was the secret of the Ambrona bones, and how did Walking Man fit into the story?

Howell decided that there was a tell-tale clue to what had happened all those years ago. He found traces of charcoal and carbon in the soil. It seemed that fires had raged over a wide area at the time the animals had died. The ground had also been marshy. What if a band of humans had set fire to the grass around a herd of mammoths? The terrified animals could then have been driven into the marsh. Their weight would make them stick fast and sink. To struggle would only make matters worse for them. As they grew tired, the hunters could wade through the mud and attack the animals with spears and heavy stones.

The animals were probably killed by a blow on the skull. Then they were cut up; one skeleton was of half a mammoth! The carcasses were torn open for soft parts like the liver and heart. Bones were broken, probably for the marrow inside. The limbs of these huge animals may have been used as stepping stones to reach dry ground. As much as possible of the meat and skin would have been dragged away to the hunters' camp or cave. Perhaps these ancient hunters celebrated with a wild dance round a person draped in the skin of a mammoth?

Cave drawings

Skulls which have been found indicate that as the years passed human brains grew larger. This suggests that human intelligence increased. In the last 100,000 years 'modern' humans arrived. These are called *Homo Sapiens*, or Wise Man, by scientists. Homo Sapiens was not content just to co-operate with others for a successful hunt. He seems to have turned to magic to help.

During the last century workmen constructing a railway line in southern France found a drawing of a mammoth on the wall of a cave. A few years later a little girl was walking through some caves at Altamira in Spain when the light of her candle revealed red and white pictures of a bison. 'Toros!' (bulls) she shouted excitedly to

Cave painting of a bison from Altamira in Spain

her father. Soon afterwards experts came to examine the drawings and found more examples of cave-dwellers' art.

Why had they been painted? Such pictures would have been difficult to see, even for the artists who painted them. The cave would have been very dark. Yet the artists had taken great trouble with these beautiful pictures. First, they had selected places which it was difficult to reach. Some are at the ends of narrow tunnels; others are behind underground lakes or springs. The artists used stone tools, brushes and sometimes hollowed-out bones to blow the colouring on the wall. The oldest pictures are just scratched outlines. Later ones are coloured black, white, brown, red and yellow.

There are several clues to help solve the mystery. All the drawings show animals which were hunted – mammoth, deer, bison. The pictures themselves show hunting scenes. At Altamira there is a dying bison, sagging as it is riddled with arrows. Swift-footed animals like deer are often shown swimming a river where their speed would be of no use to them. Sometimes the animals' insides, like the heart or stomach, are drawn outside the animal. Perhaps this was done to show the vital parts the hunter should aim to hit.

The most important clue was the fact that drawings were often painted on top of each other. If the artists had only been interested in making beautiful pictures they would not have done this. But if the drawing was a way of making magic work, or of bringing good luck, and if the drawing *had* led to a successful hunt, then it would be natural to use the same 'lucky' piece of wall again. The whole area would become a magic or sacred place. Many footprints have been found on the hardened clay floor in front of the pictures. Perhaps the hunters danced in front of the drawings to make the magic work? Perhaps they celebrated when they returned with the food? These caves may have been the first temples and their artists the first priests.

About 10,000 years ago a warmer climate caused large forests to cover some of the plains where these people had hunted. Larger animals could not survive in such conditions. They moved elsewhere or died out. Cave magic no longer produced a successful hunt so the wizard-artists gave up their work. People moved away to river valleys and marshy areas where they caught fish and hunted wild-fowl. The caves grew empty and silent until their beauties and mysteries were revealed to the modern world.

The first farmers

Stone Age humans searched for their food, either picking berries and fruits or killing animals. This *food-gathering* time is called the *Palaeolithic* or Old Stone Age. Many thousands of years later some humans discovered how to grow crops and keep animals. This *farming* stage is called the *Neolithic* or New Stone Age.

The change from food-gathering to farming may have come about as the herds grew fewer and the climate became drier. Hunters settled near a river or a lake, or by the sea, and gradually turned to farming. Some of the earliest settlers chose the coastal plains of Greece, Turkey, Iran and Syria. Others lived near great rivers like the Nile in Egypt, the Indus in India, or the Tigris and Euphrates in Iraq. Of course, one 'Age' did not follow another in every region of the world. Large numbers of people kept to the old ways, or changed backwards and forwards as conditions changed. There are still tribes of Stone Age hunters today.

. Farming is a settled way of living. A hunter follows the herds, a farmer must stay with the crops. Hunting is the way other animals still live. Farming is a step towards civilised life.

The first villages

Neolithic farmers dug the ground with pointed sticks. They reaped their crops with sickles made of wood with a sharp flint as a cutting edge. They carried water from the river or lake in pots, and dug ditches and put up fences for protection from animals or other humans. Farming produced a more regular food supply than hunting. Fewer people died of disease or were killed hunting, so the population increased.

One of the first farming villages was unearthed at Shanidar in northern Iraq. This region had been inhabited for a long time; in one cave archaeologists found skeletons 45,000 years old. The remains of the village dated from at least 8000 BC. Humans made great steps forward during this period. Wheat, barley, rice, millet and maize were first grown by Neolithic villagers. These people found out how to separate wheat from the husk, how to rub grain between two stones, how to make cloth from wool and how to *domesticate* (tame) animals. The domestication of animals probably started in western Asia where there were herds of goats and sheep.

Hunters made only limited use of animals, wearing their skins and eating their meat. They did not milk animals or use them to pull and carry, as farming people do. All these improvements in human living were carried out with cattle, sheep and horses during the New Stone Age.

A flint sickle found in Jericho

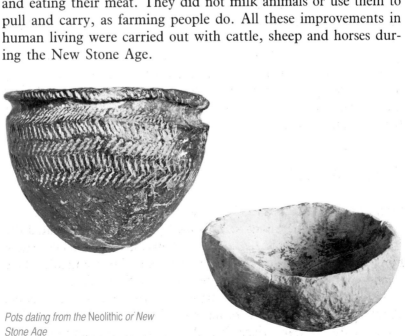

Pots dating from the Neolithic *or New Stone Age*

Sources and questions

1. Dorothy Margaret Stuart, an historian, pictures the life of a boy in the Stone Age.

> Sometimes there would be great rejoicing in the cave, and the family would utter grunts and growls that meant delight. . . . This happened when the hunters found some great beast – a mammoth, a bison – caught in a trench they had dug, or in a marsh. . . . The flesh would be roasted in the fire. . . . The hide was scraped and smoked and stretched out between stones so that the family might have rugs and cloaks of tough brown leather. One of the first things the boy learnt was to collect brushwood and fallen branches to keep the fire alive; then he would pick out from heaps of jagged blue and white flints the sharpest and best shaped from which the axe-heads and scrapers and javelin tips could be made. He had tools of his own when he was strong enough to use them, and they were laid beside him in the earth if he died.

Source: Dorothy Margaret Stuart, The Boy Through the Ages, *George G. Harrap, 1926*

(a) How could the writer have known what animals were hunted in the Stone Age?
(b) How could she have known that Stone Age people used fire?
(c) How would she have known that a boy was buried with his tools beside him? What would have been the point of this custom?
(d) Javelin tips are mentioned. How would these have been used?
(e) Can you find a sentence in which the writer describes something she could not have known but only guessed at?

2. Look at the picture on this page of the archaeological diggings in the Ambrona Valley.
(a) Why do you think archaeologists need to know *exactly* where something has been found?
(b) Why was the ground where the Ambrona bones were found a clue to solving the mystery of how they got there?

3. Can you think of any reasons why some hunters may have disliked the idea of becoming farmers and kept to their old ways? Which would you have preferred to be, a Stone Age hunter or farmer, and why?

4. Imagine you are a child in the Stone Age. Write a story called 'The Great Mammoth Hunt'.

This photograph of the Ambrona Valley diggings shows stone tools and pieces of bone left on columns of sand so that they could be mapped, drawn and photographed in the exact spot where they were found

THE FERTILE CRESCENT

Farmers depend on the weather; they must have enough sun and rain if their crops are to grow. The farmers of the New Stone Age thought the sun and rain were gods and looked upon the earth as a sort of woman whose soil produced harvests just as a real woman gives birth to babies. A bad harvest meant that the goddess was angry, a good harvest that she was pleased. In the earliest kinds of religion people often worshipped a Great Mother, rather than a 'male' god. For example, in Egypt there was Hathor, the cow-goddess, and in Sumeria, Ishtar. Such nature religions often involved yearly sacrifices of people or animals. The idea was that if seeds died and were re-born, so must the human race give up something precious to please the gods.

This fat mother goddess was found in a flint mine

Plotting the seasons

Farmers did not leave everything to the gods. They tried to learn the ways of nature and to become more skilful at getting the best out of the land. Above all, in order to plant their crops at the right time they needed to keep track of the seasons. So they had to have some kind of calendar.

There were two methods of devising a calendar, both based on watching the sky. In some places people worked out the time from one full moon to another (which is the time the moon takes to circle the earth). This calendar was split into 29–30 day periods which were called 'moonths' or months. In other places people calculated how long it took the earth to move round the sun, although they actually thought it was the sun that moved round the earth. A calendar based on the moon is called *lunar*, and one based on the sun is a *solar calendar* – from the Latin words for moon and sun.

Twelve lunar months do not keep pace with the earth's movement. They add up to 354⅓ days – about eleven less than it takes the earth to circle the sun. So the lunar calendar has to be adjusted with some 13-month years to keep it in line with the seasons. Despite this difficulty, most ancient peoples used a lunar calendar.

They probably found 'moonths' the simplest way of measuring time. We know that the Egyptians and Jews discovered a workable solar calendar, but they still made use of the moon.

The coming of cities

In Stone Age times practically every man and woman was busy catching or growing food. Only a few people could be spared for other work. But as methods of farming improved there was often a *surplus* of food (some left over). This surplus allowed new ways of life to develop. People who do not spend all their time growing or gathering food can do other things – make tools and implements, weave cloth, fashion pots, design buildings or invent ways of writing. Such activities led people to gather together to share their ideas and skills. Consequently some villages began to grow into cities. Life was starting to become 'civilised'. The word civilisation comes from the Latin *civis*, meaning citizen or town-dweller.

Conditions were particularly favourable for surplus food production in a warm region stretching through what is now Israel and Syria to the lands between the rivers Tigris and Euphrates (Iraq today). The region has its share of mountains and deserts, but in ancient times there seems to have been more rainfall and consequently plenty of good farming land. Because of its rich soil and its curved shape (see map) the region is called the Fertile Crescent. The climate was ideal for growing cereals, dates, figs

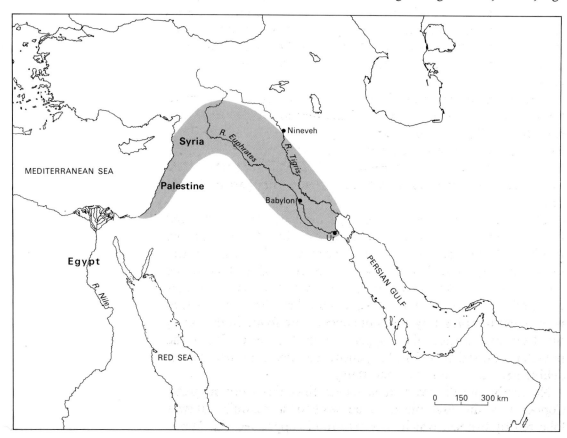

The Fertile Crescent

Lifting pots of water to irrigate the fields was a slow task. To lever up water more quickly the Egyptians invented shadoofs like the one pictured here. The bucket on the pole is balanced by a weight, like a see-saw

and olives. People multiplied in this land, filling the river valleys with their cities and temples.

The wet season was usually short in the lands of the Fertile Crescent. For the rest of the year the weather was dry and hot. So water had to be *conserved* (saved). Rain water was stored in tanks, ponds and wells. Above all, farmers dug channels so that water from the nearest river could flow through the fields where it was usually poured on the crops from pots. This way of getting water on to the land is called *irrigation*. In the upland regions, fields were cut into the hillsides, one above the other, like giant steps. Such *terraced* fields sloped inwards so that water would not run away too quickly.

New ideas and discoveries

Heavy rain during the wet season often led to floods. The rich, black mud left after a river flood was so fertile that it could sometimes produce two crops a year. Farmers soon found that their crops were better if the soil was dug before planting. Such digging was first done with stone tools. Then, after the discovery of metal (see below), bronze and iron diggers with long handles were invented. This tool became the plough, which was first pulled by hand and later by oxen.

While oxen pulled the plough, horses, donkeys and camels were used as beasts of burden – that is, to carry things. They were loaded with sacks or pots and probably made to pull heavy goods on wooden sledges. Early people probably got the idea of wheels from the common practice of rolling heavy objects on tree trunks. By about 3000 BC wooden wheels made in three pieces and fixed together with pegs were being used in the lands of the Fertile Crescent.

Pottery was essential for the development of all ancient civilisations. Without pots it would have been very difficult to store food and drink. The first pots were shaped slowly by hand. Then somebody found that wet clay could be worked much more quickly if it was thrown on to a turning wheel. The potter's wheel, like the plough and the ordinary wheel, played a vital part in human progress.

The Stone Age ended for some people when they discovered how to use metal. Metal is as hard as stone but it can be melted and bent. It does not break as easily as stone and so makes better tools and weapons. How metal was discovered will never be known for sure. An old Egyptian tale says that some travellers who had camped for the night banked up their fire with pieces of rock. Next morning tiny beads of copper were found in the ashes; the heat had melted the copper ore in the rock. When the travellers realised what had happened, they began to melt copper deliberately and use it to make things.

No doubt the discovery took longer than this story suggests. Copper was the first metal to be worked successfully. It was followed by bronze, which is a mixture of copper and tin. Meanwhile craftsmen were looking for a way of making a tougher metal. They found it when they invented iron. It improved farming tools and was particularly important in war. Soldiers with iron weapons had an advantage over those using the softer bronze swords and spears.

The spread of farmers and metalworkers

Most people in Europe and Africa were just starting to farm when the inhabitants of the Fertile Crescent were digging complicated irrigation systems and building cities. Gradually, however, superior farming skills and knowledge of metalworking spread from the Fertile Crescent, and from Egypt, to other lands (see map). The most important route into Europe was along the river Danube, which provides a great waterway from the Black Sea into Germany. People in Britain probably learned of these skills by sea, round the Mediterranean and Atlantic coasts. The interior of Africa was reached from two main directions: down the river Nile and across the Sahara, which was not the waterless desert it is today.

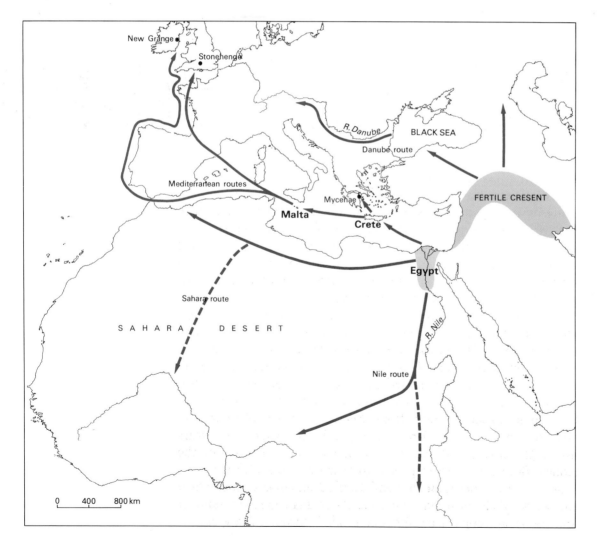

Routes showing the spread of farming and metalworking

Such routes have been worked out by archaeologists digging up settlements and searching among the remains for tools, bones and pots. Graves also give many clues because early peoples often buried the corpse with weapons, pots and jewellery which they believed it would need in the after-life. Early Europeans sometimes dug mass graves made up of a number of rooms connected by passages; a sort of house of the dead. Such tombs were often formed from rock slabs covered with earth. Examples can be seen in Malta and at New Grange in Ireland.

Not all stone monuments were graves. Sometimes massive stones, called *megaliths*, were grouped in circles for religious or other purposes. One of the best known is Stonehenge on Salisbury Plain in southern England. It was begun by Stone Age workers in about 2000 BC and completed by Bronze Age people about 500 years later. The nearest similar stone ring is in Malta. It is possible that some master-builder from Malta, or from Mycenae (in Greece), was brought to Britain to supervise the work. Some years ago a Mycenaean-style dagger was found carved on one of the stones. But why did these people go to so much trouble? Why was Stonehenge so important to them? In the *Documents* section which follows we shall try to find out more about this famous monument and see what people have thought about it through the ages.

Stonehenge from the air. Notice the bank and ditch round the outside. When this picture was taken experts were putting back some of the stones. You can see the scaffolding they were using

DOCUMENTS: STONEHENGE

The stones at Stonehenge are arranged in two circles, one inside the other. The outer circle of large stones, called *sarsens*, encloses an inner circle of smaller *bluestones*. The bluestones are arranged in threes to make a series of gateways (see picture on page 21). A circle of 56 holes was also dug around Stonehenge. These are known as Aubrey Holes after a seventeenth-century writer, John Aubrey, who first drew attention to them. The building of Stonehenge was an immense project spread over at least 500 years. Throughout the centuries people have wondered *why* and *how* it was built.

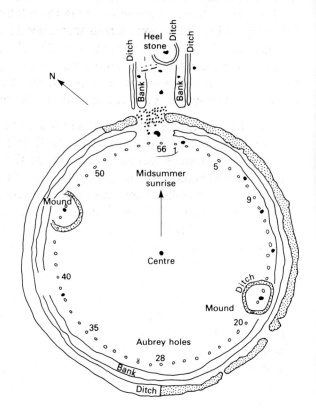

There were several Stonehenges. The first structure was changed over the years. This is how experts think it was arranged. Can you think of any reason for making it face the midsummer sunrise (21 June)?

Document 1

In about 44 BC Diodorus, a Roman historian, gave this explanation of why Stonehenge was built. He was repeating a story told by another writer who had lived about 400 years before.

> This island [Britain] is situated in the north and the land is fertile and productive of every crop. . . . Leto [mother of the Roman sun god, Apollo] was born on this island, and for that reason Apollo is honoured among the people . . . and there is a magnificent sacred spot with a notable temple which is adorned with many offerings and is round.

Source: Diodorus Siculus, The Library of History, *Book II, Chapter 47, Harvard Press and Heinemann, 1935*

Document 2

A puzzling thing about Stonehenge is how the stones got there in the first place because none of them are to be found naturally on Salisbury Plain. The nearest sarsen stones are 20 miles away at Avebury but the nearest bluestones are 200 miles away in West Wales. The people who built Stonehenge had no proper wheeled transport or suitable boats, so how did they move the stones? A twelfth-century writer, Geoffrey of Monmouth, told this tale.

> When King Aurelius [of Britain] had beaten his enemies in battle he wondered how to make the battlefield [the Mount of Ambrius or Stonehenge] memorable for he thought the green turf which covered so many noble warriors who had died for their country worthy of remembrance. He sent for Merlin, the wizard, who said, 'If you wish to honour the burial place of these men, send for the Dance of the Giants that is in a mountain in Ireland, for the stones are big and set in a circle.' So Aurelius sent an army to Ireland which beat the Irish but could not move the stones. And when all the soldiers were weary Merlin burst out laughing and put together his own machinery and laid the stones down as if they were light and told his men to carry them to the ships and return to Britain. When the King heard the news he told all his people to meet him at Ambrius. At this great gathering the King told Merlin to set up the stones around the burial place. Merlin obeyed and set them up.

Source: Adapted from Histories of the Kings of Britain *by Geoffrey of Monmouth, translated by Sebastian Evans, J.M. Dent, 1935*

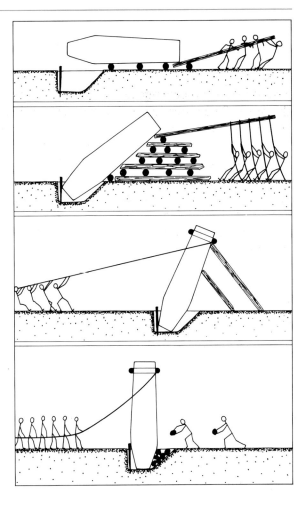

This is how we think the upright (sarsen) stones were put up. How would such stones be erected today?

Document 3

In the seventeenth century two men gave different answers to the question of why Stonehenge was built. Inigo Jones, a famous architect, wrote a report on it for King James I. John Aubrey wrote about it in a book called *The Monuments of Britain*.

> (a) Considering what magnificence the Romans used in all building works, and their knowledge, experience and skill, and also the style of their workmanship, Stonehenge in my opinion was a work built by the Romans.
>
> *Inigo Jones, in a book published in 1655*

> (b) There have been several books written concerning Stonehenge, some saying one thing, some saying another. My guess is that this ancient monument was a temple of the priests known as Druids [ancient pagan priests, see page 210].
>
> *Source: John Aubrey,* The Monuments of Britain, *1663*

Document 4

By the eighteenth century, archaeologists and other experts did not rely on guesswork so much as careful digging and calculations. William Stukeley (1687–1765), one of the first archaeologists, made a number of drawings of the site and was one of the first to notice that Stonehenge points north-east towards the rising sun on Midsummer Day. He was supported by another expert, John Smith, who in 1771, wrote:

From many visits to Stonehenge, I reckon it is a temple to the planets. I suspected the Heelstone to be the key which would reveal the uses of Stonehenge. The Heelstone points to the north-east. I first drew a circle round the ditch outside the temple and divided it into 360 equal parts. I then drew a line through the temple to the Heelstone. At the point where these lines crossed I calculated the sun's position at the summer solstice (21 June), and fixed the eastern points (of the compass) accordingly. I soon found the uses for all the detached stones, as well as those that formed the temple.

Source: Quoted in Peter Lancaster Brown, Megaliths and Monuments, *Robert Hale, 1979*

Document 5

A lot of experts since John Smith's time have thought that Stonehenge was some sort of calendar. Here are the opinions of two twentieth-century writers.

(a) ... the temple of Stonehenge pointed nearly to the sun rising at the summer solstice [Midsummer's Day]. Stonehenge was so constructed that at sunrise at the summer solstice the shadows of one stone fell exactly on the stone in the centre; that indicated to the priests that the New Year had begun.

Source: Adapted from Norman Lockyer, Stonehenge and other British Monuments, *1909*

(b) At Stonehenge move a marker, a stone in the ground, by two holes every 13 days. It will take 364 days to move the stone round the whole circle.... Move another stone marker two holes a day – this completes the circuit in 28 days. The moon takes 27.3 days to complete its path across the sky.... So the fifty-six Aubrey Holes can be used to measure the movements of both sun and moon.

Source: Adapted from Fred Hoyle, On Stonehenge, *Heinemann, 1977*

Questions

1. Why do you think people down the ages have wondered about Stonehenge and put forward theories about how it got there and what it was used for?
2. Which document seems to be the most far-fetched? Which part of it could actually be near to the truth about how the stones got to Salisbury Plain?
3. Inigo Jones and John Aubrey (Document 3) were both wrong about the origin and purposes of Stonehenge. Using pictures of Roman buildings in Parts 7 and 8 of this book, and information on the Druids in Chapter 30, can you suggest any reasons why they were mistaken?
4. Which documents suggest that people's interest in the sun's movements had something to do with the building of Stonehenge? Of these, which do you think is the *most* and the *least* likely to be true and why?
5. Could people today use Stonehenge as their calendar in the ways described in Document 5(b)? If so, how? If not, what other information would be required?
6. How do the writers in Document 3 compare with those in Documents 4 and 5 in the way they gather and use evidence?

MESOPOTAMIA

SUMER AND BABYLON

Two rivers, the Tigris and Euphrates, rise in the Armenian mountains and flow into the Persian Gulf. As they near the Gulf they move closer together. The fertile mud plain formed between them was called Sumer by ancient writers, although in the Bible it is referred to as the Plain of Shinar. Later it was known as Mesopotamia, meaning the Land between Rivers. Now it is called Iraq. This land gave rise to some of the earliest civilisations.

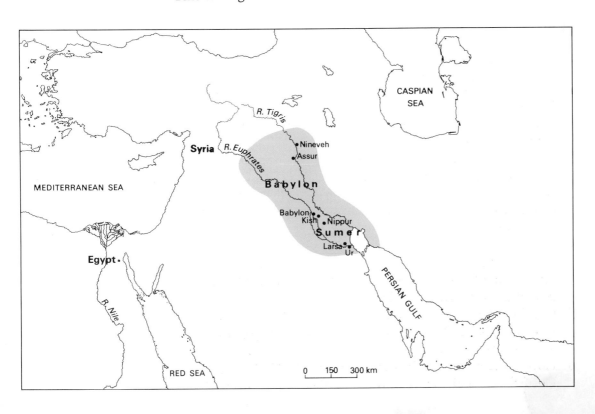

Ancient Sumer and Babylon

The Sumerians

Some time between 5000 and 3500 BC, mountain folk speaking a language called Sumerian moved into this plain. The Sumerians gave up hunting and began to farm. They learnt how to control the river floods, building earth banks, channels and ditches to direct water where they wanted it to go. This irrigation was usually successful; only occasionally did either river break its banks and cause disaster. Such happenings were remembered in folk tales of floods. The most famous is the story of Noah's Ark in the Bible.

Mesopotamian towns developed from clusters of dwellings set round a large temple. For this reason a group of people were usually named after a city, not a country. For example, Babylonians were from Babylon and Assyrians from Assur. The Sumerians founded cities at Ur, Kish, Larsa and Nippur. They became very skilled, building houses of dried mud, growing wheat, barley, vegetables and dates, spinning and weaving cloth, and slicing up tree-trunks to make some of the first wheels.

They also devised a form of writing. This was very important because writing makes it possible for people to send messages when apart and even to read the thoughts and ideas of the dead. A

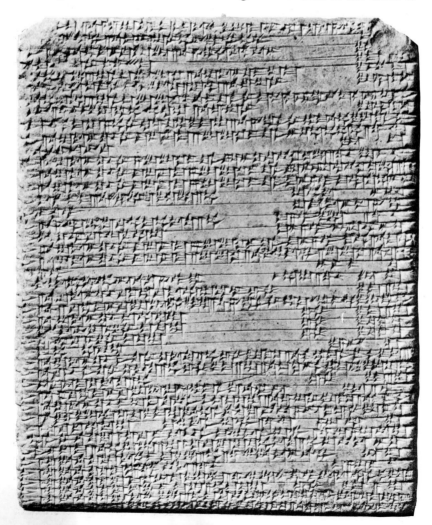

This tablet in cuneiform writing talks about the chances of a sick man recovering or dying, and the chances of victory or defeat in war

The Ziggurat of Ur. It is topped by the temple of Nannar, the moon god

great deal of knowledge is stored and passed on to later generations in this way. Sumerian writing was printed on soft clay with a nib shaped like a triangle. This nib made wedge-shaped signs which are called *cuneiform* – from *cuneus*, the Latin word for wedge. For nearly 200 years scholars struggled to decipher cuneiform carvings on stones. They finally succeeded in 1857.

In about 2300 BC the Sumerians were conquered by their northern neighbours, a people speaking a language called Akkadian. These Akkadians were not related to the Sumerians but among their descendants are the Jews and Arabs. An Akkadian conqueror, Sargon, seems to have controlled most of Mesopotamia at one time. He became a national hero and many stories were made up about him. Here is one of these tales, written as though Sargon was speaking.

Sargon, the mighty king, the King of Agade, am I.
My mother was of humble birth, I knew not my father.
My humble mother conceived me,
She brought me forth in secret,
She laid me in a basket made of reeds,
She smeared it with bitumen [tar],
She put me in the river and I did not sink.
The river carried me to Akki,
A man who watered the fields.
[He] lifted me out of the basket.
Akki brought me up as his son,
He made me his gardener,
Whilst I was a gardener the goddess Ishtar
fell in love with me and for . . . four years
I ruled the kingdom.

A later king, Ur-Nammu, (2113–2096 BC) ruled a prosperous empire. To show off his wealth and power he built a large *ziggurat*, a temple partly shaped like a pyramid. Its centre was an earth mound, enclosed by a sloping wall 60 metres high and 2½ metres thick. There were three stairways leading to the top, each with

100 steps. At the summit there was a single stairway leading to the part of the ziggurat sacred to Nannar, the moon god. This great structure loomed over the city of Ur. Farmers working in the fields up to 30 kilometres away would have seen it – and felt that Nannar, their god, watched over them.

The rise of Babylon

The Sumerian and Akkadian kings were overthrown by the Amorites, a nomadic (wandering) tribe from Syria who used a strange animal from the grasslands north of the Caspian Sea. They called it 'the ass of the mountains', and used it to pull war chariots. We know it as the horse. The Amorites broke through the line of fortresses built to keep them out and easily defeated armies untrained in chariot fighting. By 1894 BC they had reached the banks of the Euphrates and were building the city of Babylon. This city was situated where the two rivers were only 60 kilometres apart. So it was easy for the Babylonians to control most of the trade routes of the Fertile Crescent.

The Babylonians were a clever people whose ideas have influenced present-day life. They were among the first to use money to buy goods instead of swapping them (which is called *barter*). Lumps of silver of a given weight represented the articles to be exchanged. For example, a sack of corn was said to be worth so many *shekels* (ounces) of silver. They were also pioneers of arithmetic. The idea that a number changes its value if it is moved left goes back to the Babylonians, but to them it meant that it was multiplied by 60, not 10 as in our system. They liked to count in twelves. This is why today we still reckon in dozens, divide a day into 24 hours and a minute into 60 seconds. They thought the number seven was lucky, perhaps because they worshipped the seven planets known to them. This began the custom of having a week of seven days.

Signs of the Zodiac

Babylonian astronomers watched the heavens over a period of thousands of years. Their own year contained 360 days, divided into twelve 30-day months. Like the lunar calendar on which it was based (see page 17), this did not keep pace with the movement of the earth, so every now and again they added an extra month. They divided the day into six parts, beginning either at sunset or midnight. They measured these periods with a sun-clock by day and a water-clock by night.

The Babylonians were very interested in the heavens because they thought the stars were gods. It seems likely that they watched what they believed to be the pathway of the sun and planets through the sky, the so-called *Zodiac*, and divided it into twelve parts. They called each part a *constellation* and the names they gave them live on in the names of the birth signs today.

Sources and questions

1. Re-read the story about King Sargon on page 27.
   (a) Which parts of it are similar to the biblical story about the baby Moses?
   (b) Why do you think Sargon's mother decided to get rid of him?
   (c) Can you work out why, according to this story, Sargon's luck changed?
   (d) What Roman story is similar to this tale? (If necessary, you can look it up in Chapter 19).

2. Look at the picture of the Standard of Ur.
   (a) What kind of occasion is shown in the top row? What do you think the two pairs of standing figures are doing?
   (b) The middle row shows servants bringing in animals. What sorts of creatures can you see? What do you think they were needed for?
   (c) In the third row, servants are probably bringing in goods captured in war. Imagine you are carrying one of the heavy sacks. Describe some of the things inside.
   (d) How might the scenes in the three panels be connected?

3. The Babylonians believed there were seven planets. Find out (a) how many we know of today, and (b) which ones have been discovered since ancient times.

4. What advantages are there in using money and exchanging it for goods, rather than *bartering* (swapping) one article for another?

The 'Standard of Ur' – a kind of box-lid decorated with inlaid stones and figures carved from shells. It dates from about 2,700 BC and is housed in the British Museum. This panel shows scenes of life during a time of peace

ASSYRIANS AND PERSIANS

Although rich and prosperous, the Babylonians had dangerous enemies, particularly the Hittites from the north. The Hittites had discovered how to get fire hot enough to melt iron. This gave them iron weapons which were much tougher than the bronze ones used by the Babylonians. The Hittites were able to capture Babylon in 1595 BC, although they were driven out later. Then the iron-making process became known to an even more warlike people living round a city called Assur in the Tigris Valley. It was these Assyrians who destroyed the first Babylonian state.

The Assyrians were the most cruel people of ancient times.

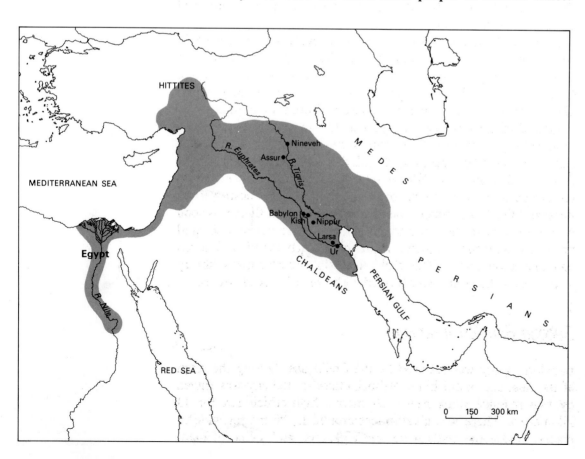

The Assyrian Empire

Their foot-soldiers and horsemen, often using chariots, captured town after town in Mesopotamia and showed no mercy to their captives. Rival kings were blinded and then burned alive. Men, women and children were beheaded or crucified, flayed alive or torn limb from limb. Even the land was sometimes poisoned so that it could not produce crops.

At first the rulers of Babylon tried to be friendly with the Assyrians and help them in their wars. Then, in 689 BC, the Assyrians turned against them. The Assyrian king, Sennacherib, besieged Babylon for nine months with a large army. When, finally, he broke in, he had the entire city destroyed. Even the mud walls which controlled the waters of the Euphrates were broken so that the ruins became no more than a marshy swamp.

The glories of Nineveh

There was a more pleasant side to Assyrian rulers. Sennacherib, for example, was very interested in farming and engineering. His capital city, Nineveh, got its water from a 300-metre long *aqueduct* (bridge for carrying water) built by its engineers. The fields were irrigated with the help of shadoofs (see page 19), and the King seems to have introduced cotton-growing to Assyria. Under Sennacherib's rule Nineveh became a splendid city with a big park and graceful squares and streets shaded with lines of trees. Its temples to the gods resembled ziggurats. Its palace walls were decorated with colourful tiles and guarded by gigantic statues of winged bulls with human heads.

Another Assyrian conqueror, Assurbanipal, was interested in education. He collected a library of 22,000 clay tablets written in cuneiform script. Some of these 'books' told the story of the Creation of the World and the Flood. Others were about medicine, science and mathematics. There was even a dictionary.

Hatred of Assyrian cruelty grew as the years passed and when weaker kings succeeded to the throne Assyria's enemies decided to strike. Two warlike peoples, the Medes and the Chaldeans, took Assur in 614 BC and Nineveh two years later. The Assyrians received a dose of their own medicine. Nineveh was destroyed by flood and fire. So complete was the destruction that there was soon no trace of where the city had stood. Its site was not rediscovered until the eighteenth century. The flames which engulfed Nineveh had one good effect. The clay tablets in Assurbanipal's library were backed hard and so survived to be read in recent times.

Second Babylonian empire

Babylon's glory was restored by the Chaldeans. During the reign of its most successful king, Nebuchadnezzar, the city was ringed by two massive walls nearly 20 metres high which ran for 13 kilometres. There was also a moat around it, 90 metres wide in places. Inside the walls were fine ziggurats, and a line of man-

Assyrian winged bull with a human head

made terraces on which there was enough earth for trees, plants and flowers to grow. These terraces were called the Hanging Gardens because they seemed to hang in the air. They were described as one of the Seven Wonders of the ancient world.

This second Babylonian empire was destroyed by the Persian king, Cyrus the Great. So unprepared were the Babylonians that there was little fighting. Indeed, the last Babylonian king, Nabonidus, is said to have been feasting when the Persian attack began. Nabonidus was disliked by many of his people. So it came as no surprise that Cyrus was greeted by cheering crowds waving date palms when he led his army into Babylon (539 BC). From then on the lands of the Fertile Crescent were destined to be ruled by outsiders – Persians, Greeks and Romans.

The Persians

The conquerors of Babylon came originally from central Asia and began to occupy the land now called Iran in about 900 BC. The centre of their power was the province of Fars, a remote and wind-swept plain ringed by mountains and desert. Such a place was easy to defend against attack, but to farm the land they had to overcome many difficulties. We can still see the stone channels

Ruins of the royal palace of Darius I and his successors – built in the dry, dusty plain of Fars. Darius started to build his capital city here in about 520 BC, but it took 150 years to complete. He called it Parsa, which meant 'Persian', but the Greeks, who later conquered it, called it Persepolis ('the city of the Persians'). This is the name by which most historians know it today

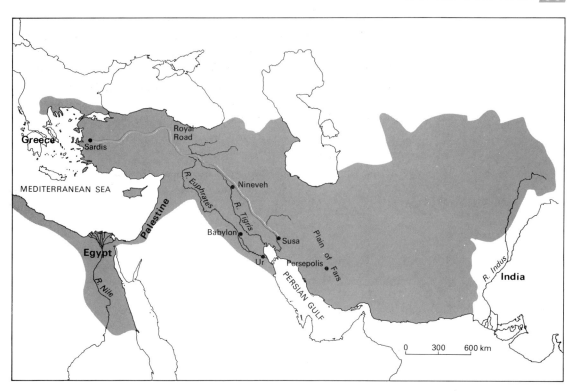

The Persian Empire at its greatest extent, under King Darius I (521–486 BC)

which the Persians built high in the mountains to carry water to irrigate their fields. This rugged land bred a hardy race of people. Cyrus the Great, conqueror of Babylon, once said, 'Soft countries breed soft men. You will never find on one soil luxurious fruits and fine soldiers.'

When the Persians followed Cyrus to war they quickly conquered an empire which the King called proudly, 'The Kingdom of the Whole World'. From the eastern shores of the Mediterranean to the borders of India (see map) Cyrus's enemies were overwhelmed by the arrows of his bowmen and the charge of his cavalry. The conquered races were treated fairly and allowed to keep their own beliefs and customs. Some even supplied soldiers to fight in the armies of the empire. But it was ruled that only Persians could hold important posts in the government, and only Persians were recruited for the empire's finest troops, the Immortals, who wore gold embroidered coats and carried spears decorated with silver.

Cyrus was killed in battle ten years after the conquest of Babylon. There were revolts against Persian rule during the reign of his son, Cambyses, but these were crushed by King Darius I (521–486 BC) who reigned at the time of Persia's greatest power. Darius was a great organiser. He divided his empire into provinces, each controlled by a *satrap* (governor), and sent round inspectors to make sure the satraps did their jobs properly. To link the provinces together, Darius built many good roads, including the 2500-kilometre 'Royal Road' from Susa to Sardis. Every 20 kilometres along it there were rest stations where messengers could change horses. A royal order could be sent the length of the road in a week.

Sir Henry Rawlinson (1810–95). He risked his life to discover the key to the Old Persian language

Most of the famous Persian kings, including Darius I, followed the religious teachings of Zoroaster, who lived around 600 BC. Little is known about Zoroaster's life. He is thought to have dwelt alone for many years before starting to preach a religion similar in many ways to Hinduism (see page 54). Zoroaster said that life was a fight between good and evil. On one side there was Ahriman, the god of darkness and evil, and on the other Ahuramazda, the god of light and truth who struggled to defeat him.

To help Ahuramazda win the fight against evil, Zoroastrians had to live good lives. They had to be honest, fair and polite, and a friend to both people and animals. When true Zoroastrians died, they went from earth to heaven along a wide bridge. Bad people, however, would find the bridge so narrow that they would fall off and never reach paradise. Belief in a battle between good and evil and in judgement after death were important to the later Jewish religion and to Christianity.

The Rock of Behistun

Our knowledge of ancient Persia owes much to words and pictures carved high up on a cliff in the mountains between Iraq and Iran. The Rock of Behistun, as it is called, tells how Darius I crushed a rebellion by rival kings, with the help of the god of light, Ahuramazda. Part of the story goes as follows:

> I sent forth an army and fought a battle.... Ahuramazda brought me help and my army utterly defeated the rebel soldiers.... I cut off the nose and ears [of one of the leading rebels] and I put out his eyes. He was kept in chains in my court.... Afterwards I crucified him.

The inscription cut into the rock is repeated in three languages, including Babylonian and Old Persian – an improved version of the wedge-shaped *cuneiform* of the Babylonians. It was necessary to compare the inscriptions in order to discover the key to the Old Persian language and so learn to translate it. This was done, in 1844, by a British army officer called Henry Rawlinson.

Ignoring the warnings of local peasants that he would fall to his death, Rawlinson edged up the cliff and copied two of the inscriptions from the top of a swaying ladder set on a narrow ledge. He completed his task with the help of a boy from a local village. First the boy clawed his way across a vertical cliff. Then he made a paper impression of the remaining inscription while hanging in a kind of cradle held against the rock wall with wooden pegs. Finding out about the past can be not only exciting but dangerous too!

DOCUMENTS: HAMMURABI'S LAWS

Between 1792 and 1750 BC the Babylonians had a king called Hammurabi. We know more about him than some other Mesopotamian kings because of a column that has been found. On it are carved 282 laws collected by Hammurabi.

Document 1

Hammurabi's column contains 16 lines of blessings for those who obey the laws, and 280 lines of curses for those who disobey them! Not surprisingly, many deal with crimes. Here are some examples.

He who steals from the temple or palace shall be killed, and the receiver of the stolen goods shall be put to death.

If a man steals an ox, or a sheep or an ass, or a pig, or a boat from the temple or palace, he shall pay thirty-fold. The poor man shall pay ten-fold. If the thief has no money, he shall be killed.

The house-breaker shall be killed and buried in the hole he dug.

The highway robber shall be caught and killed.

The man who is caught stealing during a fire shall be thrown into the fire.

If a man has stolen the son of a free man, he shall be killed.

If a man has raped the maid of the temple, or the slave or maid of a poor man outside the gate, he shall be killed.

Source: All documentary extracts in this section are adapted from E. Wallis Budge, Babylonian Life and History, *Religious Tract Society, 1925*

This carving at the top of the column shows Hammurabi receiving the laws from Marduk, the chief god of the Babylonians. Why would Hammurabi have wanted his subjects to see this?

Document 2

Women were quite well protected by these laws. Some even owned property, a rare thing in the ancient world. Here are a few of the laws concerning women. (A *dowry* is a payment in money or goods made by a bride's family to her husband when she marries.)

> If a wife spends her time out of the house, behaves foolishly, wastes her husband's goods and holds him in contempt, he can say 'I divorce you' and send her away without paying her dowry; if he does not say 'I divorce you', he shall marry another woman, and the wasteful wife shall live in his house as a servant.

> If a blameless wife has been treated badly by her husband, she shall take her dowry and return to her father's house.

> A man and woman caught in adultery shall be cast into the water, but the husband of the woman may save her, and the king may save the man.

> If a man strikes a gentlewoman and she has a miscarriage, he shall pay 10 shekels of silver for the loss of her child.

> If a gentlewoman is struck and dies, the striker's daughter shall be killed.

> If a man divorces a wife because she is childless, he shall give back double her dowry.

Document 3

The Mesopotamians believed in taking revenge for wrongs. If a member of one family was killed by another, the two families would often take a life for a life until hardly anyone survived. Kings tried to stop this *feuding* by carrying out revenge for the injured person themselves. The basis of such laws was 'an eye for an eye and a tooth for a tooth', as some of these laws show.

> If a man strikes his father, his hands shall be cut off.

> If a man strikes a gentleman, he shall receive 60 stripes with a cowhide whip.

> If a gentleman strikes another gentleman, he shall pay one *maneh* [1 lb.] of silver.

> If a man has made the teeth of another fall out, one of his own teeth shall be knocked out.

> If a man destroys the eye of another, his own eye shall be destroyed.

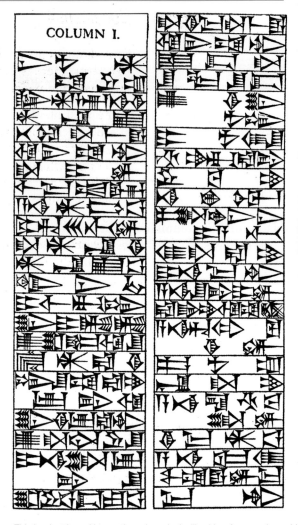

COLUMN I.

This is what the writing on the column looks like. Very few people could read in those days. How, then, would they have learned about these laws?

Document 4

Some laws seem sensible, some very strange, by modern standards. Here is a selection of laws on general matters of importance to people of the time.

If a man casts a spell on another man, and does not justify his actions, the man who is under the spell shall go down to the sacred river and throw himself in, and if the river drowns him the man who cast the spell shall take his house and his property. If the river does not drown him, the man who cast the spell shall be put to death and the innocent man shall take his house....

The mason who builds a house which falls down and kills the inmate shall be put to death.

If it be the son of the master of the house who is killed, the son of the mason who built it shall be killed....

If a lion kills a hired ox or sheep, the loss shall fall on the owner.

If a man injures or kills a hired ox, he shall restore ox for ox to its owner....

If a servant strikes a free man, his ear shall be cut off.

Questions

1. From these documents, what do you think was the Mesopotamian attitude to (**a**) fathers, (**b**) wives, (**c**) slaves?
2. Explain from these documents how Hammurabi's laws favoured the rich ('gentlefolk') against the poor.
3. Write a few sentences explaining what a husband expected of his wife in those days.
4. Which of these laws seem to you to be the most unfair? Explain why you think so.
5. What are the most common types of punishment in these laws? What punishments would be more likely for such wrongdoing today?
6. What evidence is there in these documents that farming was important to Hammurabi's subjects? What other things about their way of life do we learn from these documents?

EGYPT

THE TOMB OF TUTANKHAMEN

In November 1922 Howard Carter, an archaeologist, was digging in the valley where the ancient Egyptians had buried their *pharaohs* (kings). Most of the royal tombs had been robbed of their treasures centuries before. But one tomb, that of the boy-king Tutankhamen, had never been found. For five years Carter had searched, hoping to be the first to open it. Now he seemed near success. Underneath the burial chamber of Pharaoh Rameses VI a door had been discovered. Although shut, it had obviously been opened by robbers and then resealed. Behind it lay another door with the seal of Tutankhamen intact. Carter was about to open a tomb which had been closed for 3,270 years.

Carter needed to prevent fresh air rushing in and destroying the fragile remains inside. So he made a tiny hole and pushed a lighted candle through. 'Can you see anything?' asked his companion, Lord Carnarvon. For a time the archaeologist was too surprised to speak. 'Yes, wonderful things,' he gasped at last. In the flickering candlelight was revealed the most amazing find from the ancient world. Piled in a room 8 metres long and 4 metres wide were nearly 60,000 objects which Egyptians believed their pharaoh might need in the next world. Gold couches, chariots, painted boxes, furniture and gold statues of the King and his servants filled the room.

Nearby was a second room which contained the King's body, enclosed in four gold coffins. It was decorated with gold collars, rings and bracelets. On his face was a life-like gold mask. Nothing like this had ever been discovered in modern times. Small wonder the world went wild at the news. Women wore Egyptian-style fashions, popular songs were written about Tutankhamen and a record was made of a soldier blowing a war trumpet found in

Tutankhamen's funeral mask. It was made of gold decorated with semi-precious stones. The king is shown wearing his false beard

Howard Carter, left, pictured just after his entry into the tomb

the burial chamber. To hear this strange, unearthly sound after so many centuries thrilled people and helped to make one of Egypt's less important rulers more famous than its greatest kings. People who knew little about Egyptian history became interested. Who were these people who could bury a young man with such riches?

People of the Nile

About 10,000 years ago the climate of the Mediterranean area seems to have changed. Less rain fell, and wandering tribesmen were forced to move to the nearest water supply. The Nile is the largest river in North Africa; from its source in Lake Victoria it stretches 5,500 kilometres to the sea. As it nears the Mediterranean it spreads out to form a huge *delta* (triangle) of smaller streams. Each year, at certain seasons, heavy rains in central Africa swell its waters and cause it to spill over the land. When such a flood goes down it leaves miles of thick black mud which is ideal for growing crops.

By 3500 BC people had settled down to farm this land. In such a hot, dry country this would have been impossible without the Nile's annual flooding, or *inundation*. Each year the Egyptians watched anxiously for signs of a rise in the river level. They noticed that such floods normally occurred a few days after the star Sirius appeared at dawn in the summer sky. So they made this the first day of their New Year. Once the inundation began, special stones called 'nilometers' measured its height.

Further upstream in Egypt the deserts are closer to the river bank so there is less land for farming. For this reason the first civilised region was around the Nile delta – or *Lower Egypt*. The southern valley was settled later and called *Upper Egypt*. A King Menes of Upper Egypt united the two parts in about 3300 BC. He conquered the delta region and founded the city of Memphis. Because there had once been two Egypts, the pharaohs wore a double crown, the high white crown of Upper Egypt and the red one of Lower Egypt. Later the country was divided into 42 provinces, ruled by the pharaoh, his priests and thousands of officials.

A vulture goddess in the form of a pendant: one of Tutankhamen's jewels

Tutankhamen dressed for a religious festival

The pharaoh was very important to the Egyptians. Not only was he their priest and king. He was also thought to be a god. All important religious festivals were conducted by him. When the pharaoh appeared in public he carried a carved shepherd's staff. He dressed in a gold apron and wore an artificial beard fixed to his face with a strap. Stone carvings show pharaohs standing proud and erect, as if always young and strong. When death came to them, the Egyptians believed that they were not judged like ordinary men but went straight to heaven, sailing across the sky in a sunboat driven by golden oars. One such boat had been found in Tutankhamen's tomb.

Egyptian religion

Egyptians believed that when a person died the body and soul parted. The soul was in two parts, called Ba and Ka. Ba was the soul-bird who could take any shape and fly anywhere. Ka resembled the dead person exactly. Powerful men like pharaohs or nobles were thought to have more than one Ka. Carvings nearly always show a Ka standing behind a pharaoh protecting him. Most souls had to go on a journey after death, before being judged by the god Osiris. Good people were sent to paradise. Wicked ones had their hearts torn out by a monster.

Osiris was thought to have been killed and then brought back to life. This is why he ruled over the dead. Other powerful gods were Ra, the sun god, Isis the wife of Osiris, and Horus, who was really two gods. As god of heaven, Horus was often shown as a hawk.

The god Osiris is being worshipped by a priest

His eyes were believed to be the sun and moon. His wings were so long that they stretched to the ends of the earth. The other Horus god was the son of Osiris and Isis. Later, Amun, the sun god of the priests at the city of Thebes, became more important than Ra.

The only pharaoh who ever tried to change Egypt's religion was Amenhotep IV, who reigned in the fourteenth century BC. Amenhotep claimed that there was only one god whom he called Aten. Aten's sign was the sun and the pharaoh made himself his high priest. He changed his own name to Akhenaten, meaning 'it is pleasing to Aten', and wrote poems in honour of the god (you can read one on page 43). These poems were sung in the temples. The high priests of the old gods hated Akhenaten and after his death worship of Aten was banned.

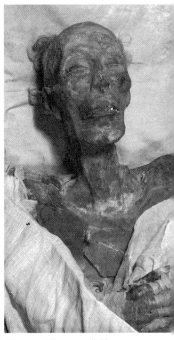

Mummy of Rameses II. You can still see the bandages wound round his fingers to preserve them

Preserving the dead

Egyptians liked to preserve the bodies of those they loved and turn them into *mummies*. Egypt has a dry climate and its soil contains preservatives like resin (a kind of gum) and bitumen (a kind of tar) so this was not difficult. After a person died, the brains and other organs were cut out and placed in special jars. The heart and kidneys were left in the body. What happened after this depended on how rich or important the dead person had been. The poor were wrapped in a thick layer of bitumen to keep out the air; the word *mummy* is Arabic for bitumen. The corpses of the rich were wrapped in linen bandage which had been soaked in resin. The bandage was criss-crossed leaving diamond-shaped spaces which were decorated with precious stones and pieces of gold.

Special care was taken to preserve the face. Egyptians believed this was necessary if the soul was to recognise its own body. For the same reason a mask of the face was made and fitted over the head. The whole *mummifying* (embalming) process could take months. The mummy of a noble would have its neck filled out and artificial eyes fixed in the eye sockets. When the body was ready it was drawn to the banks of the Nile on a wooden sledge. A boat took it to the House of the Dead on the western bank. This was a barren area used for burials because it was unfit for farming.

The pyramids

Early Egyptian stone tombs were square and flat-topped. They were called *mastabas* from the Egyptian word for bench. About 3000 BC a king called Djoser decided to be buried in a tomb made of six mastabas of decreasing size placed one on top of the other. This tomb, which is over 60 metres high, is known as the Step Pyramid. Later pharaohs built similar structures but had the steps filled in to form a sloping surface. There is one like this at Meidum built for King Snofru. His son, Khufu, usually known as Cheops, designed a true pyramid and it was put up at Giza.

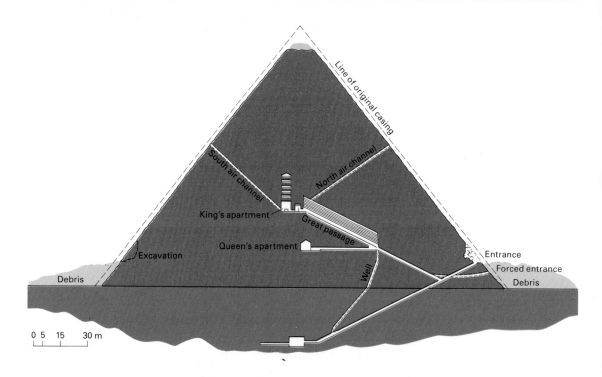

Khufu's Great Pyramid is on the right. The one on the left, with part of the casing still in place, is the Second Pyramid, built for Khafra. It is guarded by the Great Sphinx

Line of original casing

South air channel

North air channel

King's apartment

Great passage

Queen's apartment

Excavation

Entrance

Forced entrance

Well

Debris

Debris

0 5 15 30 m

A cross-section of the Great Pyramid at Giza, showing where the treasures would have been kept – until robbers got to them

Khufu's Great Pyramid, as it is called, is made of more than 2 million granite and limestone blocks. It rises to 145 metres and each side is 225 metres long. The blocks were cut in quarries on the other side of the Nile and floated across on rafts. They were dragged up earth ramps to be set in place. Two other pyramids stand nearby. The so-called Second Pyramid was built to house the body of Khafra, Khufu's son. In the hope of frightening off tomb robbers, the Great Sphinx – a large statue with the face of Khafra and the body of a lion – was built to guard it. The Sphinx represented the dead pharaoh as a god and its face was painted red. Now it is damaged and scarred by sand. It did not frighten off thieves who broke into the pyramids to get at the treasures inside. In later ages, pharaohs were buried in the Valley of Kings – a remote spot in the western desert. It was here that Tutankhamen's body was found.

Sources and questions

1. Here is one of Akhenaten's poems honouring the god Aten.
   It would have been set to music and sung in the temples.

   > Your dawning is beautiful in the horizon of heaven
   > O living Aten, beginning of life!
   > When you rise in the eastern horizon of heaven
   > You fill every land with your beauty,
   > For you are radiant, great, glittering, high over the earth.
   > Your rays encircle all the lands that you have made.

   (a) How is the subject of this poem connected with Aten?
   (b) How was the religion expressed in this peom different from the old Egyptian worship and beliefs?
   (c) What was the attitude of the priests to this new god?
   (d) In what ways was the worship of Aten similar to Christianity? How was it different?

2. Look at the picture below.
   (a) Why do you think the objects are in a muddle?
   (b) How many objects can you identify? Make a list.
   (c) What does the picture tell you about the ancient Egyptians?
   (d) Why is this particular tomb so famous?

3. There is a mystery about Tutankhamen's tomb. Even though a door on the way to the tomb had been opened by robbers it was resealed and the tomb was left intact. Can you give a likely explanation for this?

4. It has been estimated that it took about 4000 slave workers 30 years to build the Great Pyramid. Imagine you are one of those unfortunate workers and write a letter to a friend describing your experiences.

This is the scene that met the eyes of Howard Carter when he opened Tutankhamen's tomb

EGYPTIAN LIFE AND CUSTOMS

Jewelled ornament in the shape of a scarab

So much of what we know about the Egyptians concerns the dead that it is worth remembering that they were a happy people who loved life and most living things. They were particularly fond of cats. When a favourite one died the whole family went into mourning and it was sometimes mummified like a human corpse. Egyptian dogs looked rather like greyhounds. They were kept as pets or house-guards. Even the humble dung-beetle, or *scarab*, was respected because it rolled its ball of dung along in the way Egyptians believed gods rolled the sun across the sky.

The poor lived in one-storey mud or brick buildings with roofs of palm leaves. Richer people often lived in a number of two-storey buildings set around a sheltered garden. Large houses might have as many as seventy rooms and several hundred trees in the garden to provide shade. There was no need for thick clothing in such a hot country. Women wore a long linen dress, made from flax grown in the Nile delta. Men wore a loin cloth held up with a belt or, if they were of noble birth, pleated kilts and flowing robes.

Egyptian women often wore lotus flowers in their hair. This was the national flower of Egypt. Rich and noble women used heavy make-up. Their eyebrows and eyelashes were painted dark blue. Lipstick was worn and rouge put on the cheeks. Because sweating was a problem in such a climate both men and women wore perfume. The Egyptians also had a curious custom of placing a small cone of fat on their heads. As it melted a sweet-smelling liquid trickled down the forehead and cheeks.

Art and writing

The Egyptians were fine craftsmen. They turned pottery on wheels and baked their clay in a closed furnace. They were expert basket-makers, using the plentiful supply of reeds growing by the river Nile. Some baskets were lined with a clay plaster so that they could hold liquid. Egyptians could work in copper, bronze, gold, silver and iron. They carved precious stones as well as wood and it is likely that they invented glass. Although they were clever at carving on stone, Egyptian artists did not attempt to draw life-like pictures. People were often carved with their heads in *profile* (sideways) but their bodies facing the front; ship drawings often show all the oars on one side.

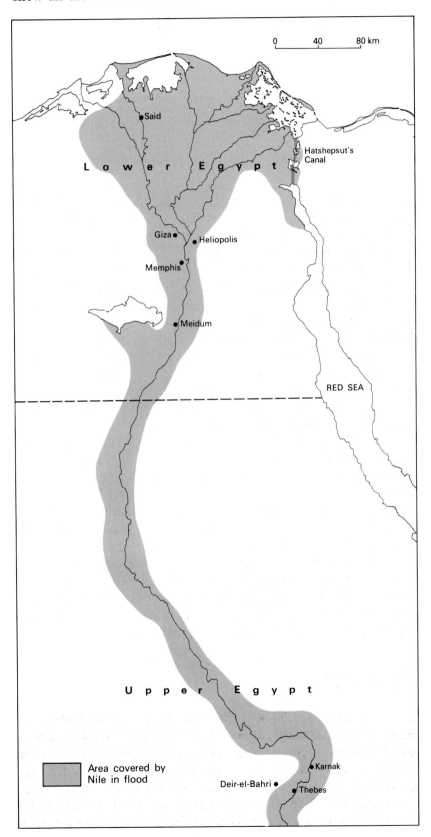

0   40   80 km

Said

Hatshepsut's Canal

L o w e r   E g y p t

Giza
Heliopolis

Memphis

Meidum

RED SEA

U p p e r   E g y p t

Karnak
Deir-el-Bahri
Thebes

Area covered by Nile in flood

Ancient Egypt

By about 2400 BC the Egyptians had invented a form of picture-writing. It is called *hieroglyphics* which means 'sacred carved letters'. At first each picture indicated a word but later it came to represent a letter. A well educated person was expected to write in this way but ordinary folk needed less complicated writing. They devised the *hieratic* version to speed up writing, and later an even simpler type called *demotic* (popular script). This was used by businessmen, court officials and traders. Writing was done with a reed brush dipped in ink made from soot, water and gum. Lengths of paper were made from papyrus reed which was stuck together in criss-cross fashion and stored in long rolls.

For centuries the secret of how to read this writing was lost. Then in 1799 some French army officers in Egypt found a stone at Rosetta near the mouth of the Nile. They realised at once that it was important because it had inscriptions in three languages: hieroglyphic, demotic and Greek. Since Greek was understood, it might be possible to learn how to translate the hieroglyphic and demotic by comparing them with the Greek – in much the same way as the secret of Old Persian was discovered from the Rock of Behistun (see page 34).

The Rosetta Stone was handed over to the British and taken to London where it is housed in the British Museum. However the French had already made copies of the inscriptions. These were sent to Paris where a brilliant French scholar, Jean Champollion, spent years studying the script along with other stone inscriptions. First he found the Egyptian letters for Ptolemy, and then those for Cleopatra – both Ptolemy's wife and sister had this name. Gradually it became possible to translate the many papyrus rolls and stone carvings left by the ancient Egyptians and so learn about their history.

Education, medicine and law

Egyptian schools were tough places by modern standards. A favourite saying of Egyptian schoolmasters was, 'The ear of a boy is on his back and he listens when he is beaten.' Pupils learnt to write on fragments of broken pottery called *ostraka*; papyrus was too expensive to be wasted! When their writing improved they used a reed pen, ink and paint which they kept in a wooden palette like a pencil box. Pupils learnt mathematics and a great deal about the movements of the planets (astronomy), but writing was their main task. A lot of time was spent copying out folk tales which the teacher dictated.

The Egyptians were very interested in healing and had medical schools at Said, Thebes and Heliopolis. Doctors spent a lot of time trying to cure eye complaints, many of them caused by the swarms of flies which infest the country. They sometimes used quite modern methods but they also relied on spells and magic. One treatment required the doctor to recite a spell to some ointment seven times before applying it to the wound!

Lawyers were looked upon as priests serving Maat, the goddess of justice. Egyptian trials were well-organised. There was a judge and a clerk who wrote down the evidence. The accused were allowed to defend themselves. Serious punishments were usually decided by the pharaoh, not the judge. They ranged from death to loss of limbs or a severe beating.

Egyptian boats

The ancient Egyptians were a river people who travelled mainly by boat. Land travel was hot, dusty and tiring. It was much better to row or sail on the Nile's cool waters. Early Egyptian boats were made of reeds tied together. The bunched reeds at each end pointed upwards, giving the vessel a half-moon shape which was copied when larger, wooden craft were developed.

Egypt has few tall trees. The most common tree, the acacia, can only be cut into short lengths. This meant that Egyptian boats had no long tree-trunk, or *keel*, on which to build the hull. So small pieces were pegged together on a frame, rather as bricks are laid to make a wall. To strengthen the vessel, a cable of stout rope was

This tomb painting shows an Egyptian nobleman hunting wildfowl in marshes

Cleopatra's Needle on the Thames Embankment, London

tied to each end and supported along the deck on wooden holders rather like props for a washing line. Sailors twisted this tight if the boat began to sag at the ends. It seems a clumsy and fragile way to make a sea-going ship but Egyptian vessels were sturdy, fast craft which often survived storms because they were flexible and could bend with the waves.

When the horse became known in Egypt, chariots and two-wheeled carts were used as well as boats for transport. Horses were used for pulling but they were not ridden, although poor people sometimes travelled astride donkeys. But boats were always more important. It was in a boat, not in a chariot or on a horse, that the Egyptians believed their dead pharaoh voyaged to heaven.

Warrior pharaohs

The earliest period of Egyptian history was a time of peace. It is known as the Old Kingdom and was the period when the pyramids were built. The Old Kingdom collapsed in a series of rebellions against weak pharaohs. Stronger royal *dynasties* (families) gained control. The most famous of these were the pharaohs of the so-called Eighteenth Dynasty who made Thebes, their capital, the finest city in the country. They also built the largest of all Egyptian temples, at Karnak on the east bank of the Nile. Great pillars from the temple still survive; some are so thick that 100 people could stand on top of them. The long rule of the Eighteenth Dynasty, which historians call the Middle Kingdom, was a time of prosperity. Trade expanded and many beautiful shrines and temples were erected.

The Middle Kingdom was destroyed by foreign invaders. In about 1670 BC, a people the Egyptians called the Hyksos, meaning either 'Shepherd Kings' or 'Rulers of the Uplands', swept into Egypt from Asia. Little is known about these warriors except that they fought in chariots drawn by horses. After nearly a century of wars the Hyksos were driven out of Egypt. These years of fighting made the Egyptians a more warlike people. In later centuries their soldiers, riding in chariots and armed with bows, arrows and spears, conquered an empire which at one time stretched from the river Euphrates to the Sahara (see map on page 45).

One of the most famous warrior-pharaohs, Thotmes III, won so many wars that the temple at Karnak was enlarged to celebrate his victories. Many *obelisks* (pointed columns) are carved with the stories of his battles in words and pictures. One was brought to England and put up in London. It is known as 'Cleopatra's Needle' but it has nothing to do with that queen.

Ancient Egypt was weakened by many years of foreign wars. Trade was upset and there were frequent famines. Nevertheless, the land of the pharaohs remained independent until 341 BC when it was overrun by the Persians. As we shall see in later chapters, Egypt was conquered again by Alexander the Great (333 BC), and, finally, by the Romans who added it to their empire after overthrowing Queen Cleopatra (31 BC).

DOCUMENTS: THE REIGN OF QUEEN HATSHEPSUT

Queen Hatshepsut ruled in Egypt 3,500 years ago (from about 1505–1483 BC). She is one of the best remembered of all Egyptians because of the great temple she had built at Deir el-Bahri on the west bank of the Nile. Inside the temple, which served as her tomb, there were many inscriptions on the walls. Historians have used these to piece together an account of her reign.

In recent years archaeologists, many of them from Poland, have begun restoring Hatshepsut's temple at Deir el-Bahri. This picture shows the progress made by 1990. Two separate groups of workers constructed the largest columns – and do not seem to have agreed on the measurements. Can you see any differences between the left and right sides?

Document 1

When Hatshepsut's husband, Pharaoh Tuthmosis II, died, his only son was six years old. Although the boy was declared Pharaoh, in practice it was his stepmother, Hatshepsut, who became the most powerful person in the kingdom. Later she claimed to be Pharaoh, the only woman ever to do so in ancient Egypt. The following inscription from Deir el-Bahri tells of her rise to power.

> The Pharaoh (Tuthmosis II) mounted triumphantly to the sky and took his place among the gods. His son took his place as ruler of the Two Lands and became Pharaoh upon his father's throne. . . . The divine wife Hatshepsut managed the affairs of the country according to her own desires.

Source: All documentary extracts in this section are adapted from J. M. White, The Reign of Queen Hatshepsut, in History Today, Vol. II, No. 12, 1952.

Document 2

Wall carvings at Deir el-Bahri, made on the orders of the Queen's chief architect, show Hatshepsut being crowned by the gods. Amon-Ra (God of Thebes) and her father both declare her Queen.

My daughter's name shall be Hatshepsut. She shall have supreme power over the entire land. . . . You [the Egyptian people] shall carry out her wishes. You shall act together to serve her. The man who worships her shall live. The man who speaks against her shall die.

Statue of Hatshepsut. On the chin you can see the remains of a beard. Why do you think she has been given a beard, like a man?

Document 3

In this inscription from Deir el-Bahri, Hatshepsut explains the erection of two large *obelisks* (pointed columns) at Karnak. Each was 30 metres high and weighed 350 tonnes.

Future generations will know of my devotion to Amon-Ra. They will enquire about this monument which I raised for my father the god. . . . The two great obelisks which I have tipped with *electrum* [a mixture of gold and silver] are for my father Amon-Ra. They will make sure that my name will be remembered for ever and ever. Each obelisk is made of a single granite stone without any joints. . . . They can be seen on both sides of the valley. The Two Lands are bathed with their splendour. The sun rises between them in the way that it rises from the horizon of heaven.

Document 4

One of the most famous events in Hatshepsut's reign was the sending of eight large ships to Punt (probably present-day Somalia) to bring back sweet-smelling myrrh trees for her temple and other riches. An inscription at Deir el-Bahri describes some of the cargo brought back from Punt.

> The ships returned heavily laden with marvels of the country of Punt, all goodly fragrant woods of the East, gum and young myrrh trees, ebony and spotless ivory, green gold, cinnamon, incense, eye-paint, baboons, monkeys, dogs, skins of the southern panther and natives and their children. Such a treasure was never brought for any king who has ruled since the beginning of the world.

This drawing was copied from a wall in the temple at Deir el-Bahri by Howard Carter, who later became famous through the discovery of Tutankhamen's tomb. It shows one of Hatshepsut's ships being loaded in Punt. What does the drawing tell you about ancient Egyptian ships (for instance, how they were made, driven or steered)?

Questions

1. Tuthmosis II's son, who ruled after Hatshepsut's death as Tuthmosis III, hated Hatshepsut and had her name erased from all inscriptions at Deir el-Bahri. How does Document 1 help to explain this?
2. Hatshepsut's father could not have spoken the words in Document 2 because he could not have foreseen that she would rule Egypt. What, then, was the purpose of this inscription?
3. What do these documents tell you about the religious beliefs and practices of the ancient Egyptians?
4. Hatshepsut hoped that her temple and its inscriptions would make people remember her. In what ways might famous people today try to make sure they are not forgotten?
5. Give reasons why it was easier to trade by sea than overland at this time?
6. What does the cargo described in Document 4 reveal about the way of life of rich Egyptians 3,500 years ago?

INDIA AND CHINA

LOST CITIES OF THE INDUS

Until recent times little was known about early Indian civilisations. In the last fifty or sixty years, however, the ruins of dozens of ancient settlements have been found – mostly in the valley of the river Indus (see map on page 53). Some have still to be investigated thoroughly, but two cities in particular, Harappa in the Punjab, and Mohenjo-daro in Sind province, have been excavated by archaeologists.

Both cities cover about 8 square kilometres. Although they are 650 kilometres apart, they are similar in design. Each had long straight streets which cross at right angles, making the grid pattern found in modern American cities. Many streets had brick drains emptying into main sewers down the centre. New houses seem to have been built on the ruins of older dwellings. This may have been because the river level rose as the years went by. Both cities had large granaries for storing corn and were protected by fortresses built on man-made hills.

The Dravidians

Mohenjo-daro and Harappa are not the only major discoveries that have been made by archaeologists. It seems that between about 2500 and 1500 BC the Indus valley region, stretching from the Arabian Sea to the Simla Hills, was dotted with cities and villages built by people known as Dravidians. The Dravidians were farmers whose main crops were wheat, barley, melons and possibly dates and cotton. They kept cattle and pigs and used camels and horses to carry people and goods. From the coast they traded with places as far afield as the Mesopotamian cities. Gold from southern

A street in the ancient city of Mohenjo-daro – uncovered by archaeologists. Notice the brickwork

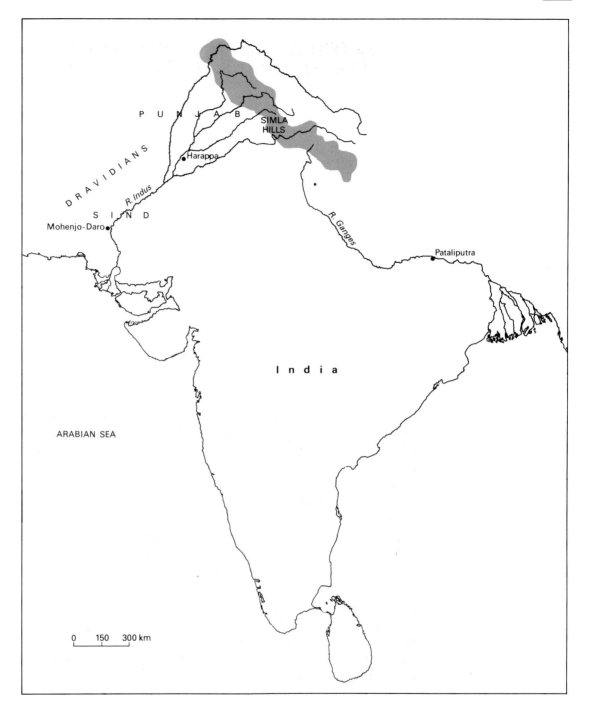

Ancient India

India and turquoise (a blue-green stone) from Persia have been found at Harappa and Mohenjo-daro, while Indian pottery, made on a wheel, has been unearthed in Mesopotamia.

There are still a lot of unanswered questions about the Dravidians. Both Harappa and Mohenjo-daro stand in dry, treeless plains. Yet a huge amount of wood must have been burnt to make the millions of bricks used to build the houses. Rain must have been much more plentiful at that time than it is now or the trees would not have grown. Moreover, without plenty of rain, the countryside would not have been able to produce sufficient crops to feed such large populations. The climate certainly seems to

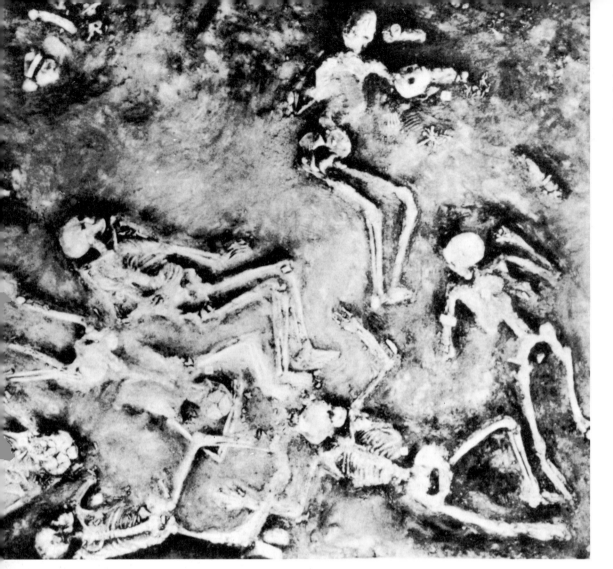

have changed since those far-off times. Perhaps the Dravidians themselves helped to change it by cutting down the trees?

We can only guess at the way the Dravidian civilisation ended. In about 1500 BC people called Aryans moved into India from Asia. It seems they attacked and destroyed many Dravidian cities. Skeletons have been found in disordered heaps in Harappa and Mohenjo-daro, which probably means that people were massacred and left unburied. Apart from conquest, there is also evidence that the cities may have been destroyed by floods. Perhaps the Aryans occupied 'ghost' towns inhabited by only a few survivors.

Many Aryans settled in the Ganges valley where their language, religion and way of life survive to the present day. Their language was Sanskrit, which is still studied by scholars, though very few people speak it. Their religion grew out of hymns chanted by holy men called *Brahmins*. The popular name for this creed is Hinduism and it is the chief religion of India (not Pakistan).

Hindus believe that each soul goes through a number of lives, through being *reincarnated* (re-born) each time. To be born again into this world of pain and sorrow is not thought to be desirable, so good deeds on earth reduce the number of rebirths while bad deeds increase them. Good deeds also affect a person's position in the world. Those people who have been good in a previous life are born into four privileged groups, called *castes*. Of these, the most saintly are the Brahmins. People not born into these castes are known as out-castes or *Untouchables*. They do hard, rough jobs or take up trades forbidden to other castes and are forced to live in special quarters away from the rest of the population.

The Buddha

Some holy men disliked the caste system, claiming that it was wrong and unfair. One of these was Prince Gautama, the founder of Buddhism. Gautama was born in about 500 BC, the son of an Indian king. Many legends grew up about him. When he was a baby, wise men predicted that he would give up being a prince and become a holy man when he saw an old man, a sick man and a corpse. We are told that his father, worried by this strange prophecy, shut him away in a beautiful palace to avoid such sights. But, as he grew up, Gautama saw all three. This led him to wonder why people grew old and died. Hoping to find the answer, he decided to leave his wife and child and live alone like a monk.

Gautama wandered from place to place, trying to find the secret

These golden figures of Buddha are in the Chapel of the Emerald Buddha in Thailand

of life. At last the answer came to him as he sat under a tree. He became the Buddha, or Enlightened One. The Buddha thought the reason people were reborn was because they kept wanting things. If they could give up their desires they would cease to be reborn and disappear 'like a drop of water in the sea' of Brahma, the Great Spirit. This happy state Buddha called *Nirvana*. He suggested eight ways, the Eightfold Path, which would lead to the end of all desires. Chief among these were right living, right thinking and right doing.

The Buddha said the Eightfold Path was like a journey where more views unfold to the travellers as they go on their way. After more than forty years of teaching the Buddha died at Oudh. His wife took up the Buddhist way of life and so did millions of others. Buddhism was a simple and peaceful belief. It taught people to be satisfied with very little and to help and love others.

Asoka the Good

After Gautama's death, Buddhism continued to spread throughout India, especially during the reign of King Asoka (274–236 BC). Asoka began life as a conqueror. During one invasion his soldiers slaughtered thousands of his enemies. The sight of the tortured bodies and the screams of the dying made the king a changed man. He felt ashamed of his cruelty and soon afterwards became a Buddhist. Instead of going to war he went on pilgrimages to holy places. Instead of having hundreds of animals killed each day for his kitchens he reduced the amount to two peacocks and one gazelle. Finally he became a vegetarian.

Asoka also became a kind and more just ruler. Roads were built all over north-west India. Laws were fair and had to be obeyed. Buddhist missionaries were sent as far afield as Persia. When he died, this great king had helped to spread the teachings of the man who refused to be a king. Today few Indians are Buddhists but the faith is strong in many parts of the Far East, particularly Burma and Tibet.

The Mauryan empire

Asoka reigned over the Mauryan empire – Maurya was the name of the royal family. His rule extended north and south from the valley of the river Ganges. In previous centuries these lands had been overrun by the Persians. The conquerors had left their mark. Indian artists and architects copied Persian methods and designs. Asoka's grandfather built a great hall in his capital city of Patali-putra which looked like the palace of the Persian kings at Persepo-lis. Its pillars were highly polished and bell-shaped at the top, in the Persian style. A similar column with lion carvings at the top belonged to Asoka. It is now the badge of the republic of India.

Like an Egyptian pharaoh, a Mauryan king was looked upon as a god. Each year he ploughed the first furrow of land with his own

King Asoka's column

hand. If the crops were poor he was blamed; it was thought he had angered the other gods. He also judged his subjects personally, using, it was said, 7,000 law books to help him. Punishments varied from fines to being trampled to death by elephants or thrown head first over a cliff. Prisons were grim places in which not only the criminal but also his family were sent for long periods.

The key to Mauryan prosperity was farming, particularly rice and sugar growing and cattle-breeding. Fields were divided up by small embankments or narrow water channels. Cattle were so valuable that a family's wealth was measured by how many they owned. These beasts were kept for food, milk, skins, horn and hair. Peasants paid a quarter of their crops in tax to the government. This made possible the building of good roads connecting the main towns. Roads encouraged trade. The Mauryan people sent ivory, perfume, diamonds, rare animals and valuable woods abroad, in exchange for goods from as far away as Italy, Egypt and China. In many ways, the Mauryan Empire was one of the best organised and most successful in India's history.

Sources and questions

1. Here are ten commandments for Buddhists.

    1. Do not destroy life.
    2. Do not take what is not given.
    3. Do not be unfaithful in marriage.
    4. Do not lie or deceive.
    5. Do not drink alcoholic drinks.
    6. Do not eat too much and never after midday.
    7. Do not watch dancing, singing, music or plays.
    8. Do not wear garlands, perfumes, ornaments and jewellery.
    9. Do not sleep in high or luxurious beds.
  10. Do not accept gold or silver.

Here are the ten commandments for Christians.

    1. Worship no god but me.
    2. Do not make for yourselves images of anything in heaven or on earth.... Do not bow down to any idol or worship it, because I am the Lord your God and I tolerate no rivals.
    3. Do not use my name for evil purposes.
    4. Observe the Sabbath and keep it holy.
    5. Respect your father and your mother.
    6. Do not commit murder.
    7. Do not commit adultery.
    8. Do not steal.
    9. Do not accuse anyone falsely.
  10. Do not desire another man's house; do not desire his wife ... or anything else that he owns.

Source: Adapted from L. Adams Beck, The Life of the Buddha, *Collins, 1946, and* The Good News Bible, *Collins/Fontana, 1976*

(a) List the main similarities and differences between these two sets of commandments.
(b) Buddhist monks have to obey all ten of their commandments. Buddhist men and women have to obey only *five*. Can you work out which rules are for monks only?
(c) In your opinion, which set of commandments, Buddhist or Christian, if obeyed, would be most likely to make a person live a better life? Give reasons for your answer.
(d) The word God is not mentioned in the commandments of Buddhists. What important difference in the attitude to life of Christians and Buddhists does this indicate?

2. What does the skeleton pictured on the next page tell you about:
(a) the position in society of the person when alive;
(b) the burial practices of the people?

This skeleton was uncovered by archaeologists working at Harappa

3. The climate of the Indus Valley region (Punjab and Sind) must have been very different in the days of the Dravidians. One possible explanation of the change is that there were trees 3,500–4,000 years ago but the Dravidians cut too many of them down.
   (a) Why would the Dravidians have wanted to cut down the trees?
   (b) How might cutting down trees affect the climate?
   (c) Can you name any part of the modern world where experts fear that tree-felling is having the same effect today? How would you explain the problem?

4. The tale of the Buddha seeing an old man, a sick man and a corpse is not likely to be true in every detail. Can you work out why it was made up and what it is meant to tell us about the Buddha as a person?

THE CHINESE

Chinese civilisation began in three valleys, those of the Yellow, Yangtze, and Huai rivers. Along their banks farmers produced plentiful crops of wheat and especially rice which grows in flooded fields. By about 1000 BC these regions were sufficiently well irrigated to support large populations. The Chinese were cut off from other parts of the world by mountains, deserts and the Pacific Ocean. Such barriers prevented them from mixing freely with other peoples and exchanging ideas and inventions. Few invaders came and those that did were soon cut off in a similar way and so copied Chinese customs.

The First Universal Emperor

Chinese history, like that of Egypt, is divided into periods named after royal families or *dynasties*. Some of the earliest rulers are known to historians as the Shang (or Yin) kings. Their remains, including buildings, tombs, bronze pots and treasure pits, have been found near An-Yang in Hunan province. They date from 1500–1000 BC and show that the people of this region were skilled bronze workers. They also used chariots in war and scratched signs on bones when they wanted to ask their gods questions. These scratched bones show the first traces of what later became the Chinese language.

It took a long time for the people of such a vast country to form one state. At first, large cities controlled the countryside around them. Then some of the more powerful ones conquered their neighbours until there were just seven kingdoms in China. Eventually the most powerful state, called Ch'in, overran the others in 221 BC. Its warrior leader called himself Shih Huang Ti (First Universal Emperor) and founded the Ch'in or Chinese empire which lasted until 1911. Shih Huang Ti wanted to give the country a new start. He gave the peasants the land they worked, melted down the weapons of his enemies and destroyed any books he did not like. Every time he defeated a rival prince he had an exact copy of the conquered man's palace built in his own capital, Hsien-Yang.

Great Wall

HUNAN

An-Yang

SHAN TUNG

Hsien-Yang   Yellow R.

HIMALAYAS

Huai R.

Tibet

Yangtze R.

C h i n a

PACIFIC OCEAN

0   250   500 km

Ancient China

Chinese achievements

The Chinese were the first to do many things. By about AD 100 they had found a way of turning tree-bark into a paste and spreading it out to make paper. A few hundred years later they invented a way of printing with ink-covered blocks – long before this was thought of in Europe. They also used gunpowder before anybody else and invented the clock and the wheelbarrow. Meanwhile, Chinese craftsmen carved beautiful animals and dragons from a green stone called jade and Chinese artists found a way of drawing landscapes in black ink on pots, paper and walls.

This whole civilisation depended upon its farming. Growing rice is a difficult job. It involves back-breaking work while stand-

The Great Wall of China – the only human structure that can be seen from Outer Space. Originally there were a number of separate earth walls built to keep out invaders from central Asia. Shih Huang Ti and those who ruled after him joined the walls together and strengthened them with stone. The resulting Great Wall was 2,900 kilometres long, 7 metres high and 6 metres wide

ing for hours in water. Weeds spring up quickly in a hot climate and these have to be cut away. An ancient Chinese book on farming gives the worker this advice :

> When the rice shoots are [about 20 centimetres] long the old weeds will have sprung up again. You must plunge your scythe into the water and hack at them at the root; then they will rot and die.

China's climate is unreliable and crops were often ruined by drought. When this happened, large numbers of people starved to death.

Lao Tse and Confucius

Since ancient times the Chinese have been greatly influenced by the teachings of Fu-Tzu (Confucius) and by ideas linked with a mysterious figure called Lao Tse. Lao may never have existed. He was said to have been born 81 years old and to have been known

When Shih Huang Ti died he was buried with this 'stone army' (it is actually modelled from terra-cotta, a kind of pottery with a dull surface). There are 6,000 soldiers, 500 horses and many chariots. All the figures are life-size and lined up for battle. The Emperor hoped that this 'army' would remind people of his conquests

as the 'Old Teacher'. The ideas and beliefs of his followers are called Taoism from the Chinese word *Tao*, meaning a way or path.

Taoism teaches people to stop wanting things, to forget about pride, ambition or even goodness and to take as their motto 'Leave alone'. Followers are encouraged to imitate nature. A tree does not want things; it does not struggle to control other trees. It just grows. Taoism encourages people to live simple lives and to love trees, flowers and the countryside. Some of the finest Chinese artists have been Taoists who spent their lives drawing and painting the beautiful Chinese landscape.

Picture by a Taoist artist. It shows a demon-killer on his travels

Confucius's teaching was different. He was born in Lin province in 551 BC at a time when there were constant wars between the different Chinese kingdoms. Such disorder horrified him and he became convinced that people could only lead better lives by following strict rules of behaviour. People could be taught to be kind and polite, to obey their elders and to be considerate to others, Confucius claimed. A good start could be made if everyone followed his Golden Rule : 'Never do to other people what you do not want them to do to you.'

Confucius was not a religious teacher. He did not talk about God or life after death. 'How can we know about death when we have learnt so little about life?' he once asked. His aim was to show people how to behave properly, hoping that this would improve their characters. For example, he said a boy must always call his father 'honourable' and refer to himself as 'an unworthy son'. A subject should not just bow before his king but touch the ground with his forehead in what the Chinese call the *kow-tow*. Confucius did not think much of soldiers and their violent ways. He said people should admire scholars because of their knowledge. Confucius wrote down old tales and poems but altered them

Future mandarins took their examinations in these cells about a century ago

so that they contained a useful lesson, or *moral*. They are to be found in a book called *Spring and Autumn Annals*.

According to Confucius, people's behaviour could be improved either by advice or example. In particular, a king or emperor must set a good example to his subjects. Only then would he be worthy to rule. Although Confucius stressed the importance of the family in teaching good behaviour, he had the traditional attitude of the Chinese to women which was that they are inferior to men. This is shown in the following poem from the *Book of Songs*, a collection which may have been the work of Confucius.

> Sons shall be born to him –
> They will be put to sleep on couches;
> They will be clothed in robes. . . .
> Daughters shall be born to him
> They will be put to sleep on the ground
> They will be clothed with wrappers.

Later generations altered both Taoism and Confucianism. Magical ceremonies crept into Taoist beliefs. Temples were built where Confucianism was studied as though it were a religion. Sensible rules about politeness and good behaviour were mixed up with rules about never sitting on a mat that was not straight or wearing a coat that was not wider at the bottom than at the waist.

When China became a single empire her rulers found they needed a large number of officials, called *mandarins*, to help them govern. Those wanting to be mandarins had to pass long and difficult tests to qualify. Each year thousands of candidates took food, candles and writing materials into special little cells and struggled for days and nights trying to answer questions about the writings of Confucius and other scholars. Only a few passed. Yet a mandarin's job was so pleasant that thousands more tried next year. At the same time dishonest men tried to dodge the examinations by getting to know friends of the emperor or buying a post with bribes. We can imagine how such things would have displeased Confucius.

DOCUMENTS: THE WISDOM OF THE CHINESE

Document 1

The first two of these sayings are by Confucius; the third comes from Hsun Tsu, one of Confucius's followers.

(a) Attack the evil that is within yourself; do not attack the evil that is in others. Never do to others what you would not like done to you. Love your fellow men.

(b) Those who in private life behave well towards their parents and elder brothers, in public life are seldom inclined to resist the authority of their superiors.

(c) The nature of man is evil – his goodness is only acquired by training. The original nature of man today is to seek for gain. If this desire is followed, trouble and greed result and politeness dies. Man is envious and naturally hates others. Hence the civilising influence of teachers and laws is absolutely necessary.

Source: Adapted from The Analects of Confucius, *translated by Arthur Waley, George Allen and Unwin, 1938, for (a) and (b); (c) quoted in Hilda Hookham,* A Short History of China, *Longman, 1969*

This temple was built in honour of Confucius at Chufu in Shantung province. Confucius is buried nearby. Do you think he would be pleased if he knew about the temple?

Document 2

Taoism had very clear views about the way governments should behave, as these extracts show.

(a) The ancients who practised Tao did not use it to make them clever but to make them simple and natural. If you have difficulty in governing people it is because of too many rules and regulations. He who tries to govern the kingdom by too many laws is only a nuisance to it; while he who governs without them is a blessing. To know these two things is the perfect knowledge of government...

(b) Wealth and snobbery often lead to a man's downfall. If we stop looking for perfect people to put in power, there will be no more jealousies among the people. If we cease to desire goods that are hard to get, there will be no more thieves.... Without law and compulsion men would dwell in harmony.

Source: Adapted from The Way and Its Power, *translated by Arthur Waley, George Allen and Unwin, 1935*

Document 3

Here are two extracts from the teachings of Mo Tsu, who lived shortly after Confucius. His followers are known as Mohists.

(a) There are three things the people worry about; that when they are hungry they will have no food, when they are cold they will have no clothing, and when they are weary they will have no rest.... Now let us try sounding the great bell, striking the rolling drums ... and waving shields and axes in a war dance. Does this do anything to provide food and clothing for the people?

(b) The rulers and ministers must appear at court early and retire late, hearing lawsuits and attending to affairs of government – that is their duty. The gentlemen must employ to the full their minds, directing ministers within the government and abroad, collecting taxes on the products of the hills, forests, lakes and fish weirs, so that the granaries and treasuries will be full – that is their duty. The farmers must leave home early and return late, sowing seeds, planting trees, and gathering large crops of vegetables and grain – that is their duty. Women must rise early and go to bed late, spinning, weaving, producing large quantities of hemp, silk and other fibres, and preparing cloth – that is their duty.

Source: Adapted from Mo Tsu, Basic Writings, *translated by Burton Watson, New York, 1963*

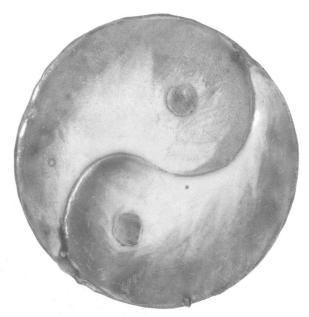

This is the emblem or badge of Taoism. It shows the dark, still side of life balanced by the light, active side. How did the Taoists hope to achieve this balance?

Document 4

Chinese emperors liked to have wise men as their advisers, sometimes listening to Taoists, Mohists and Confucianists. But another group, the Legalists, often had the greatest influence on the way the country was governed. Here is a Legalist *decree* (a command which had to be obeyed by law) issued in the name of one of the emperors of Ch'in, the Chinese state which eventually united all the others into one country.

The people are to be organised into groups of families which should be responsible for each other's good behaviour, and share each other's punishments. Anyone who did not denounce a wrongdoer would be cut in two at the waist; anyone who denounced a wrongdoer would receive the same reward as if he had cut off the head of an enemy soldier. A family which includes two adult males would be divided, or pay double taxes.

Source: Quoted in Hilda Hookham, A Short History of China, *Longman, 1969*

Questions

1. In what ways are Christian teachings similar to the Confucian ideas in Document 1?
2. Imagine you are a Chinese emperor and you have been given all the advice in Documents 2, 3 and 4. Which advice would you follow and which would you reject? Give reasons for your answer.
3. Re-read Document 3 (b) and then write out what you think would be the Mohist teaching on the duties of the staff and pupils at your school!
4. What do the Mohist and Legalist teachings (Documents 3 and 4) tell you about the way the Chinese people lived at this time?
5. Can you find evidence in any of these documents to show that **(a)** the Chinese respected old people, and **(b)** men and women were not equal in ancient China?
6. Re-read the Documents section on the Laws of Hammurabi of Babylon (pages 35–7). Which of the Chinese teachings are most like the Babylonian laws and which would have been against them? Give reasons for your answer.

THE AMERICAS

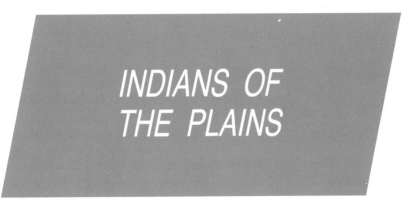

INDIANS OF THE PLAINS

These sharp points, all less than 8 cm long, were chipped from beer bottles by 'Ishi', the last known survivor of his tribe

In 1911 men working in the Californian desert found a lone Indian. They were surprised because it was thought the Indians of that region had died out forty years before. The stranger was starving and miserable. He had burnt his hair, a sign that he was mourning the loss of a relative. The men took him back to the nearest town where he was fed and made comfortable. News of their discovery spread quickly and teachers from the University of California came to talk to the Indian. They hoped to find out the man's tribe from lists of Indian words. As there are thousands of Indian languages they knew that their task would be difficult. At first the Indian did not respond. Then one teacher began to read words of an Indian language called Yahi. The Indian reacted at once. First, he murmured the Yahi words for 'wood' and 'man', then followed these with a stream of other Yahi words. It would now be possible for the Indian and his American friends to understand each other.

The Indian went to live at the Berkeley museum in California. For a person who had probably never seen even a small town, it was surprising that he did not seem worrried by the big city of San Francisco. He learnt some English, dressed in American clothes and enjoyed riding on the trams which climbed the city's steep streets. While he was learning about the modern world, he was also teaching the experts a way of life at least 20,000 years old. He showed them how to make stone tools and weapons, how to twist strands of tough weed into rope, how to choose the best juniper trees for bows and the finest hazel branches for arrows. Quickly, with practised skill, he carved pieces of bone into harpoon tips, burnt holes through dried wood and chipped stone spear-points until they were razor sharp. Because his ancestors had been food-

This is Ishi's 'death mask' – a cast taken from his face after he died

gatherers, he was able to pick out over a hundred different plants and seeds which his people had used for food and medicine.

Most important of all, the Indian told tales and legends and talked about the customs and traditions of a people who had left no written accounts. But he would not tell anyone his name because by Yahi custom only others could speak your name. The staff at Berkeley museum called him 'Ishi', the Yahi word for 'man'. Ishi died in 1916, five years after he had been discovered. He had taught the Americans a lot about their Stone Age past.

By land to America

We call Ishi's ancestors 'Indians' because the explorer Columbus made a mistake. When he reached America in 1492, he thought he had landed in the 'Indies' (islands in the Indian Ocean now called Indonesia). As it happened, people from Asia – including the 'Indians' – had come to the American continent about 25,000 years ago. This was a time when much of the earth was covered in vast sheets of ice. The ice froze the sea and caused the water-level to drop. Land 'bridges' were formed between America and Asia across what is now Canada and the Bering Sea (see map). Today, the United States's Little Diomede island and Russia's Big Diomede island in the Bering Strait are separated by about three miles of sea. In those far-off times the two islands were the tops of mountains which rose above a grassy plain. The first Americans – 'Indians' – crossed these regions from Asia in search of food. When, thousands of years later, the ice melted and the water-level rose, they were cut off from their original homeland.

Once in America, the Indians hunted camel, bison, reindeer, mammoth, woolly rhinoceros and the small American horse. Experts have traced their movements by an important clue – a thin, two-edged spear-point or dart. It does not look very dangerous compared with modern weapons but it proved deadly to animals unprepared for this new threat. We know that animals were killed in very large numbers because of the bones which have been found. At one site in the State of Colorado over a hundred bison skeletons were found in a pit, remnants of just one 'kill'.

Bands of Indians trapped animals in specially dug holes, drove them over cliffs or lured them down ravines where they trampled each other to death. Such mass slaughter reminds us of what was found at Ambrona in Spain (see page 12). By 7000 BC the large American bison and the small horse had been wiped out. The loss of the horse held back the development of the Indians. They had no means of wheeled transport, no beast of burden to carry people and goods, and no suitable animal to pull a plough.

The mound-builders

Indian hunters were always on the move. For this reason they spread across the continent more quickly than a settled farming people might have done. However, by 5000 BC some tribes had begun to add to their food supply by picking plants and seeds. Food-gathering led to food-growing and this, in turn, led to a settled way of life. Traces of Indian houses and graves have been found scattered all over North America. On such sites, archaeologists have also found stone tools, pottery and basket-work, linen and other clothing, tobacco pipes and small statues. The pipes remind us that tobacco is a plant that comes from the Americas. Indians often smoked it as part of religious ceremonies. Their stone pipes often had unusual designs – as we can see from the one pictured here.

A lot of these objects were dug out of earth mounds which had been made by Indians to honour their dead. The bodies or ashes of the dead were placed in holes lined with logs. These log-tombs were then covered with earth. After a time the tomb collapsed, as the wood rotted, but the mound remained. This was then used as a platform to worship the gods. At Poverty Point in Louisiana archaeologists discovered a fine example – a large circle of mounds, set one inside the other with the largest in the middle.

Indian settlements were not all the same. In Wisconsin they were made of wood with a fence and watchtowers round them. The settlement pictured here is much grander. This 'city' was carved out of the cliff face at Mesa Verde in about AD 900. As well as living rooms for four hundred people, Cliff Palace, as it is called, has twenty-three round chambers used for religious ceremonies. The walls were made with uncut stones piled up and held together with mud mortar. Such sites tell us a lot but we often have to rely on guesswork because the Indians had no written language.

This thirteenth-century stone carving found in the state of Oklahoma shows a warrior cutting off his victim's head in some sort of sacrifice. It is part of a pipe which would probably have been smoked only on special occasions

Cliff dwellings at Mesa Verde, in the present-day state of Colorado

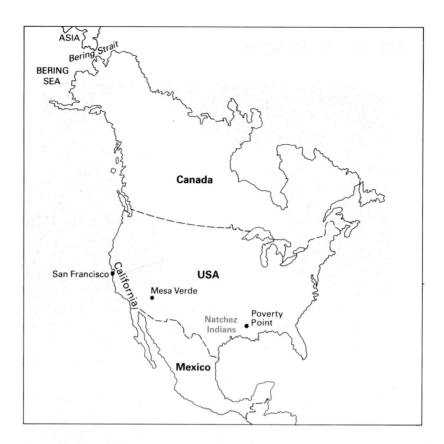

North America. Former 'land bridges' to Asia now lie under the sea

The Natchez Indians

One early North American Indian society survived long enough to be described by French settlers in the eighteenth century. These were the Natchez who seem to have flourished from about AD 1000 onwards. The Natchez lived in groups scattered over what are now the states of Louisiana, Arkansas, Oklahoma and Texas. Some Natchez moved north to the Great Plains region where they were known to the European settlers as the Wichita and Pawnee.

The Natchez appear to have been divided into classes, including lordly 'suns' and 'honoureds', and to have been ruled by a Great Sun. Every noble, whether man or woman, had to marry an ordinary person. A great Sun inherited his crown from his mother who was called the White Woman. Great Sun's brother, if he had one, was called Little Sun and was usually the Great War Chief. When a Great Sun died a number of people were killed or killed themselves as a mark of respect. Later their bones or ashes were dug up, placed in a temple and worshipped. When a White Woman died her husband was strangled by his eldest son. Such executions took place after dancing and pipe-smoking when the victims were probably in a trance.

When the Spanish brought the horse to the Americas in the sixteenth century the lives of many Indians changed. They gave up farming and became hunters again like their ancestors, chasing the smaller bison and other animals on their horses. This is how many people think of the North American Indian but it is only part of the story of Ishi's ancestors.

Sources and questions

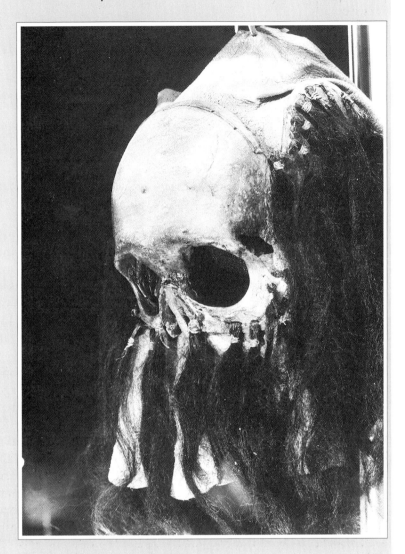

This head-dress was made from part of a human skull. It would have been worn at certain times by a witchdoctor

1. Look at the picture above.
   (**a**) What sort of person do you think might have had their skull used in this way?
   (**b**) What effect do you think this head-dress was meant to have?
   (**c**) For what sort of ceremony might the head-dress have been worn?
   (**d**) Describe other activities that might have taken place at such a ceremony.

2. Look at the picture of Cliff Palace on page 71. What does it tell you about the people who built it?

3. Imagine you are Ishi. Describe what happened when you were found in the Californian desert. Explain how you felt when you were taken to the big city of San Francisco.

4. Compare the view of Indians given in 'western' films with the ways of life described in this chapter.

EL MIRADOR – THE LOST CITY

Pilots flying north from Guatemala City in central America pass over a green mass of jungle. In order not to go off course into Mexico, they keep a low range of hills on their right wing. Only recently it was discovered that these hills are not natural parts of the landscape. Buried under them are houses, palaces, pyramids, streets, stairways and avenues. For these 'hills' are really the lost city of El Mirador, wrapped in vegetation, hidden from the sun and empty for over a thousand years.

El Mirador was one of the first cities built by an Indian people called the Maya. It was founded over two thousand years ago. Some of the city's buildings are large even by modern standards. The biggest pyramid, called the Tigre after the Indian name for the jaguar, is eighteen storeys high. Its base covers an area equal to three modern soccer pitches. The second largest pyramid, called the Danta, is actually taller than the Tigre but narrower at the base. Both are surrounded by groups of buildings. Beside the Danta are two temples, ten or twelve storeys high, and a vast platform

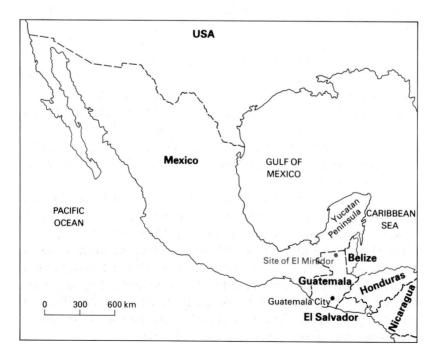

Central America today

The Tigre temple, built by the Maya at El Mirador

extending north and south for 300 metres. A round stone altar is set in its centre.

Pyramids of the gods

The Tigre pyramid faces the rising sun, the Danta the sun when it sets. This is not surprising because the Maya thought they were 'keepers of the sun'. Both pyramids have steep sides with hundreds of steps leading to their tops. At dawn and dusk Maya priests climbed them to worship, perhaps to thank Chac, the raingod, or bow down before Itzamna, their chief god. Maya worship could be bloodthirsty. Sometimes the king or high priest would cut himself, or tear the heart out of a human victim. The Maya believed that such bloodshed was essential because without regular supplies of blood their gods would die. Blood and its colour were often used in Maya art and workmanship. Most walls and statues were painted with a red chemical taken from the earth. This helped preserve the stonework but its colour had religious importance as well.

Most of El Mirador's buildings are made of earth and broken stones held in place by carved stone blocks set in lime-mortar and plaster. They are decorated with *hieroglyphic* letters (see page 46), called glyphs for short, which tell the history of the Maya kings of the city. These glyphs are partly picture-writing and partly based on sounds like a modern alphabet. Unfortunately, they are complicated and have never been properly understood. No 'Rosetta Stone' key has been found to unlock them and what the Maya could have told future ages remains unknown.

The Maya region

Although El Mirador keeps many of its secrets, regular work by archaeologists since 1978 has answered some questions about the buried city. At the height of its power El Mirador housed thousands of people, including architects, engineers, craftsmen, astronomers, artists, priests, warriors, merchants, and peasants. It lay like a spider at the centre of a web of roads, canals and rivers which led to smaller towns such as Tintal and Nakbe (see map). Through this network flowed the essentials for Maya civilisation – granite and marble from Belize, salt and pottery from Yucatan, seashells and coral from the Pacific and Caribbean. These goods were moved by canoe or on the backs of men and women, for the Maya had no wheeled transport or beast of burden. In about AD 150 something went wrong. Either famine or war destroyed the city's wealth and power. El Mirador began a slow decline into emptiness and silence.

Maya art and science

El Mirador marked a beginning, not an end. Other Maya cities sprang up in central America and Maya civilisation spead through the Yucatan and into parts of present-day Mexico, Honduras, El Salvador and Belize. The basis of this prosperity was the farming of maize, beans and chilli peppers. The Maya were skilful farmers who controlled the landscape; the jungle only took over after they had gone. Swamps were drained and turned into fertile land, dams

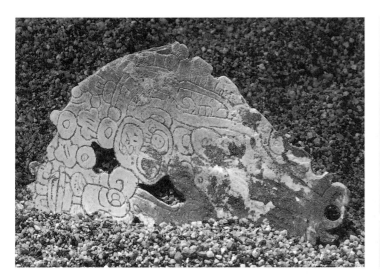

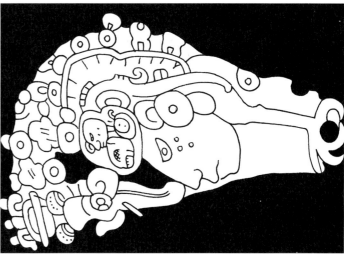

and irrigation ditches constructed and man-made fields set on platforms. A key to Maya success was the way they saved water in a hot climate. Water was stored in reservoirs and household containers. There were even carefully-placed tanks taking rainwater from the sloping sides of temples and pyramids.

The Maya were fine craftsmen who made statues, pottery and jewels. Their carving on jade (a beautiful green stone) is thought to be among the finest produced in ancient America. All this was done with stone tools. Glyphs, which were often painted on walls, were also carved on stone or inked on folding books made from deerskin or lime-coated paper. Those which have been translated show that the Maya were clever astronomers and mathematicians who worked out the number of days in the year correctly.

The Maya calendar was made up of eighteen 'months' of 20 days each, plus a five-day period (believed to be unlucky) to make up the 365. This calendar was more accurate than the one used in Europe until the sixteenth century and in Britain until 1752. There was also a 'sacred year' invented by the priests. It lasted 260 days and every fifty-two years the sacred year and the actual year started together. This was treated as an important occasion with feasting and ceremonies.

Maya designs made clever use of animals and birds, as we can see from this piece of Caribbean shell which has been carved into a pendant. The drawing of the design shows how a long-beaked cormorant is curled round the face of a man. On top of his head is a cluster of glyphs which have not been translated

The city by the blue river

Maya cities prospered until about AD 900. One city from this period has been named Rio Azul, the Spanish for blue river. It lies in northern Guatemala and seems to have ruled a small empire. The city itself has massive memorial temples, the tallest of which is 47 metres high. Palaces for the ruling families were encircled by smaller houses in which workmen, scribes (secretaries) and priests lived.

Some very interesting tombs have been uncovered in Rio Azul. The grave of a king or noble pictured here was opened in 1985. The corpse was important enough to be buried with pottery and other objects. These showed that he had been wealthy when alive

Grave of a Maya king or nobleman. It was uncovered in the 1980s at Rio Azul

and may have been intended for his use in the after-world. The glyph on the boulder above the skeleton tells us about the moon goddess. Below is what looks like the head of a monster.

The Maya religion probably started with some kind of nature worship aimed at bringing good harvests. It had lots of gods of the earth, sky and underworld, including gods of fire, rain, wind and the maize – the crop on which the whole civilisation depended. Some gods were bad and some were good. The Maya thought that the earth was square, with each corner having its own colour and religious importance. The colours were red for east, yellow for south, black for west and white for north. Two symbols of Maya power were the jaguar and the snake. They were shown on walls, statues, pottery and masks.

Archaeologists found signs that Rio Azul was abandoned in about AD 535 but reoccupied later. We do not know why but a war with a rival city may have been the reason. About AD 830 the city was captured by invaders from the north who killed the ruling families and ransacked and damaged the buildings. It is possible that most of the people living in the city who survived were taken away as slaves. Rio Azul, like El Mirador, was left to the jungle.

At its height, the Maya civilisation probably extended to between three and four million people. But by AD 900 quarrels, wars and perhaps famine or disease, led to its collapse. Later Indian peoples of this region, particularly the Toltecs and Aztecs, copied the customs, art and ways of life of the Maya.

DOCUMENTS: THE DISCOVERY OF THE MAYA

Document 1

Two of the first people to start looking for Maya cities were John Stephens (1805–52), an American lawyer, and Frederick Catherwood (1799–1854), a British artist and architect. In 1839 they went to Central America where they had many adventures, including being captured by soldiers in a civil war. Stephens described their journey in a book called *Incidents of Travel in Central America*. They were very excited by their first sight of a Maya city which was known as Copan. Stephens later bought it for 50 dollars from a local Spanish official!

> Soon we came to the bank of a river, and saw directly opposite a stone wall, perhaps a hundred feet [30 metres] high, with furze growing out of the top.... [Later] we came upon a colossal stone figure about fourteen feet [4½ metres] high.... It was the figure of a man curiously and richly dressed ... the face was solemn, stern and frightening ... at a distance of three feet was a large block of stone which we called an altar.

Source: John Stephens, Incidents of Travel in Central America.

Catherwood made this drawing (left) of the stone statue mentioned in Document 1. Stephens wrote later, 'Catherwood found difficulty in drawing. He made several attempts but this idol seemed to defy his art.' Look at the drawing and compare it with this model of the original figure (right). Do you think Catherwood should have been dissatisfied with his drawing?

Document 2

Later Stephens and Catherwood were very impressed with the ruins they found at Chichen Itza. This is possibly the greatest Maya city so far found.

> We lived in the ruined palace ... we went to the desolated temples and fallen stairways and wherever we moved we saw evidence of Maya taste and Maya artistic skill ... we looked back to the past, cleared away the gloomy forest, and imagined every building when it was perfect, with its terraces and pyramids, its grand, lofty and imposing statues and ornaments. We imagined the strange people who gazed at us sadly from the walls; pictured them, in fancy costumes and dressed in plumes of feathers, climbing the terraces of the palace and the steps leading to the temples ... nothing ever impressed me more than this once great and lovely city, over-turned, desolate and lost ... overgrown with trees for miles around and without even a name.

Source: As for Document 1

This Maya vase (20 centimetres high) is decorated with a picture of a Maya god. He is known to experts as 'L' and is shown sitting on a throne. Women kneel before him and a rabbit writes down what he is saying. Can you think of another ancient people who drew pictures on their vases?

Document 3

Modern explorers have followed in the footsteps of Stephens and Catherwood. This extract is from Ray T. Matheny, an American archaeologist, who has worked at El Mirador since 1979.

> I resolved to spend my career studying this superb Maya site.... In the first season we took advantage of work done by unlikely helpers – looters. They had been quite active in El Mirador in recent years, excavating dwellings and public buildings, searching for ancient burials containing coloured vessels adorned with hieroglyphs and human and animal figures. Such vessels command big ... prices.

Source: R. T. Matheny, 'El Mirador: an early Maya metropolis uncovered', in National Geographic *magazine, September 1987*

Document 4

In this extract an historian sums up the Maya achievement.
Aboriginal means 'primitive' or 'first known' and Neolithic refers
to the New Stone Age.

> Of the five basic steps in human advancement – (1) the control
> of fire; (2) the invention of agriculture; (3) the domestication of
> animals; (4) tools of metal; (5) discovery of the wheel – the
> Maya knew only two. When their whole achievement is judged
> in the light of their limitations, which are equal to those of
> Neolithic Man, we may safely say that the ancient Maya were
> the most brilliant aboriginal people on this planet.

Source: Adapted from Sylvanus G. Morley, The Ancient Maya,
Stanford University, 1946

Questions

1. Why do you think Stephens and Catherwood decided to call a
   large block of stone an altar? Why do you think Maya cities
   have Spanish names?
2. In Document 2 what does Stephens mean when he says, 'the
   strange people who gazed sadly at us from the walls'?
3. What are looters? Why would they be interested in ancient
   burials? How can they sometimes be of help to archaeologists?
4. Using your knowledge of what the Maya had *not* mastered,
   what were the two 'steps in human advancement' they had
   mastered (Document 4)?
5. What evidence is there in these documents that Maya ruins
   were not thought to be of any value in 1839 but are regarded as
   valuable now? Why do you think opinions have changed about
   them?
6. What other ancient people built pyramids? In what ways were
   they different from Maya pyramids?

GREECE

CRETE AND MYCENAE

This wall painting shows the sport of bull-leaping, which may have suggested the Minotaur story. The man in the picture (coloured red) is about to be caught by the woman (coloured white) behind the bull

A famous poet of ancient Greece called Homer told a story about the nearby island of Crete. The son of King Minos of Crete was said to have been killed by the king of the Greek city of Athens. In revenge, Minos captured Athens and ordered seven young men and seven young women to be sent to Crete every nine years. These prisoners were driven into a *labyrinth* (a maze of tunnels) where they wandered lost until they were eaten by the Minotaur, a monster with a bull's head and the body of a man.

According to Homer's story, after some years Theseus, son of a

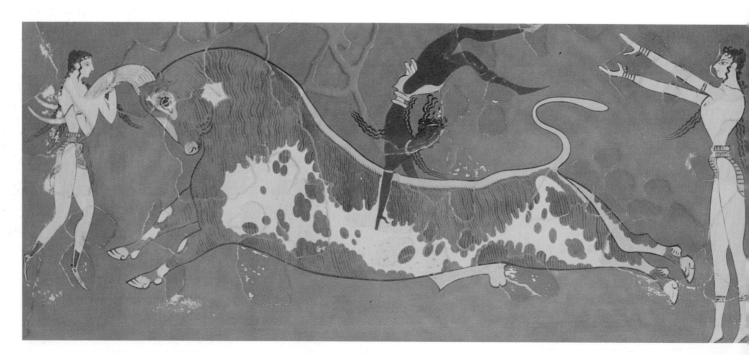

later king of Athens, offered to go as one of the victims and try to kill the Minotaur. The Cretan king's daughter Ariadne, fell in love with the prince. Before he entered the labyrinth she gave him a sword and some string. Theseus laid this string behind him and when he met the Minotaur he killed it with his sword. Then he found his way back to the entrance by following the trail of string. Theseus sailed back to Greece in triumph but forgot that he had arranged to hoist white sails on his ship if he was successful. When his father, King Aegeus, saw black sails instead of white he thought his son was dead. Overcome with grief, he threw himself into the sea and drowned. This is how the Aegean Sea was named.

The palace of Knossos

What could have given rise to the legend of the Minotaur? Some clues began to emerge at the turn of the twentieth century when Sir Arthur Evans, an English archaeologist, went to Crete to look at some ancient walls and other remains which had been dug from a mound at Knossos. Beginning in 1900, Evans's team of workers uncovered the remains of a large palace set round a central courtyard. The palace contained many passages and tunnels as well as a complicated underground drainage system.

Most of the rooms in the palace of Knossos had been used to store grain. Others were full of precious stones and one contained a throne. A staircase of brilliant white stone was decorated with beautiful columns which tapered at the bottom. The walls were covered with brightly coloured paintings showing dark-haired women and athletic men. The women wore long gowns and had thick make-up and jewelled combs in their hair. The men were dressed in short trousers and had feathered head-dresses. In some pictures the men and women were somersaulting over bulls in an arena. Here were some of the ingredients of the old story – the labyrinth, the bulls and the great palace of a king.

A great deal of this ancient Cretan world lies buried forever under farmland. Its full story will never be known. But the size of the palace suggests that a population of at least 40,000 once lived at Knossos. Evans's discoveries showed that Cretan civilisation had flourished since at least 3000 BC. Because some of its kings were named Minos, he called this civilisation Minoan.

Minoan life

The Minoans were mainly fishermen and sailors who lived by trading or piracy. The island had large forests which supplied wood for shipbuilding and long beaches on which it was easy to drag a boat ashore. No traces of their ships or dockyards have been discovered but as there are no forts on land it seems they relied mainly on a fleet for defence. Crete stood conveniently on ancient trade routes between Egypt, Palestine, Asia Minor and Greece.

This snake-goddess figure is made out of ivory and gold. Minoans seem to have believed that a goddess of this kind 'protected' their houses

The Cretans were the first Europeans known to have been civilised. They grew corn and fruit and made articles from gold, silver, copper and tin. Their pots and jugs were decorated with pictures of octopuses, plants and, sometimes, a curling 'S' line. They also made tiny statues from ivory or wood. Their religion seems to have been partly based on an Earth Mother (see page 17) who was worshipped in woodland shrines. She was offered fruit, poppies and perhaps bulls as a sacrifice.

In a warm, sunlit land, the Minoans lived a generally peaceful life threatened only by earthquakes. About 1500 BC for example, the island of Thera, now called Santorini, 100 kilometres from Crete, blew up. Enormous waves, travelling at great speed, destroyed many Cretan coastal towns while other earth tremors shattered the palace of Knossos. Evans himself experienced a slight earthquake in 1926. 'A dull sound rose from the ground, like the muffled roar of an angry bull', he wrote. Perhaps this was the sort of sound that gave rise to the legend of the Minotaur?

While digging at Knossos, Evans found thousands of clay tablets with symbols and signs carved on them. There were two different kinds which experts called Linear A and B. Each seemed to have developed from the outlines of an earlier picture-writing. Linear A remains a mystery even though examples of it have been found all over Crete. It is probably the language of the ancient Cretans. In 1953 an English architect, Michael Ventris, discovered that Linear B was a shorthand form of Greek. This provided a link with the mainland of Greece because Linear B tablets had been found in several Greek cities, including Pylos and Mycenae.

Mycenae and Troy

The Linear B discovery confirmed the view of historians that one of the earliest of Greek peoples, the Mycenaeans, had conquered Crete in about 1450 BC. This conquest was very important because the Mycenaeans copied the ways of the more civilised Cretans. As a result Minoan civilisation entered the mainland of Europe.

The chief Mycenaean cities – Thebes, Pylos, Tiryns and Mycenae itself – were all defended by forts. These were strongly built, as we can see from the picture on page 87 of the Lion Gate at

A linear B tablet, made of clay baked hard by fire

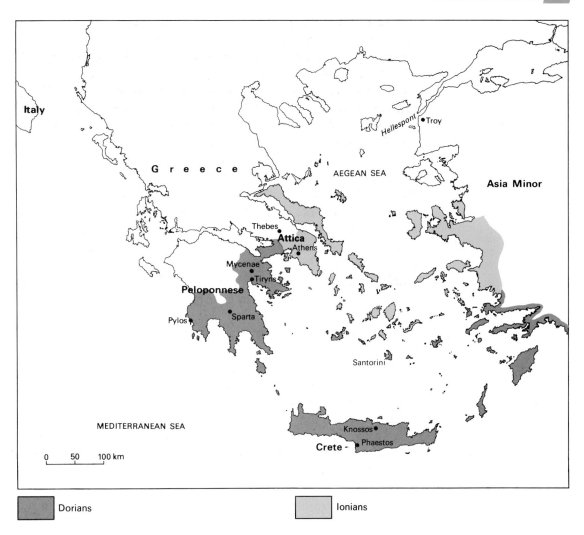

The early Greek world

Dorians

Ionians

Mycenae. The Mycenaeans were keen fighters who painted war scenes on their palace walls, not beautiful women as the Minoans had done. They hunted the wolf and wild boar and grew wheat, barley, millet and peas. They also cultivated vines and made a wine that was sweetened with honey.

Mycenaean soldiers were well armed with bronze swords and spears and large 'tower' shields which protected them from head to foot. When their warrior-kings died they were sometimes buried in a stone tomb shaped like a beehive. One of the largest tombs of this kind, at Mycenae, is known as the Treasury of Atreus after one of their kings. It is called a treasury because a Mycenaean king was buried with gold belts, weapons, precious rings and necklaces. His face was covered with a gold mask.

Mycenaean merchant ships sailed all over the eastern Mediterranean, to Syria, Palestine and Egypt. Trading brought them into conflict with other merchants and sometimes led to war. It seems that in about 1150 BC the Mycenaeans fought a long trade war with Troy, a city in Asia Minor (modern Turkey). A story from this so-called Trojan war was made famous by Homer in his long poem, *The Iliad* – meaning the story of Ilium, another name for Troy.

Homer and Schliemann

According to Homer, the Mycenaeans fought battles outside the walls of Troy for ten years but failed to take the city. In the end they pretended to sail away, leaving a large, hollow wooden horse outside the city walls. One Greek stayed behind to tell the Trojans that the horse was a gift to the gods and must not be taken into the city or the gods would be angry with the Greeks. The trick worked. When the Trojans heard this tale they broke down part of their city wall and dragged the horse inside. But the horse was full of Greek soldiers led by Odysseus, who had thought of the scheme. After dark, the Greeks climbed out, attacked the guards and opened the gates. The rest of the Greek army returned and Troy was taken and destroyed.

Like the Minotaur legend, much of Homer's *Iliad* is far-fetched. However it contains some very detailed descriptions of events and of the Mycenaeans' way of life. In the last century a German called Heinrich Schliemann decided to follow up the clues in *The Iliad* in the hope of finding the lost city of Troy. After teaching himself Greek and other languages to help him in his search, Schliemann went to Turkey and organised an archaeological expedition. Using Homer's words as a guide, he made his way to a large mound at Hissarlik. Here his workmen uncovered the remains of nine cities, one on top of the other. The Troy about which Homer wrote stood on top of six earlier ruins.

Schliemann also led expeditions to Mycenae where he found more clues to the Greek past. In his poem, Homer tells how Agamemnon, the Greek leader, had been murdered on his return from the capture of Troy. His body and the bodies of some of his nobles were said to have been buried by the Lion Gate. Schliemann dug near the gate and found six graves containing nineteen bodies. The skeletons wore clothes and armour of the kind described by Homer. Schliemann even thought that one body was that of Agamemnon. Excitedly he gazed upon the face behind its gold mask. After a few seconds it crumbled to dust. We now know it was not the corpse of the Greek hero but of a soldier who lived 250 years before Agamemnon's time.

Around 1250 BC wars and piracy made trading in the eastern

The mask Schliemann thought belonged to Agamemnon

The Lion Gate leading into the fortress at Mycenae. The idea of carving two animals facing each other comes from Crete

Mediterranean more difficult. As a result the Mycenaean cities grew poorer. When the Dorians, a fierce mountain people, invaded from the north, armed with superior iron weapons, the Mycenaeans were overthrown. The Dorians were a stern, disciplined race who treated those they conquered as slaves. Many Mycenaeans fled to Attica to escape them. These refugees are known as Ionians after the Greek dialect they spoke. Dorians and Ionians became the two most famous Greek races. The chief Dorian city was Sparta; the most important Ionian city was Athens.

Sources and questions

1. Towards the end of his life, Sir Arthur Evans looked back on his achievements at Knossos.

   > It is now some forty years since – lured [attracted] by the earliest folk traditions of Greece and encouraged by . . . signs of an unknown script – I first explored the site [of Knossos], at a time when there was nothing to be seen above ground apart from the tumbled remains of a wall. The work of the spade has now brought out the truth of the old traditions that made Knossos – the home of Minos – the most ancient centre of civilised life in Greece.

   Source: Sir Arthur Evans in his Foreword to J. D. S. Pendlebury, Knossos and its Dependencies, Macdonald, 1954

   (a) What does Evans mean by 'work of the spade'? Why was such work so important in Crete?
   (b) What folk stories or traditions had 'lured' Evans to Crete in the first place?
   (c) Evans claims to have shown the 'truth' of the old traditions. How much was fact and how much was fiction?
   (d) In what form did Evans find the 'unknown script' which interested him? Did he discover what it meant?

2. Look at the painting of bull-leaping on page 82.
   (a) Why do you think this wall-painting was called 'The Toreador' by the archaeologists who uncovered it?
   (b) Can you think of any reason why the man is coloured red and the women white?
   (c) How does this sport seem to be different from modern versions of such contests?

3. Can you guess how quarrels might have broken out between merchants of different nations – and how such quarrels could have led to full-scale wars?

4. Look at the picture of the Lion Gate on page 87.
   (a) Why do you think the Mycenaeans chose a lion for a badge? What does it suggest about them?
   (b) Does this picture tell you anything about Mycenaean building methods?
   (c) What kind of old buildings in Britain remind you of this gate and wall?

THE CITY STATES AND THEIR GODS

Today if you look at a map of the Mediterranean region you will see the boundaries of a country, Greece, with its capital city, Athens. In ancient times, however, most Greek towns were self-governing and independent; there was no state called Greece. The Greeks knew that they belonged to a race with a shared homeland and a language of its own. But generally they were loyal only to the *polis* (city state) they came from.

The Greek polis

When Greeks spoke of a *polis* they could mean the people as well as the place. A *polis* was a small community by modern standards. Only Athens and two Greek settlements overseas, at Syracuse and Acragas in Sicily, ever had more than 20,000 citizens. Women and slaves have to be added to this figure as only free men with the right to vote were called citizens. Most city states were much smaller than Athens and some were tiny. Mycenae, for example, after its decline, once sent an army of eighty-four men to a battle!

A *polis* had enough farmland to feed its people and was usually near the sea so that its citizens could earn a living by trade or fishing. In earliest times these cities were normally ruled by kings. Such monarchies were often followed by the rule of a few noble families (called an *aristocracy*). Some cities were ruled for a time by a *tyrant*. The word did not mean that he was necessarily wicked or unpopular, only that he had seized power and not been elected. The city states eventually gave voting rights to either all their citizens (a *democracy*) or just the richer ones (an *oligarchy*). Political rights were never given to women.

The most freedom-loving *polis* was Athens. Here every man was encouraged to help govern the city by attending its assembly. Voters came by boat or horse from outlying districts and the streets were empty by the time the assembly met. A long rope was swept across the *agora* (market-place). Any citizen who lingered there and was brushed by the rope was fined for not being on the Pnyx Hill, the meeting-place of the assembly. A citizen of a *polis* like Athens would never feel forgotten or ignored. His rulers

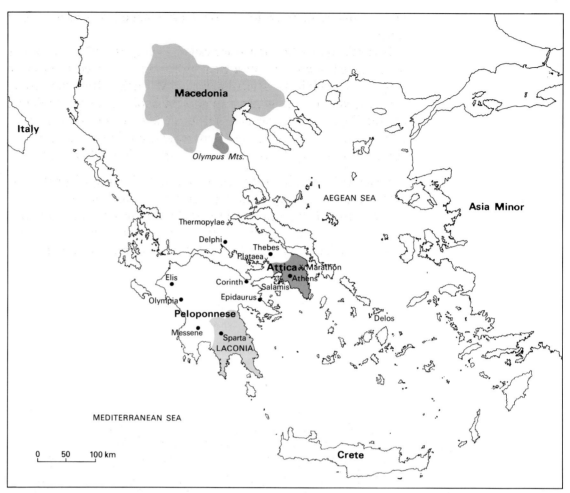

Ancient Greece

would be known to him personally and he could argue with them if he disagreed with what they were doing. Nearly all government jobs were filled by drawing lots each year. In this way power was shared amongst as many men as possible instead of being concentrated into the hands of a few.

Sparta

Most of the interesting or beautiful things about the Greeks were at their best in Athens. Its sculpture and pottery, its buildings, its plays, its ways of government are still copied and admired today. Its great rival, Sparta, was very different. Few ancient cities even looked like Sparta. Travellers approaching it noticed at once that it had no walls. This was to make its soldiers fight harder when attacked! Similarly, no lights were to be seen after dark – in order to make its soldiers skilled night-fighters.

The Spartans did not mix with other Greeks if they could help it. The only true Spartan citizen was called a *Spartiate*. Most outsiders or prisoners-of-war were made slaves – called *helots*. The helots were very badly treated. They were beaten if they did not work hard enough and killed if they protested. The Spartans were able to live on the labour of slaves because they were soldiers.

Only a tough fighting force could have hoped to crush a helot rebellion.

It is said that a Spartan ruler called Lycurgus – who may never have existed – worked out a training scheme designed to produce magnificent soldiers. Selection began at birth. Only the strong were allowed to live. Weak or deformed babies were left to die on Mount Tygetus or thrown off its steep sides. At seven years of age all boys were taken from their families and put in special barracks. Here life was very hard, as a Greek writer, Xenophon, tells us:

> Instead of softening their feet with shoes, [Lycurgus's] rule was to make them hardy by going barefoot.... Instead of pampering them with a variety of clothes, his rule was for them to wear ... a single garment the whole year through ... so they would be better prepared to withstand extremes of heat and cold.

Ruins of the agora (market place) of ancient Athens

During their training, young Spartans were also kept short of food and forced to steal rations from grown-ups. Boys not caught stealing were admired; those who were discovered were beaten severely. Even after he was grown up and married, a Spartiate had his meals in a military club and spent very little time with his family. Meals consisted of barley bread, figs, cheese and a kind of haggis. The haggis was so revolting that after one dinner a foreigner remarked, 'Now I understand why Spartans do not fear death.'

It was easy to laugh at the Spartans – and many Greeks did. But there were things to admire about them. They were very loyal to their leaders. They allowed girls as well as boys to do physical training, something few other Greek cities would permit. Spartans also respected old people. At one Olympic Games an elderly man was unable to find a seat because of the crowds. Everyone ignored him until he reached the section where Spartans were sitting. Then every man rose and offered him a seat. Thankfully he murmured, 'All Greeks know what is right but only Spartans do it.'

Even the bravest enemy felt fear when the red-coated Spartiates moved into battle, performing their complicated drill. Spartans were rarely defeated; those that were, died where they stood. Any retreat to safety was out of the question. It was said that Spartan soldiers never turned their backs upon the enemy so all their wounds were in the front. Sparta's citizens left no beautiful temples, fine plays or poetry, but today a rough, hard and disciplined way of life is often called Spartan.

The Pantheon

The Greeks learnt a lot from the people they met on their travels. This is shown in their religion. Some of the gods they worshipped were very similar to those of Egypt, Crete and other places. Like most ancient peoples, they explained nature by saying it was the work of a god or goddess. The sea was controlled by one god, the land by another. A rich harvest meant that the earth goddess was pleased. Storms, famine and disease were signs that the gods were angry.

To the Greeks, all virtues and skills were gifts from the gods. Consequently there were gods of wisdom and beauty, of laughter and dancing. Any gifts which the gods had given could be taken away. This frightened the Greeks who were always trying to find out what a god wanted, or what might have angered him or her. When they wanted to find out a god's wishes, the Greeks consulted the *Pythia*, or priestess, at Delphi. This woman sacrificed animals and kept an eye open for strange signs. For instance, a mouse gnawing through a bag or a cock crowing were bad signs. While in a trance, she was thought to be able to tell what the gods wanted. However such *oracles* were often in riddles which were difficult to understand.

Homer's writings were the basis of Greek ideas about the gods.

Statue of a Spartan soldier. Their helmets were beaten from single sheets of bronze. Today no one knows how this was done

Bronze head of a Greek god. It may be Poseidon (ruler of the sea) or Zeus (father of the gods)

Homer described gods and goddesses who were almost human. They spoke to people through dreams and sometimes took on human shape to join in a battle or play a trick on someone who had annoyed them. They lived, it was said, on Mount Olympus, the peak of which could be seen from many parts of Greece. Here they behaved very much like the Greeks themselves, quarrelling, scheming, loving and hating.

The following gods and goddesses, known as the *Pantheon*, were worshipped as a sort of heavenly family.

Zeus, father of the gods and men.
Poseidon, ruler of the sea.
Apollo, god of sun, music and fortune-telling.
Athena, goddess of wisdom and the arts of peace.
Demeter, goddess of the earth.
Hera, Zeus's wife and goddess of marriage.
Hephaestus, god of fire and metalwork.
Hermes, messenger of the gods and ruler of the winds
Artemis, goddess of the moon and hunting.
Hestia, goddess of the home.
Ares, god of war.
Aphrodite, goddess of love and beauty.
Dionysus, god of wine and plays.

Only the chief gods, or *Olympians*, belonged to the Pantheon. There was also Pan, the god of flocks and woodlands, and numerous semi-gods such as *Naiads*, who lived in the water, and *Dryads*, who lived in trees. At times there seem to have been as many Greek gods as there were people! Most cities had favourite gods and even important families sometimes claimed to have a god as their founder.

Gods and sportsmen

The Greek year was full of religious festivals. These could take many forms, including processions, solemn sacrifices and sporting events. The most famous sporting occasion was the Olympic Games. Every four years sportsmen from all over the Greek world gathered at Olympia, where temples and stadiums were built from the ruins of an old city. At first only foot races were held. The runners ran up and down in a straight line, not round a circular track as they do today. In later times jumping and throwing events, boxing, wrestling, chariot and mule racing were added.

Some contests involved more than one skill. The *pentathlon*, for example, combined running, long jumping, wrestling, javelin and discus throwing. Some events were very rough. The *pancration* was unarmed combat with eye-gouging, arm-twisting and kicking allowed. Men occasionally died as a result. The five-day festival ended with the winners being crowned with sacred olive wreaths. Their names were recorded in a golden book and they were allowed to wear purple robes like a king. To the Greeks such champions represented the power of the gods on earth. They believed that only those whom the gods loved could win at the Olympics.

Statue of an athlete using an instrument called a strigil. To remove dirt and sweat after exercising, oil was put on the skin and then scraped off in this way. Why do you think the Greeks (and the Romans after them) chose this method of cleaning themselves?

DOCUMENTS: GREEK SPORTS

Document 1

To the Greeks sport was a way of worshipping the gods. Sporting contests, called games, were held on special occasions such as festivals and funerals. They were also held at particular places such as Delphi and Olympia. This extract from Homer's *Iliad* describes a contest during funeral games held in honour of Patroclus, friend of the Greek hero, Achilles. Patroclus had been killed in battle by the Trojans.

> Achilles announced the prizes for the boxing match. The winner would get a strong, six-year old mule . . . the loser a two-handed goblet. Huge, tough Epeius sprang up. Laying hold of the mule, he shouted, 'Anyone is welcome to the goblet, but the mule must be mine! . . . I have yet to meet the Greek who could outbox me. My challenger's friends should stand ready to carry him away when he has been battered. . . .'
>
> There was a deep silence. Gallant Eurylus alone dared face him. Diomedes prepared him for the fight, tightening his boxing belt, winding rawhide straps across the flat of each hand, all the while giving encouragement. . . .
>
> Epeius and Eurylus advanced towards each other. Both raised their weighted fists and the match began. They were soon sweating hard, grinding their teeth and going at it hammer and tongs until, at last, Epeius rushed in. . . . Eurylus, crouching to block his leading fist, caught a powerful uppercut on the cheekbone. Up went Eurylus, and then down, like a fish! . . . They fetched him a goblet, while he spat blood from his torn mouth.

Source: Adapted from The Anger of Achilles, *Homer's Iliad, translated by Robert Graves, Cassell, 1959*

Document 2

The first Olympic Games were held in 776 BC as funeral games for Hippodamia, the daughter of a Greek king. They grew into the most important sporting event in Greece. The modern Olympic Games copy them, although in ancient times no women were allowed to compete or watch and most athletes ran, wrestled or boxed naked. These extracts are about spectators at such events.

(a) Some unpleasant and hard things happen in life... And do they not happen at the Olympics? Do you not swelter? Are you not cramped and crowded? Are you not bathed in sweat and drenched whenever it rains? Do you not have enough of noise and shouting and other annoyances? But I fancy you put up with it because of the memorable spectacle.

Source: *Epictetus*, Discourses, *Leob Classical Library*

(b) Aristonicus was cheered by the crowd because he had the courage to stand up to Clitomachus, the champion. As the bout continued, Aristonicus showed himself Clitomachus's equal. When he landed a well placed punch, there was a burst of applause and shouts of 'Keep up your courage, Aristonicus.' Clitomachus then stepped back, caught his breath, turned to the audience and asked why they were cheering Aristonicus and supporting him as hard as they could. 'Have I committed a foul or broken the rules? Do you not know that I am fighting for the glory of Greece, Aristonicus for that of Egypt? Would you prefer an Egyptian to carry off the Olympic wreath by beating Greeks?' When the spectators heard these words, it is reported, they changed their attitude and cheered Clitomachus so much that Aristonicus was eventually beaten.

Source: as above

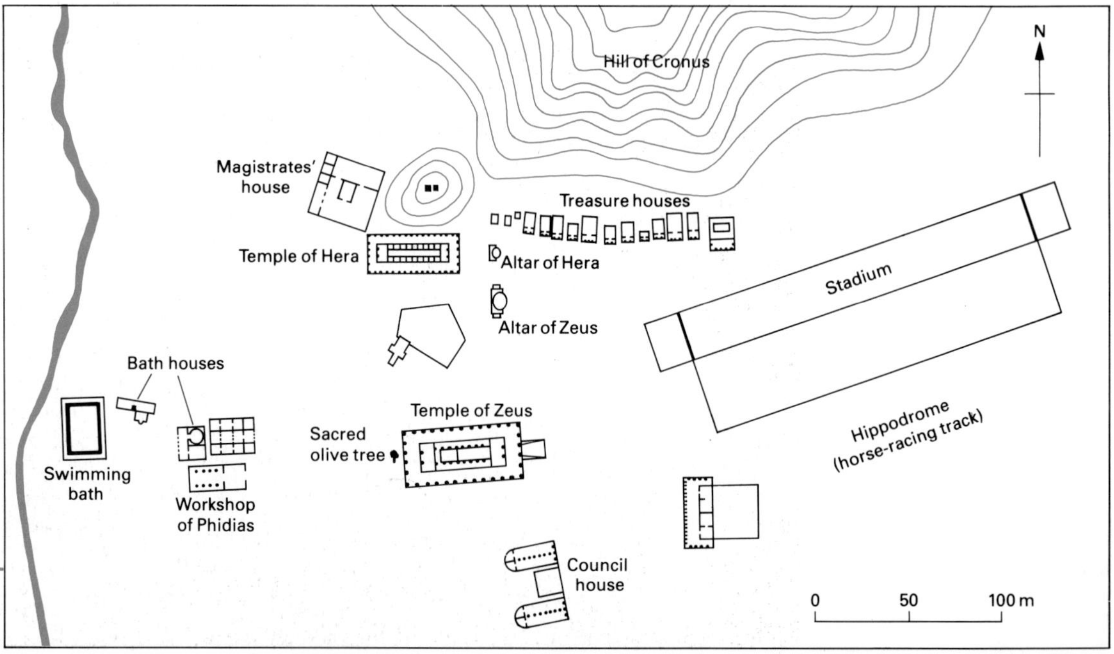

A plan of the Olympic stadium about 500 BC. Phidias, whose workshops are shown on the left, was a famous Greek sculptor. Can you work out what he might have been doing at the Olympics? What evidence is there in this diagram of a connection between Greek sport and religion?

Document 3

Here are two different views of why men competed in the Olympic Games. The first is from Alcibiades, a rich Athenian, who was trying to persuade the city assembly to give him command of a military expedition. The second is from a famous Greek poet, Pindar, describing the victory of a youth in a wrestling bout at Delphi.

(a) Think of the magnificent showing I made at the Olympic Games. I entered seven chariots for the chariot race, a larger number than any private individual before. With these chariots, I took first, second and fourth places, and did everything in suitably grand style. It is the custom to honour such successes and at the same time they give an impression of power.

Source: Adapted from Thucydides, Peloponnesian War, *J. M. Dent, translated by R. Crawley, 1910*

(b) He who wins, of a sudden, some noble prize,
In the rich years of youth.
Is raised high with hope, his manhood takes wings;
He has in his heart what is better than wealth,
But brief is the season of man's delight. . . .
Yet when god-given splendour visits him,
A bright radiance plays over him, and how sweet is life!

Source: Pindar, quoted in H. D. F. Kitto, The Greeks, *Penguin, 1951*

Delphi today. Its sportsground is set on a mountainside and is one stadion *(about 185 metres) long. Notice the starting line. What modern word connected with sport is derived from 'stadion'?*

Document 4

Not every Greek approved of sports and sportsmen. In the second century AD, a writer called Lucian invented two characters, Anacharsis, who disliked sportsmen, and Solon, who admired athletic skills and training. This is part of their conversation.

Anacharsis: Why do your young men behave like this, Solon? Some are grappling and tripping each other, some throttling, intertwining in the mud like so many pigs wallowing. They put down their heads and begin to push, and crash their foreheads together like a pair of rival rams. . . . We shall surely see these poor fellows spit out their teeth in a minute. . . . Now what I want to know is what is the good of it all? To me it looks more like madness than anything else. . . .

Solon: I regret there are no games at the moment for you to see. You should be there sitting in the midst of the spectators, looking at the men's physical courage and beauty, their marvellous condition. . . their unconquerable spirit and their determined pursuit of victory. This makes them good guardians of our country and defenders of our freedom.

Anacharsis: I see, Solon, when an enemy invades, you anoint yourselves with oil, dust yourselves over and go forth sparring at them. . . . Why, if I were to draw this little dagger they'd all run away.

Source: Adapted from Lucian of Samosata, Anacharsis or On Physical Exercise, *Loeb Classical Library*

Questions

1. Using these documents as a guide, summarise the reasons why the Greeks held athletic games. Which do you think was the most important reason?
2. In what ways were the boxing matches described in Document 1 and Document 2 (b) different from modern contests? Are there any similarities with boxing matches today?
3. From these documents do you think the Greeks were amateur or professional sportsmen? Do you think they competed fairly? Give reasons for your answer.
4. Would Solon or Anacharsis (Document 4) have agreed with the writer of Document 2 about the Olympic Games being 'a memorable spectacle'?
5. How might Solon have answered the point made by Anacharsis in his second speech? Write Solon's reply.
6. In what ways does a modern Olympic Games depart from Greek traditions? What do you think the ancient Greeks would have thought of the modern Olympics?

THE PERSIAN WARS

The Greek city states enjoyed many centuries of self-rule before they were conquered, first by Macedonian Greeks (see Chapter 17) and later by the Romans. Before this the only serious threat to their freedom came from Persia. By 500 BC the empire founded by Cyrus the Great (see page 33) had spread as far as Asia Minor, where some Greek settlements were overrun. In the 490s these settlements rebelled against the Persians, helped by Athens and another Greek city state called Eretria, but they were defeated. Soon afterwards King Darius, Cyrus's grandson, demanded obedience from the cities of Greece. These cities, led by Athens, refused, so Darius sent an army to punish them.

Marathon

The Persians landed near the plain of Marathon, a coastal region to the north-east of Athens. The Athenians, together with men

On this decorated bowl made in the fifth century BC we can see Greek hoplites (footsoldiers) fastening on their armour. One man is taking his shield from its wrappings. In ancient Greece all but the poorest men were trained and experienced soldiers

from the city of Plataea, marched out to meet them. We know a great deal about the wars which followed because a Greek historian, Herodotus, wrote an account. Herodotus tells us that the Athenians sent a runner – a trained athlete called Pheidippides – to ask the Spartans for help. The Spartans were in the middle of a religious festival. They promised to come as soon as it ended, which would be at the next full moon.

The Greeks and Persians faced each other for some days without fighting, each army playing a waiting game. The Athenians, greatly outnumbered, were hoping that the Spartans would arrive. The Persians delayed attacking because they hoped that traitors inside Athens might open the city gates to them. Finally, Miltiades, the Athenian commander, decided to attack. At dawn on the sixth day he formed his *hoplites* (foot-soldiers) into a long line, four deep in the centre and eight deep on each wing.

The Greeks came down the hill at a run, chanting a war hymn to the god Apollo. They broke into the Persian ranks and began to hack and stab at close quarters with their short, heavy swords. It was a dramatic moment. 'Until this time no Greek could hear the word Persian without terror,' comments Herodotus. The Persians tried to counter-attack but when they drove forward into the weak centre the two powerful Greek wings closed in on them like a vice; this is what Miltiades had hoped would happen. The Persian bowmen were massacred while the horses of their cavalrymen slithered and got stuck in the marshy ground. The Persians lost 6,400 men, the Greeks only 192. It was a great and unexpected victory.

This burial mound is on the field where the battle of Marathon was fought. It contains the bodies of the 192 Athenians who were killed in the battle

The soldier on the left is having an arm wound bandaged. He seems to be in pain

The whole Greek world rejoiced at the news. Pheidippides, after delivering his message to Sparta, is supposed to have returned to fight in the battle and then been the first to run back to Athens with the news of victory – before dropping dead with exhaustion! This is the origin of the Marathon race of just over 26 miles – roughly the distance from Marathon to Athens. The Spartans, meanwhile, had finished their festival. Herodotus tells us,

> After the full moon two thousand Spartans came to Athens. . . . They came, however, too late for the battle; yet, as they had a longing to behold the Persians, they continued their march to Marathon and viewed the slain. Then, after giving the Athenians all praise for their achievement, they departed and returned home.

Thermopylae

King Darius was furious when he heard the news of Marathon. He decided to lead a larger expedition against the Greeks but died before he could do so. His son, Xerxes, was as determined as his father to gain revenge. The army he gathered amazed the civilised world. Herodotus says it was drawn from 46 nations and amounted to 5,283,000 men! These numbers are greatly exaggerated; Xerxes probably had no more than 150,000 soldiers. Nevertheless, it was clear that by 481 BC a very large Persian army and fleet had been assembled at Sardis in Asia Minor.

Next spring this force crossed the Hellespont on a bridge made of boats tied together. It was said that the Persian king watched his men march across for seven days and nights. The Spartans entered the fight quickly this time. Leonidas, their king, led 300 of his men, together with troops from other Greek cities, to a

In this wall carving from the Persian royal palace of Persepolis, Xerxes stands behind his father, Darius, who is seated on the throne

place called Thermopylae (meaning Hot Springs) – a narrow pass through the mountains which divide northern and central Greece. Xerxes sent his best soldiers, the Immortals, into the pass but time after time they were driven back. For three days Leonidas and his men held out. Then a traitor showed the Persians a secret pathway through the mountains.

As the Persians poured into the valley behind him, Leonidas ordered all the Greeks, except his own Spartiates, to escape. Most went, but the Thespians and Thebans decided to stay. Of these three, the Thespians and the Spartans fought to the end, first with their spears and swords and, when these were broken, with hands and teeth until they were all dead. Years afterwards the Greeks erected a stone over their graves. On it were carved the words, 'Stranger, tell the Spartans that we lie here obedient to their laws.'

Salamis and victory

The stand of the Spartans at Thermopylae only delayed the Persians. Now the entire Greek world was in danger. The Athenians consulted the oracle at Delphi. At first the priestess was discouraging: 'Save yourselves and bow your heads in grief,' she moaned. When questioned a second time she was more hopeful, saying,

Safe shall the wooden wall continue for you and your children.
Do not wait for the tramp of the horse, nor men on foot moving
   mightily over the land, but turn your back to the foe and retire.

This led to much discussion. Some Athenians were sure it meant they should build a wooden fence around the city. Themistocles, the Athenian leader, thought the priestess meant ships.

Athens had a fine fleet. Perhaps the priestess meant they should give up the city, retire to the islands nearby and fight the Persians in a sea battle? This seemed to be their only chance, so they abandoned the city. Athens was soon occupied and burned by Xerxes's troops. Sadly, the Athenians watched the flames light up the sky as they positioned their ships in the narrow waters between the island of Salamis and the mainland.

By fighting in the narrow straits chosen by the Greeks, Xerxes failed to use his larger fleet to advantage. The Persian war-galleys were often so crushed together that they either sank each other or provided an easy target for the battering-rams of the Greek ships. Vessels rolled over or broke in two. Greek javelins, arrows and even stones added to the panic and slaughter on the crowded Persian decks. All day the struggle continued until the sea was littered with wreckage. An Athenian poet, Aeschylus, fought in the battle. Afterwards he described how:

The sea vanished
Under a clogged carpet of shipwrecks,
   limbs, bodies,
No sea, and the beaches were cluttered
   with dead.

The Greek warship (right) appears to be overtaking a merchant ship

Seated on a special throne, Xerxes watched with horror. When evening came the proud Persian fleet had suffered such a severe defeat that it could no longer guard the army's supply routes back into Asia Minor. Xerxes was forced to retreat from Europe. For forty-five days his troops marched wearily back into Asia. Only a picked force of Immortals led by Mardonius remained in northern Greece.

Salamis had saved the Greek world from foreign domination. But the Greeks were soon quarrelling among themselves and were slow to gather an army to deal with Mardonius. It was only after the Persians cut off their food supplies that the Greek soldiers prepared to attack them at Plataea. At first things went badly for the Greeks. Waves of fierce Immortals shattered their battle-lines. In this crisis only the Spartans stood firm. Through the din of clashing swords, shouts and groans, the Spartiates could be heard chanting a war hymn.

> Come now young men, do battle, each keeping his place in the line . . . . Forget love of life when you confront the foe. Let each man withstand the attack . . . his two feet planted firmly on the ground, biting his lip with his teeth.

In spite of their courage and determination, the Spartan army might well have been destroyed but for a stroke of luck. Mardonius could be seen clearly on his white horse. Suddenly a Spartan broke through the Persian General's bodyguard and smashed his head with one blow. As the news of their commander's death spread, the Persians broke ranks and fled. The war was over and the Greeks gave heartfelt thanks to their gods. At Delphi a column was erected to commemorate the victory. At Plataea the battle was celebrated for centuries in a special festival. Each year the Plataeans would drink a toast, 'to those who lost their lives for the freedom of Greece'.

Sources and questions

1. After the Persian defeat at Salamis, Xerxes offered Athens the chance to be his ally against the other Greek states. Herodotus tells us that the Athenians made this reply.

   If we were offered all the gold in the world, or the most beautiful and fertile land, we would never be willing to join you and help in making the Greeks slaves. First, there is the burning and destruction of our temples and the statues of our gods. This forces us to take vengeance on you rather than come to terms. Then there is . . . the bond [between Greeks] of blood and language, our holy altars and sacrifices, and our common way of life, which it would be wrong for Athens to betray . . . as long as a single Athenian survives we will make no agreement with you.

   Source: Herodotus, Histories, 8. 144

   (a) How did the Persians get the opportunity to destroy the Athenians' temples and statues of the gods?
   (b) What were the 'holy altars and sacrifices' which bound the Greeks together?
   (c) This was written by a Greek historian after a Greek victory. Do you think this makes it a more or less reliable account of the Athenian attitude at the time?
   (d) Why was such a defiant attitude likely to be successful after the battle of Salamis?

2. Look at the picture of a Greek warship overtaking a merchant ship on page 103
   (a) What is the warship's main attacking weapon?
   (b) What would have been the purpose of having sails as well as oars?
   (c) Why do you think the merchant ship has only a sail?
   (d) What other differences can you see between the two ships?

3. When Spartan soldiers went off to war their womenfolk said to them, 'Come back either with your shield or on it.' What exactly did they mean, and how might this have affected the fighting spirit of the men?

4. Imagine you are King Xerxes. Write the letter to which the passage quoted in Question 1 was the reply.

THE GOLDEN AGE OF ATHENS

The Athenians were overjoyed at their victory over the Persians. However, to a visitor to the city there must have seemed little to rejoice about. The Acropolis hill was covered with the blackened ruins of temples burned down by the enemy. The goddess Athena was being worshipped in a temporary wooden shrine. Wild dogs roamed free, rubbish was left to rot in the streets, pigs lived in the gardens, and the marshes to the south of the city were infested with mosquitos. Yet the victory let loose the talents and energies of the Athenians. Their achievements in the fifty years after the Persian Wars have led to this period being called a Golden Age.

Athens had led the Greeks in war. Now it forced many other Greek cities to follow it in peacetime. An alliance of Greek cities, called the Delian League because its treasury was kept on the island of Delos, was set up by Athens. Eventually the League included the islands of the Aegean Sea and most of the coastal cities around it. Sparta, however, kept apart. Worried by the growing power of Athens, it formed its own Peloponnesian League which dominated the Greek mainland. There was a clear danger of war between the two rival Leagues. Realising this, the Athenians took precautions. Piraeus, the port of Athens, is about six kilometres from the city, so defensive 'long walls' were built between the two. In this way the Athenians hoped to avoid ever being cut off from their fleet by an enemy on land.

Bust of Pericles

Pericles and the rebuilding of Athens

The most famous Athenian leader at this time was Pericles, a rich, well-educated man who was also a fine public speaker. Like most Greeks, Pericles was ready for war if necessary. But he hoped for peace so that he could make Athens the most beautiful city in the world. He told the citizens:

> What I desire is that you should fix your eyes every day on the greatness of Athens as she really is, and that you should fall in love with her.

As far as Pericles was concerned, this was a religious mission.

Every stone laid, every statue carved, was to be in honour of the gods who had given Athens victory in the Persian Wars.

Pericles helped to organise the rebuilding work, together with Ictinus and Callicrates, two architects, and a sculptor, Phidias. Almost every Athenian craftsman helped in some way or other. On the Acropolis, the Parthenon, a temple to Athena, was erected. It was 20 metres high with 58 columns and over 500 carved figures of men, gods and animals. Its lines appear straight but, in fact, all are curved. This is because Ictinus knew that really straight lines would appear to sag. So every column bulges out slightly and all slope inwards. Today, its ruined yellow stones shine bare and bright in the sun. When it was built it was a blaze of colour. Its stone figures were painted with gold hair, pink faces and scarlet and emerald clothes, all set against a blue background.

The Parthenon was surrounded by other beautiful buildings, including a small blue and white temple called the Erechtheum which housed sacred relics. A huge bronze statue of Athena stood on a high point so that sailors out at sea could spot the sun flashing on her helmet. At the foot of the Acropolis graceful walks were set around the *agora* (market-place). Overlooking the agora, on a small hill, was the Theseum. This temple was built in honour of the god Hephaestus, but it got its name because in later years the citizens thought it had been built in honour of another god

The Acropolis hill. The most prominent building is the Parthenon

Porch on the south side of the Erechtheum

called Theseus. The Theseum is the best preserved of all ancient Greek buildings.

Before Pericles died the greatest days of Athens were coming to an end. Plague had struck its citizens and it was beginning a long and disastrous war with Sparta and her allies. But Pericles had his wish. For centuries visitors have gazed at the fine buildings of his day and most have fallen in love with Athens.

Athenian life

What was life like for the people of this famous city? Greece is a sunny land so there was little need to make homes warm and comfortable. The poorer Athenians mostly lived in small, box-like dwellings with few windows and a single door opening on to the street. Town houses were usually one or two storeys high. They were built of brick set on a stone base and had tiled sloping roofs. The larger ones had courtyards. The rooms in the upper storey were for the women's use because they were rarely allowed out. Men, on the other hand, were often out, so a guard or porter was employed to protect the house and its womenfolk.

Greek food was simple, but the rich made their meals last a long time. Few races have loved conversation as much as the Greeks. To prevent all the diners talking at once, a president was usually elected for the evening. His job was to organise the discussion and to keep order. Although this dinner-table talk was called the *symposium*, which means 'drinking together', the Greeks drank

Dining scene painted on a pot. Notice that the diners are reclining on couches rather than sitting at a table

Here we see Greek women spinning yarn (left) and weaving cloth. How is the method of weaving shown here different from that on a modern loom?

little except at festival times. Wine was nearly always mixed with water because, as one Greek wrote,

> The first cup means health, the second pleasure, the third is for sleep and then wise men go home. The fourth means rudeness, the fifth shouting, and the sixth disorder in the streets, the seventh black eyes and the eighth a police summons.

Ancient Greece was very much a man's world. Greek women played an important part in festivals and religious ceremonies but they took no part in politics. They did not belong to the assembly and could not vote. Girls of well-to-do families were educated at home by their mothers. This education did not amount to very much. One Greek writer, describing the childhood of a certain girl, said she was brought up 'under the strictest control, in order that she might see as little, hear as little, and ask as few questions as possible'.

The education of boys was taken much more seriously. The main subjects of study were Homer's two long poems, the *Iliad* and the *Odyssey*. As well as teaching a boy Greek history, these books told him about the gods. Homer's lines were learned by heart and frequently recited aloud. Writing was scratched on a wax pad with a *stylus*, a pointed stick tipped with iron or bone. Its top was sometimes flattened for smoothing out mistakes on the wax surface. In their free time, Greek children played games similar to those of today. They spun tops and rolled hoops, enjoyed many kinds of ball games and tossed five small bones in the air, catching them on the backs of their hands.

Soon after her fifteenth birthday a girl was usually married to a man chosen by her parents. Greek wives were kept busy indoors, as far away from male strangers and other mischief as possible! In this passage from a book by a Greek writer, Xenophon, a husband says what he expects of his wife.

> Your business will be to stay indoors and help to despatch the servants who will work outside, while supervising those who work indoors. You will . . . allocate the necessary expenditure . . . and see that the money for the year's expenses is not spent in a month. When wool is delivered to the house you will see that garments are made for those who need them, and take care

A blacksmith sits at his forge heating and shaping a piece of iron. Notice his long pair of tongs

that the dried grain is kept fit to eat. . . . You will also have to see that any of the servants who is ill gets proper treatment.

Soldiers and craftsmen

After school a boy went for military training. The Greeks believed that no city was entitled to be free if it was not ready to fight. Therefore war played an important part in their lives. In Athens, men became adults at eighteen and for two years had opportunities of service at home and abroad. Then they retired to civilian life but could be called up for military service at any time up to the age of sixty.

Although they were always capable of a warlike attitude, the Athenians devoted as much time as possible to peaceful occupations. Athens was a city of craftsmen. Numerous sword-makers, sculptors, stone-masons, potters and blacksmiths lived and worked in its noisy streets and market places. Pottery was a particularly important trade. The clay of Attica turns an orange red colour when baked. This is called *terracotta*. Patterns and figures were very striking when painted black on the red background.

The Greeks liked to have pots of different shapes and sizes, each for a particular purpose. There was, for example, a pot for wine, another for water and yet another for mixing the two before meals. Other *amphorae*, as they were called, were used for the storage of food and oil. Many are beautifully shaped and their decorations tell us a great deal about Greek dress, religion and ways of life.

DOCUMENTS: GREEK EDUCATION

Document 1

Greek boys went to school between the ages of 7 and 14, if their parents could afford to pay. Here Plato, the Greek writer (see page 114), describes the first steps in a child's schooling. This comes from a book about a wise man called Protogoras.

When a boy knows his letters and is ready to proceed from the spoken to the written word, his teachers set him down at his desk and make him read the works of the great poets and learn them by heart; there he finds plenty of advice, and many stories and much praise and glorification of great men of the past, which encourages him to admire and copy them.

Source: Plato, Protogoras, *quoted in* The World of Athens, *CUP, 1984*

Document 2

A great deal of Greek schooling, even wrestling and boxing, took place to the sound of music. Plato, in his book *The Republic*, explains why this was done.

We attach supreme importance to a musical education, because rhythms and harmony sink most deeply into the mind, and take the most powerful hold of it, making a man graceful. He that has been brought up in this way will have a keen eye for faults, whether in nature or art, and will love beautiful objects and gladly receive them into his soul, and feed upon them and so grow to be noble and good; whereas he will hate and condemn ugly objects, even in his childhood.

Source: Adapted from Plato, The Republic, *Book 3, 401–2, Macmillan, 1943*

Here is a picture of a Greek school painted round a bowl by an Athenian artist. How does this picture fit in with what you have read in Document 2?

Document 3

The Greek aim in education was to produce a healthy body *and* a healthy mind. So a lot of school time was taken up with athletic activities. Our word gymnasium comes from the Greek word *gumnoi*, which means naked, because the boys did their PE without any clothes on. Here Plato explains why Greeks thought physical education so important.

> Gymnastics will hold next place to music in the education of our young men . . . careful training in gymnastics, as well as in music, ought to begin in childhood, and go through all their lives. My belief is, not that a good body will make a good soul, but, on the contrary, that a good soul will by its excellence make the body perfect.

Source: Plato, The Republic, *Book 3, 403*

Greek children learned to write with a pointed stylus on wax-covered wooden boards. These were well suited to young writers liable to make mistakes. Can you explain why?

Document 4

Here Plato condemns the man who does not strike a balance between mental and physical education but concentrates on one at the expense of the other.

> When a man surrenders himself to music and flute-playing, and allows his soul to be flooded with sweet and soft harmonies and spends his whole life warbling and delighting himself with song, such a man begins to waste away. . . . On the other hand, if he devotes himself to hard labour in gymnastics but avoids music and *philosophy* [the search for truth], even if he at first had some capacity for learning, he will become a hater of discussion . . . and unintelligent . . . with no use for reasoned argument, and determined to settle everything by brute force.

Source: Plato, The Republic, *Book 3, 411*

Questions

1. Using these documents, make a list of the qualities the Greeks expected in an educated man.
2. Do you think the Greeks had any other purpose for gymnastics besides making boys fit? Give reasons for your answer.
3. What sort of person did the Greeks hope a musical education would produce? Do you think they were right?
4. From the information in these documents, describe what you imagine might have been a typical day in the life of a Greek schoolboy.
5. Plato was an Athenian. In what ways do you think Spartan views of education would have differed from those of Plato?
6. Imagine that Plato was an inspector visiting your school and observing classes. Write a report that he might have produced at the end of his visit.

PLAYWRIGHTS AND PHILOSOPHERS

The Greeks had many festivals. Often these were in honour of particular gods or to celebrate events in the year such as the spring and harvest. Some, like the Olympic Games, were festivals of sport. Others stressed music, dancing, acting and mime. From these developed theatrical performances. At first there were no individual actors, only a number of people, a *chorus*, who chanted or recited a story. Later an actor, usually the poet who had written the play, helped to tell the tale.

Greek drama

The first plays were probably performed in market places. Then special theatres were built. These were in the open air because of Greece's dry, sunny climate. The actors performed in a circular space called the *orchestra*. Around it seats were set in a series of semi-circles, each raised above the one in front so that all spectators could see clearly. Early theatres were built of wood but after several serious fires the Athenians decided to use stone. As a result some have survived to the present day.

Greek theatres were generally much larger than modern ones. But they were so well constructed that people in the back row could hear clearly. However, actors needed to speak loudly and wave their arms if they wanted the audience to follow the story. Actors wore large masks because their faces could not be seen at a distance. Consequently, an actor would have to shout 'I weep' if he wanted the spectators to know he was in tears! Masks meant that an actor could perform several different parts in the same play. Actors wore costumes to show who they were meant to be; a king or a messenger could be easily identified in this way.

The first Greek play of which we have a complete copy is *The Persians* by an Athenian dramatist called Aeschylus. It was produced at a festival in 472 BC and tells the story of the Persian Wars, in which Aeschylus had fought. The play has two characters as well as a chorus so Aeschylus was able to use conversation, or *dialogue*, as the following extract shows. Here the Persian queen-mother, Atossa, is asking about Athens.

A tragic actor. Notice his mask on the right

ATOSSA	But tell me, friends, where is this Athens reported to be?
CHORUS	In the far west, where the Sun-god's rays grow dim and set.
ATOSSA	But why should my son be so anxious to make it his prey?
CHORUS	If Athens were won, all Greece would be subject to him.
ATOSSA	Has it so plentiful a supply of fighting men?
CHORUS	It has, and it has done much damage to the Persians.
ATOSSA	What else has it? Are its people wealthy?
CHORUS	There is a spring of silver which the earth treasures for them.
ATOSSA	What leader and commander have they?
CHORUS	They are no man's slave and take no man's orders.
ATOSSA	How can they withstand invading enemies?
CHORUS	So well that they destroyed Darius's great and splendid army.
ATOSSA	Dread words to those whose sons are with the army now.
CHORUS	Soon, I think, you will know the full truth. This man is surely a Persian messenger bringing news, good or bad.

Aeschylus's plays were tragedies – plays with a serious subject and often an unhappy ending. The Greeks loved such plays, especially during solemn religious festivals. They also liked comedies which poked fun at the people and customs of the day – like the plays of Aristophanes which are named after the character given to the chorus, such as *Wasps*, *Clouds* or *Frogs*. Nevertheless, most Greek

Marble statue of Socrates

plays are tragedies. Aeschylus, for example, uses his play about the Persian Wars to show how disappointed Xerxes was at the failure of his invasion. Rather than celebrate a Greek victory, he tells how the proud Persian failed because he dared to behave as if he were a god. Another dramatist, Sophocles, told the Greek legend of Oedipus, whom the gods doomed one day to kill his father and marry his mother because he did not recognise them. When he discovers his mistake he blinds himself.

Socrates, Plato and Aristotle

The Greeks loved to ask questions about life and nature, knowledge and truth. A questioning search for the true meaning of things is called philosophy. The greatest Greek philosopher, Socrates, was an ugly, clumsy man who would stop passers-by in the street and ask questions like 'What is love?' or 'What is justice?' Some people were merely annoyed and hurried on. Others found themselves forced to think deeply about such matters.

Socrates did not write any books, but a lot of what he said was written down by his pupils, particularly Plato. Plato's writings are not always an accurate account of Socrates's opinions but thanks to him we can get some idea of the fascinating conversations the philosopher had with his friends. Such an outspoken man made enemies as well as friends. Eventually Socrates was accused of leading young people astray with his talk. He was sentenced to death and, although he could easily have escaped, he refused to do so because it would have meant breaking the city's laws. He died bravely, talking to his friends as he sipped a cup of poison.

Plato was different from his famous master. He wrote poems and plays, and also studied science. He had a keen interest in politics and this led him to found a school for statesmen. However, his only attempt to train a real statesman, Dionysius of Syracuse, was a failure. His book, *The Republic*, describes what he thought to be a perfect city-state. Plato did not believe in democracy. He favoured the rule of 'philosopher-kings' who would spend many years being specially educated for the task. Plato's book, which is written in the form of discussions between Socrates and his friends, has influenced people ever since, especially on the subject of education.

Another famous Greek philosopher, Aristotle, set out to gather as much information as possible about the world around him. 'All men possess by nature the desire to know,' he wrote. It was certainly true of Aristotle himself. Altogether, he is said to have written 146 books, although some were almost certainly written by his pupils. The few which survive show the great variety of his interests. For example, there is one *On Alexander*, a military conqueror (see Chapter 18), who was his pupil for three years, and others *On drunkenness* and *On being given in marriage*. He also wrote important books on politics and *oratory* (the art of public speaking). Aristotle founded a school in Athens. It was called the Lyceum because it was near a temple called the Apollo Lyceius.

Aristotle was thought to be always right and was called '*the* Philosopher'. Actually, in small matters he could be wrong. He thought, for instance, that goats breathed through their ears.

Eureka!

The Greeks' curiosity led to many discoveries in mathematics and science. For example, Pythagoras and his pupils established a number of important rules for geometry. Pythagoras also declared the world to be round when most people thought it was flat. Aristarchus was the first man known to have suggested that the earth and planets moved around the sun, instead of the other way round. Another Greek scientist, Archimedes of Syracuse, realised as he sat in his bath that a body placed in water displaces the same volume of water as itself. Delighted, he jumped out naked and ran through the streets shouting 'Eureka, Eureka!' (I've found it).

Hippocrates was the first famous Greek doctor. He founded a hospital and wrote books on medicine. His habit of keeping a careful watch on a patient and recording every symptom is the basis of the way doctors work today. Hippocrates described how he believed a good doctor should behave:

> Carry out your treatment in a calm and orderly way ... What is needed is often not reasoned diagnosis but practical help. So you must predict the outcome from your previous experience.... Be brief, be encouraging and sympathetic, show care and reply to objections, meet any difficulties with calm assurance, forbid noise and disturbance, be ready to do what has to be done.

Few doctors of Hippocrates's day would have lived up to such standards. Indeed, many of them relied on herbs, magic spells and superstition. Hippocrates once said it was fortunate that serious illnesses were in the minority because the same was true of good doctors!

This statue of Hippocrates stands in the museum on the Greek island of Kos

Sources and questions

1. The following passage was written to be acted in the theatre. It presents a different view of Greek education from that in the Documents section on pages 110–11.

   > Lampriskos, hoist up this wicked boy and thrash him.... Every day things go from bad to worse. He'd be hard put to find his writing master's door, but school bills arrive each thirtieth of the month. Yet ask him where the gambling den is ... and in a breath he'll tell you. His wretched writing tablet that I spread and smooth so carefully each month with wax slips down between the bedposts and the wall. He scowls like death if he sees it,

won't write a proper word, but scrapes it clean. Yet in his satchel rattle lots of dice. . . . You've got to scream at him five times before he'll learn the first letter of the alphabet.

Source: From an ancient Greek mime quoted in J. Lindsay, The Ancient World, *Weidenfeld and Nicolson, 1968*

(a) Lampriskos was not a teacher. What do you think his job was?

(b) Can you work out from this passage how the boy liked to spend his time?

(c) Why did monthly bills have to be paid?

(d) What does this passage tell you about methods of teaching and learning in ancient Greece?

This painting from the fourth century BC shows two actors at a window

2. Look at this picture. How would actors today perform differently?

3. Re-read the extract from the play by Aeschylus on page 113. How can you tell, just by reading it, that it was written by a Greek rather than a Persian?

4. Find out how the 17,000 seating capacity of the theatre at Epidaurus (pictured on page 113) compares with:
   (a) a modern theatre,
   (b) your nearest professional football or other sports stadium.
   What do your answers tell you about the ancient Greeks?

THE FALL OF ATHENS

The later years of Pericles saw the start of a long war between Athens and Sparta, which had grown jealous of each other's power. The Peloponnesian War, as it is called, lasted twenty-seven years. It divided the Greek world because most Greek cities were forced to take one side or the other. We know a lot about this war because a very detailed history was written by Thucydides, who served as an Athenian admiral during the fighting.

Disaster in the Hellespont

Pericles felt sure that if the Athenians avoided a battle on land with the Spartans, and kept control of the sea, they would win. Athens was well defended by its long walls down to the port of Piraeus. It was richer than Sparta and so could hold out longer. But Athens had a weakness. It depended on corn supplies from Russia. Should this life-line be cut its citizens would starve. Every time the Athenian assembly met during the war it discussed this vital problem.

Early in the war a plague broke out in Athens and Pericles was one of the many who died from it. The Athenian leaders after Pericles did not follow his advice. They fought battles on land, in which they were defeated, and a large army sent to attack a Spartan ally, the city of Syracuse in Sicily, was wiped out. Of this disaster, Thucydides wrote,

> The Athenians were beaten at all points . . . their fleet, their army, everything was destroyed, and few out of the many returned home . . . for a long while [the Athenians] would not believe even the most respectable of soldiers who had escaped from the scene of action and clearly reported what had happened. . . . When the truth was forced upon them, they were angry with the politicians who had suggested the expedition, ignoring the fact that they themselves had voted for it.

Even worse was to follow for the Athenians. In 405 BC the Spartan admiral Lysander smashed the Athenian fleet in a battle in the Hellespont and so cut the city's corn supply. Only nine

Athenian galleys escaped Lysander's ships and of these, only one, the *Paralus*, reached Athens. An eye-witness described the sad scene when the ship returned.

It was night when the *Paralus* reached Athens with her bad news, and a bitter wail of woe broke forth. From Piraeus, following the line of the long wall up to the heart of the city, the wailing swept and swelled, as each man passed the news to his neighbour. On that night no man slept.

The rule of The Thirty

Corinth, an ally of Sparta, wanted to destroy Athens completely, killing all the men and selling the women and children as slaves. The Spartans, however, remembered how the Athenians had saved the Greek world at Marathon and Salamis and refused to allow such a massacre. Nevertheless, Spartan troops occupied the city, destroyed the long walls, and reduced the once mighty Athenian navy to twelve ships. For a time the Athenians were ruled by a Spartan-controlled government called The Thirty. It was this regime which put Socrates to death (see page 114). But in the following year a more democratic rule returned to Athens.

Although Athens never again became as great as before the war, it remained one of the most important cities of Greece. The long walls were rebuilt and trade was brought back to Athens. It

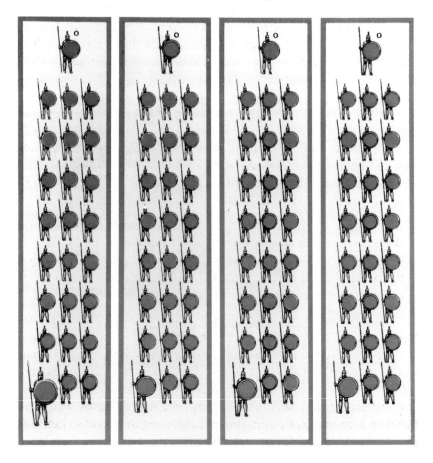

A phalanx formation, in files eight-deep, of the kind used by the Thebans. When a man in the front rank fell, his place was taken by the man behind and the whole file moved forward to fill the gap. The commanding officers stood in the front and the 'rear rank officers', called ouragos, made sure that the men at the back did their job

The lion of Chaeronea. This statue was put up on the site of the battle to commemorate the brave band of Thebans who fell there in 338 BC

remained famous for all time for its art and architecture, its philosophy and literature. Sparta, meanwhile, tried to dominate Greece but failed. In 371 BC, at the battle of Leuktra, the Spartan ranks were broken by the troops of Thebes fighting in a *phalanx* (close formation) eight rows deep. These phalanxes cut through the enemy like a modern tank, leaving gaps which could be entered by the cavalry. The Greek world was astonished at the total defeat of the Spartans. For a while Thebes became the leading city in Greece.

Philip of Macedon

While the Greek city-states wasted time and energy fighting among themselves, a new power arose in the north. Macedon was a mountainous land inhabited by a tough shepherd people. Its king, Philip, had spent some years in Thebes and had seen the army which beat the Spartans. Philip copied the Theban phalanxes. He also gave his foot-soldiers a spear 5½ metres long – much longer and heavier than the spears of the Greeks. With the addition of his fierce cavalry, the Companions, Philip's army soon proved unbeatable.

Philip must have been a frightening sight. He limped from an old wound, was blinded in one eye and had a hunched back caused by a broken collar bone. Yet he was more than just a rough warrior. The Macedonian King admired the civilised ways of cities like Athens. He was also a cunning politician who was determined to gain control of Greece by setting one city against another. It was some time before the Greek states realised the danger. When they did they formed a league to fight Macedon. It was too late. Philip destroyed their independence once and for all at the battle of Chaeronea in 338 BC.

Two years later Philip was murdered. The whole Greek world sighed with relief at his death. In fact, as one wise man remarked, Philip's death had only reduced the Macedonian army by one! Years afterwards, his son, Alexander, is reported to have said this about his father. He was speaking to his soldiers.

> He found you homeless and in poverty, most of you dressed in skins, feeding a few sheep up the mountain-sides.... Instead of skins he gave you cloaks to wear, and from the mountains he led you down into the plains, and made you capable of fighting the neighbouring tribes ... from being slaves and subjects he made you rulers.

Alexander was only twenty years old when he succeeded his father as king of Macedon. Within months he had crushed a revolt in northern Greece after cutting steps up a mountainside to get his troops behind the enemy. Then Alexander beat some Balkan tribes by ferrying his soldiers across the river Danube on leather tent covers stuffed with hay. When rebellious Thebes was captured and destroyed by Alexander, people began to realise that the son was even more dangerous than the father.

This ivory head was found on a tomb in Macedonia. Experts think the tomb is that of Philip of Macedon and the face a likeness of the king himself. The deep cut in the right eyebrow is a clue as we know Philip was blinded in one eye

Sources and questions

1. Here Demosthenes, a Greek writer and politician, describes events in Athens as Philip of Macedon's troops neared the city.

   It was evening when the Committee got the news that Elatieia [a city in alliance with Athens] had fallen. They at once left their suppers, sent for the generals and called the town crier to spread the news. The whole city was in wild commotion. Next day at dawn the Committee summoned the Council to the chamber while the citizens went off to the Assembly. Indeed, the whole people were there seated on the hillside before the Council had done any business.... And then the messenger was brought forward and gave his account – and the herald called out, 'Who wants to speak?' No one came out. The herald kept on repeating the question. Still no one stood up, though all the generals and orators were present, and our country was crying out for someone to speak on her behalf.

   Source: Quoted in Jack Lindsay, The Ancient World, *Weidenfeld and Nicolson, 1968.*

   (a) What does this passage tell you about the way Athenian government was organised?
   (b) What does the passage tell you about the way in which Athenians made decisions? How was this different from the way the Macedonians made decisions?
   (c) What is an orator? What would have been his purpose in a Greek assembly?
   (d) Why do you think nobody had anything to say at this meeting?

2. Look at the picture of the ivory head of Philip of Macedon on page 119. What, if anything, does it tell you about,
   (a) Philip's character?
   (b) the artist's knowledge of Philip?
   (c) the attitude of the artist towards Philip?

3. Re-read the extract from Alexander's speech to his soldiers about his father (page 119). What do you think the soldiers would have thought of it? What else might they have said about the effect of Philip's rule upon their lives?

4. Imagine you are a TV reporter in Athens in 405 BC. Write a news report describing the return of the *Paralus* from the battle in the Hellespont.

ALEXANDER THE GREAT

Philip of Macedon had conquered Greece and was dreaming of invading Persia when he died. Alexander set out to complete his father's work. In 334 BC he left Pella in Macedon with a force of 35,000 men. It was an unusual army. As well as soldiers, it had clerks who kept daily accounts of everything that happened. In addition to siege towers and battering rams, it had historians, geographers and poets. From his teacher, Aristotle, Alexander had learned to love everything Greek. The Persian empire was about to be invaded by Greek learning as well as armed men.

'This is being a king'

Alexander was faced by the so-called 'Kingdom of the Whole World', stretching from Egypt to the Caspian and Black Seas. The

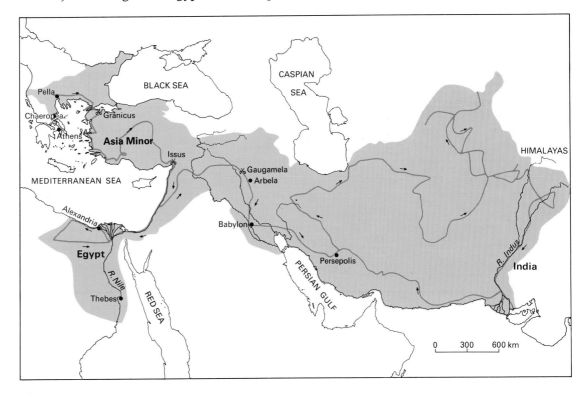

Alexander's Empire

This wall mosaic of the battle of Issus is a Roman copy of a Greek painting. Alexander is on the left, bareheaded, and Darius is on the right, rising above the rest of his soldiers

Persian empire was well governed, connected by good roads and able to assemble enormous armies for war. Its bowmen and cavalry were famous and feared; its fleet was first class. Young Alexander, looking magnificent in full armour topped by a white-plumed helmet, sacrificed a bull to the Greek god Poseidon as his fleet crossed into Asia. His troops must have wondered whether even the gods could bring victory in such a dangerous adventure.

At first, Darius III, the Great King of Persia, did not take the Greek invasion seriously and left his generals in command of the army. The first major battle was by the river Granicus (see map). When the fighting started, an attack by the Macedonian right wing led the Persians to expect that the real assault would come on the left. But, to their surprise, Alexander's right kept pushing on. This attack was led by Alexander himself, who cut down man after man, including Mithridates, Darius's son-in-law. Only once was Alexander in danger. This was when a Persian cut open his helmet with a sword thrust. The King's friend, Cleitus, killed the man and so saved his master's life. Soon afterwards, the Persians retreated from the battlefield and Alexander was able to occupy most of Asia Minor.

Granicus was a defeat but not a disaster for the Persians. Darius's answer was to recruit a far larger army and challenge Alexander in person at Issus in 333 BC. Although they were slowed down by the sheer weight of numbers on the enemy side, the Macedonian cavalry slaughtered thousands of Persians. Many others were captured, including Darius's wife, mother and two daughters. When the news spread that Darius had fled the Persian resistance crumbled. The night after the battle, Alexander occupied Darius's war-tent, a domed structure of gold cloth, delicate embroidery and precious stones. 'This, I believe, is being a king,' he remarked, as he was served with Darius's food and wine. Alexander now claimed to be the new Great King of Persia. He sent a letter to Darius containing these proud words:

Coin showing Alexander wearing the horns of the Egyptian god Amun

Whenever you send to me, send to me as King of Asia . . . and if you dispute my right to the kingdom, stay and fight another battle for it; but do not run away.

After Issus, Alexander entered Egypt where he was welcomed as the enemy of the unpopular Persians. The Egyptian priests received him with special honours because he wore ram's horns, the sign of the god Amun, in his hair. This was a clever thing to do. It won him the favour of the Egyptians who, for centuries afterwards, called him 'The Two-Horned'. In fact, Alexander was truly interested in Egyptian religion and may really have believed he was the son of an Egyptian god! He also showed a liking for Egyptian ways and founded the city of Alexandria while he was there.

The end of the Persian empire

Meanwhile Darius assembled his greatest army, equipped with chariots and elephants. When the Macedonians lined up against him at Gaugamela, near Arbela, in 331 BC, the noise of his army was said to sound 'like the distant roaring of a mighty ocean'. Yet Alexander again proved too clever for the Persian king. First, he chose to fight on rough ground where the Persian chariots could tip over at speed. Then, when the Persian chariot attack did come, he arranged for his troops to stand aside and let them through their ranks so that his bowmen could kill the drivers. As the battle reached its climax, Alexander fought his way towards the Persian king. For a brief moment the two deadly enemies looked at each other. Then, before Alexander could strike, Darius hurled his spear, missed, and fled.

The slaughter which followed was greater than that at Issus. Afterwards the victorious Macedonians marched south to Babylon and on to the royal city of Persepolis, which they ransacked and burned in revenge for Xerxes's destruction of Athens (see page 102). The battle of Gaugamela finally destroyed the Persian empire. In the following year a few horsemen led by Alexander found Darius in the desert. He had been abandoned by his bodyguard and lay dying from a spear wound given him by a traitor. A

Macedonian soldier gave him a drink of water but he was dead before Alexander galloped up.

Alexander had conquered the Persian empire with the sword. In another way, however, it was conquering him. Its wealth and luxury were slowly changing his character. One of his followers, called Ephippus, wrote this about him:

> He had . . . a golden throne and couches with silver feet, on which he used to sit with his companions. . . . Sometimes he would put on the purple robe . . . and horns of Amun, as if he had been the god. . . . He used also to have the floor sprinkled with delightful perfumes and with fragrant wine; and myrrh and other kinds of incense were burned before him.

Each day Alexander acted more like an Eastern tyrant. He expected his subjects to bow and touch the ground with their foreheads when they approached him. Each day he became more cruel to those who opposed him. Rebellious towns were ruthlessly destroyed and their inhabitants massacred. Even his friend Cleitus was murdered by him in a drunken fight and two of his most trusted generals were executed.

The invasion of India

Even though Persia had been occupied, Alexander wanted to go on fighting. So the weary march east went on. In 327 BC the Macedonians entered India over the Himalayan mountains. High among the tallest mountains in the world, Alexander's men suffered terribly from cold and hunger. When they came down into the plains they were tormented by thirst and heat. One day they discovered a smelly and undrinkable liquid which gushed out of the ground and easily burst into flames. Alexander offered sacrifices to the gods to save his men from what was, in fact, oil! Then he defeated the army of an Indian king called Porus in a hard-fought battle.

At last the Macedonian troops grew tired of their wanderings. When they reached a spot near where the city of Delhi stands today they refused to go on. Alexander was furious but there was nothing he could do about it. He erected a pillar for each of the chief Greek gods, to show where he had been, and then began a slow retreat. Soon after reaching Babylon, Alexander died of marsh fever, just before his thirty-third birthday, in 323 BC. When asked who should rule after his death he whispered 'The best'. Not surprisingly, his generals had different ideas of who was best. In the years of fighting which followed Alexander's empire was divided into three parts, each ruled by one of his generals.

Although Alexander's empire only lasted a short time, it did much to spread Greek ideas and the Greek language far beyond Greece. It is thought that Alexander may have founded as many as seventy Greek-style cities in the East. On the north-west frontier of India craftsmen made statues in the Greek manner. Back in Greece people learned of the customs and religion of the Indians.

In this Indian painting, Alexander is supervising the building of a defensive wall. It shows how Alexander's fame lived on in India because it was painted more than 1000 years after his death

Even today some Indian craftsmen make wooden carvings of Macedonian horsemen, while other people talk of Alexander as though they had known him. Year by year the legend of Alexander has grown. In many stories he appears as a god. One can imagine how pleased he would be if he knew.

Sources and questions

1. Alexander was responsible for some spectacular destruction during his campaigns. Here is a description, written nearly 400 years after the event, of the burning of the Persian palace at Persepolis.

> When a farewell party was held in Xerxes's palace the men and women became very drunk. One of the women present, an Athenian named Thais, shouted that the finest deed Alexander could do in Asia was to lead them in triumphal procession round the palace and then set fire to it. Her words excited the younger men, who were already very drunk, and someone shouted out to lead on, snatch up torches and revenge the wicked deeds of the Persians against the Greeks. Others took up the cry, saying that Alexander should do it. The King was excited by their words and all leapt up from their drinking to form a procession. Flares were collected and with women singing and men playing flutes and pipes they advanced on the palace. Thais followed Alexander in throwing her blazing torch into the palace which rapidly took flame.

> *Source: Adapted from* The Works of Diodorus Siculus, *Loeb Classical Library, Heinemann and Harvard University Press, 1965*

   (a) Why were Alexander and his companions in Xerxes's palace in Persepolis?
   (b) The story of the burning of the palace was probably told first by some of Alexander's generals. Why do you think this event still interested people hundreds of years after it happened?
   (c) Why do you think the writer mentions particularly that an Athenian suggested burning the palace?
   (d) Do you think this is likely to be a reliable account? Are there any reasons to suspect that it might be inaccurate or biased?

2. Look at the picture of the mosaic on page 122.
   (a) Try to describe the expressions on the faces of Alexander and Darius.
   (b) Do these expressions tell you anything about the intention of the artist who painted the original picture?
   (c) Alexander has armour on his body but no protection for his head. Why do you think the artist showed him like this?

3. There is a famous story told about Alexander and his war-horse, Bucephalus. Try to find out what it is.

4. Imagine you are Darius after the battle of Gaugamela. Write a letter to a close friend – someone you can trust – in which you give your real views on Alexander.

ROME

THE CITY ON SEVEN HILLS

The short-lived empire of Alexander was the biggest the world had known up to that time. But before long a greater and much more long-lasting empire began to grow up around the shores of the Mediterranean. Its centre was the city of Rome, on the west coast of Italy. At the time of Alexander's conquests, in the fourth century BC, Rome was little more than the centre of a busy farming area. But a great expansion of Roman power was about to occur.

The beginnings of Rome

Little is known about the earliest history of Rome. We have to rely on legends, a few findings of archaeologists and a lot of guesswork. The only thing we can be fairly sure of is that it began as a collection of mud huts built on the south bank of the river Tiber by a tribe known as the Latins. Like the Greeks, the Latins originally came from Asia.

On the fertile plains surrounding the city, plentiful crops of corn, olives, grapes and other fruit ripened in the warm climate. There was also good pasture for cattle and sheep. The Romans began to trade, first with neighbouring tribes and then with merchants sailing from other parts of the Mediterranean. A port called Ostia grew up at the mouth of the Tiber, a few miles from Rome. Its streets filled with merchants, shopkeepers and craftsmen who learned to make tools and weapons, pots, pans and furniture.

The people of Rome grew proud of their city and began to make up stories about its beginnings. These were written down by historians hundreds of years later. It was said that Rome had been

This bronze statue of a she-wolf, probably made by an Etruscan craftsman, dates from about 500 BC. It can now be seen in a museum on the Capitol Hill in Rome. The figures representing Romulus and Remus were added about 2,000 years later

founded in 753 BC by Romulus, son of Mars, the god of war. The story goes that when he was a baby, Romulus, together with his twin brother Remus, had been abandoned in a basket on the river Tiber – at the orders of their wicked uncle. But the twins were saved when their basket was washed ashore. A Roman historian, Livy, who was born in the first century BC, tells us that,

> a she-wolf, coming down out of the surrounding hills to quench her thirst, turned towards the cry of the infants, and allowed them to suck her milk so gently that a shepherd . . . found her licking them with her tongue . . . he carried the twins to his hut and gave them to his wife . . . to rear.

It was said that when the twins grew up they founded a city at the spot where they had been rescued. Following a quarrel in which Remus was killed, Romulus called the city Rome, after his own name. Rome's first settlements were on the slopes of what was later called the Palatine Hill, but gradually the six surrounding hills were also included within its walls. This explains why Rome is often called 'the City on Seven Hills'.

We are told that Rome was ruled by kings for about 250 years from its beginnings. This is probably true, and it is likely that some kings were Etruscans from the other side of the river. The Etruscans, who probably came by sea from Mesopotamia, were more civilised than the Latins; they were skilful metalworkers, builders and artists. The largest Etruscan town, Veii, was only a dozen miles from Rome. The two peoples almost certainly mixed and influenced each other.

SPQR

The last king of Rome seems to have been an Etruscan called Tarquin the Proud. His rule was harsh and unpopular, and he was driven out in a rebellion (509 BC). Leading Romans now decided that they would have no more kings. Instead, they set up a *republic* – a type of government in which rulers are usually chosen by the people.

From now on, the Romans were determined to prevent any one person having too much power. So they divided the former kings' duties between two equal magistrates called *consuls*. These were

expected to keep a check on each other. If they disagreed it was possible for either one of them to cancel the other's decisions. This was called a *veto*, which is Latin for 'I forbid'. To make doubly sure that the consuls did not get too powerful, they were only elected for one year.

Consuls were chosen by an assembly of Roman citizens which met at certain times of the year. This assembly also elected other ruling magistrates, including those who had the task of enforcing the laws. When their period of office was over, magistrates usually became life members of the *senate* – a kind of parliament or council which got its name from the Latin *senex*, meaning 'an old man'. This reminds us that Roman women were not allowed to hold positions of power; they were not even allowed to vote in elections.

The senate was a permanent body. This meant it was in a strong position to advise consuls who held office for only a short time. It also meant that the senate gradually became more important than the citizen's assembly. Even so, members of the senate knew that in the first place their power had come from the people as whole.

This wall painting in an Etruscan tomb of the fifth century BC shows a scene from a banquet

Coin with the inscription SPQR

For this reason, the government of Rome is summed up in the words *Senatus Populus-Que Romanus* (SPQR for short) which means 'the Senate and People of Rome'. The letters SPQR are found on Roman coins and were proudly displayed on the battle standards carried by the armies of Rome.

Patricians and plebeians

From early times, there were two quite distinct classes of people in Rome – the patricians, or nobles, and the plebeians (common people). The plebeians were mostly ordinary peasant farmers, merchants and craftsmen. The patricians, on the other hand, were the descendants of the original founders of the city. They owned the largest estates and had the best herds of cattle and sheep.

Even though they were greatly outnumbered by the plebeians, the wealthy patrician families kept many privileges for themselves. They had more votes in the assembly than all the plebeians put together. Only members of patrician families were allowed to become magistrates, and therefore senators as well. As plebeians were not allowed to marry patricians, there seemed to be no way of breaking down the barriers between the classes.

The common people protested about the unfairness of their position. We are told that in 494 BC they walked out of Rome and threatened to start a rival plebeian city nearby. This alarmed the patricians because they could not possibly manage on their own. To get the plebeians to return they had to give way to some of their demands.

It was agreed that in future the plebeians could choose from among themselves two magistrates called *tribunes* (the number was later raised to ten). These tribunes, who held office for one year, protected ordinary people against unfair treatment. They could not give orders or make laws, but they could veto the action of any citizen or magistrate, even a consul. This gave them great power. According to Plutarch, a Greek writer born in the first century AD,

> The tribune does not pride himself above the rest of the people, but is like an ordinary citizen in appearance, dress and way of life. . . . It is the custom that not even the door of his house shall be closed, but it remains open both night and day as a place of safety for those who may need it. The more humble he is in outward appearance, the more he is increased in power.

In the next 200 years or so the patricians were forced to give up many more privileges. Ordinary people were allowed to become magistrates and sit in the senate. By 342 BC plebeians could be consuls. It was further agreed that one consul at least should be a plebeian. Finally, men and women from different classes were allowed to marry. This, more than anything else, helped to reduce the differences between the nobles and the rest. But they would never be equal. In practice, power remained in the hands of a limited number of rich families.

Remains of an iron model of an axe and bundle of rods known as the fasces. In Rome, the chief magistrates got attendants to carry the fasces to remind the people of their power to beat or put to death wrongdoers. It is a symbol of power that was probably copied from the Etruscans

Sources and questions

1. A complaint of the plebeians in the early years of the Roman republic was that the magistrates kept the laws secret. This allowed dishonest patricians to take advantage of them. The plebeians got their way when, in about 450 BC, the chief laws of Rome were written on twelve bronze tablets and set up in the *forum* (market place). Here are some extracts.

   Quickly kill . . . a dreadfully deformed child.

   If a person has broken another's limb, he must lose his own limb unless some other compensation is agreed.

   For pasturing on, or cutting secretly by night, another's crops . . . there shall be punishment by death.

   Any person who destroys by burning any building or heap of corn beside a house shall be bound, flogged and put to death by burning at the stake, provided that the misdeed was deliberate; but if he did it accidentally, that is, through carelessness, it is ordered that he repair the damage.

   A dead man shall not be buried or burned within the city.

   The penalty shall be death for a judge . . . who has been found guilty of receiving a bribe for giving a decision.

   (a) What do these laws tell you about Roman life at that time?
   (b) Compare these laws with those of Hammurabi (see pages 35–7). What similarities and differences can you find?
   (c) Four of these laws lay down punishments for wrongdoing. How would the punishments for the same offences in our own society be different? Can you think of any reasons to explain the differences?
   (d) Some crimes are easier to prove than others. From these extracts can you pick out any examples of laws that would have been difficult to enforce? In each case, say why.

2. Look at the picture of the Etruscan wall painting on page 129.
   (a) Can you describe what is happening in the picture?
   (b) What would have been the point of decorating a tomb in this way?
   (c) What sort of person do you think would have been buried in a tomb with painted walls?
   (d) What information can we get from this painting about the way the Etruscan people lived?

3. Start off your own *Glossary of Roman History* by listing the meanings of the following words: republic, consul, veto, senate, patrician, plebeian, tribune.

4. Re-read the quotation from Plutarch on page 130. Can you explain how the power of a tribune could have been affected by his outward appearance?

ROME GOES TO WAR

The early Romans had no desire to become conquerors. They wanted peace so that they could get on with their farming and trading. But tribes from the hills and mountains were attracted by the rich soil and pleasant climate in the valley of the Tiber. They often tried to seize land or steal animals and crops. The Romans were forced to fight back. They soon discovered that attack was the best method of defence.

The conquest of Italy

There were no full-time soldiers in the early Roman republic. At the request of the consuls, men left the land and brought their own weapons – usually spears and swords. Wealthy Romans who could afford to keep horses would ride into battle. At first, soldiers were not paid, but as the Roman state grew in size taxes were collected to provide wages for the army. Soldiers also began to receive some military training.

During the fifth century BC the Latin cities led by Rome fought many battles against the Etruscans and other neighbouring tribes. The power of the Etruscans was broken in 396 BC when the Romans captured their capital city of Veii after a long siege. But the Romans suffered a setback six years later when Rome was ransacked and burned by a large force of Gauls who came down from the north. The Romans bribed them with gold to return to their homeland in the region of the river Po (see map).

The last Italian tribe to hold out against Rome was the Samnites from the mountains of central Italy. After three hard-fought wars, they were finally overcome and made *allies* (friends in time of war) in about 290 BC. Even then, the Romans did not control all of Italy. Along the southern coasts there were a number of wealthy Greek settlements, or 'colonies', at places like Naples and Taranto. Alarmed by the spread of Roman power, the Greeks of Taranto called to their assistance a famous Greek king called Pyrrhus.

Pyrrhus landed in 280 BC with 25,000 men and twenty elephants – which were probably used like tanks in ancient warfare. The Roman army did not seem to be a match for the

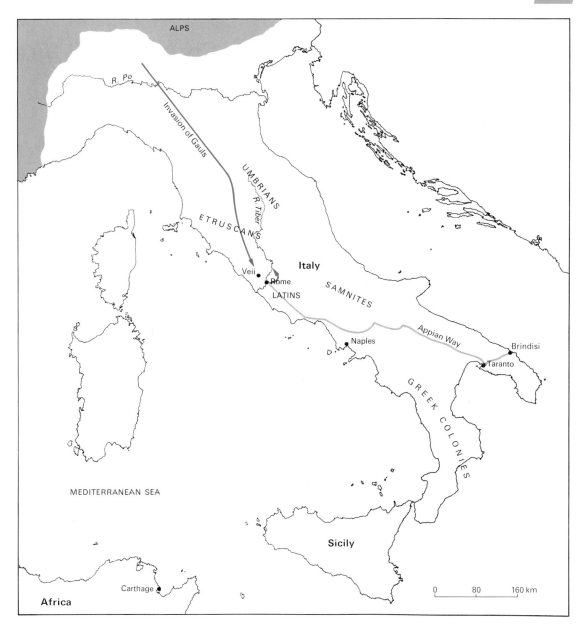

The position of Rome was a good one. It was surrounded by low hills, making it easy to defend, and the river Tiber was shallow enough at that point to be easily crossed. Rome's climate is similar to that of Greece – hot in summer, mild in winter – with enough rain to make the soil fertile

invading forces. But what they lacked in equipment they made up for in courage and the strictest discipline. If any man questioned an order he was flogged. If a company of soliders failed to stand up to the enemy it was *decimated* (one man in ten was executed). It is therefore not surprising that the Romans fought like tigers.

Although Pyrrhus won two battles, his losses were so heavy that he is reported to have said, 'If we win one more battle against the Romans we shall be ruined.' People still speak of a 'Pyrrhic victory' when it harms the winning side more than the losers. According to the Greek writer Plutarch,

> Pyrrhus ... had lost a great part of the force he had brought with him and almost all his friends and commanders ... while, like a fountain continually flowing out of the city, the Roman army was quickly filled up with fresh men who did not lose courage because of their defeats.

Pyrrhus was defeated and gave up the struggle in 275 BC, returning to his homeland. The Greek colonies in Italy were forced to accept Roman control. Rome was now master of all Italy south of the river Po.

Wise government and good roads

In past ages, people who won wars against their neighbours usually helped themselves to land, cattle, crops and anything else of value they could lay hands on. They often made slaves of the people they had conquered. But the Romans did not behave in this way. Defeated peoples were required to supply troops for Rome, but otherwise they were usually treated fairly – in the hope that they would become allies for the future.

The privileges of Roman citizens were granted to other Italian peoples, beginning with the nearby Latin cities. When a man became a full citizen, no matter where he lived he could go to Rome to help elect the magistrates and make laws in the citizens' assembly. The Romans gained a reputation for justice and good government. It was not long before the Roman language and way of life were spreading throughout Italy.

To link up the Italian cities and make it easier to move armies from place to place, a network of fine, straight roads was built. The most famous of these was the Appian Way, which ran 376 km south-east from Rome. As well as soldiers on the march, the traffic on roads like this included chariots, covered wagons, four-wheeled carriages and farmers' carts. Roman roads were so well made that they still provide the basis of many modern highways.

The struggle with Carthage

Nearly 640 km south of Rome, where the African coast juts out into the sea, lay the great city of Carthage. It had been founded by Phoenicians, seafaring people from the eastern Mediterranean, in about 850 BC. Carthage was a republic, like Rome, but in practice it was governed by a small group of rich merchants. Their main aim was to increase trade and this often brought them into conflict with Roman merchants in the western Mediterranean.

A full-scale war between Rome and Carthage broke out in 264 BC as a result of a quarrel in Sicily. The Carthaginians, with a large fleet of warships, were masters of the sea and therefore confident of victory. But with their usual determination the Romans began to cut down whole forests and build ships in large numbers. A Carthaginian vessel that had been wrecked on the coast of Italy was used as a model.

The Carthaginians were the better sailors, but the Romans had a way of making sea battles similar to those on land. Standing upright against the mast of each Roman warship was a wooden 'drawbridge' with an iron spike on the end. This was called a *corvus* (the Latin word for crow) because it looked like a bird's

Cobblestones from the original Appian Way. Roman methods of roadbuilding were similar to those we use today, even though they had no machines for earth-moving. They dug deep trenches and filled them with layers of cobblestones and crushed rubble. The finishing touch was a cambered (curved) surface of large paving stones. Rainwater ran off into drainage ditches along the roadside

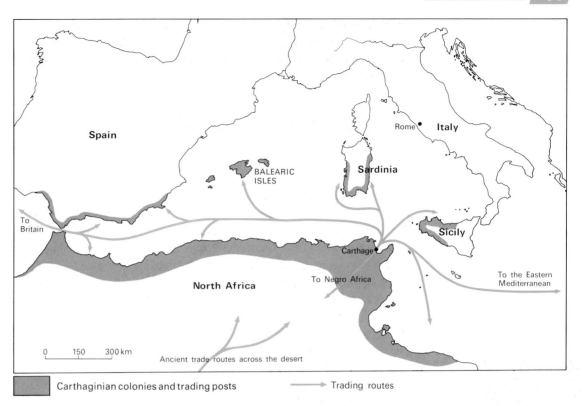

Colonies and trade routes of Carthage. Its fine harbour and central position in the Mediterranean made it an ideal trading city. Carthaginian ships carried silver from Spain, silk and perfumes from the East, papyrus from Egypt and even tin from far-away Britain. Through contact with Negro peoples beyond the Sahara desert, gold, ivory, hides and ostrich feathers were obtained and sold in the Mediterranean lands

■ Carthaginian colonies and trading posts   → Trading routes

beak. When an enemy vessel came close, the drawbridge was dropped so that the spike sank into its deck and locked the two ships together. This provided a gangway for soldiers to cross and force the enemy to fight hand-to-hand.

The war dragged on for more than twenty years, with enormous losses on both sides, until the Romans gained the upper hand with a naval victory near Sicily (241 BC). As part of the peace agreement they took over Sicily, but they did not treat the Sicilians in the same way as the Italian peoples. They seized most of their land and made them pay heavy taxes. The island became a *province* of Rome, governed by a Roman magistrate.

Hannibal

The Carthaginians were still rich and powerful and determined to gain revenge. Hamilcar, their leading general, made his son, Hannibal, swear an oath never to be a friend of Rome. After his father's death, Hannibal became a general at the age of 26. When a fresh war broke out with Rome he was ready with a daring scheme. Hannibal realised that the enemy controlled the sea routes, so he prepared to march his army out of Spain, through France and into Italy from the north.

In the spring of 218 BC, Hannibal set out with nearly 100,000 soldiers and three dozen elephants. The hardest part of the journey was the crossing of the Alps. The mountain passes were narrow and strewn with boulders. High up, the ground froze and there were frequent blizzards of snow. Thousands of men and animals fell to their deaths or perished from cold and hunger.

A coin minted in Spain shows one of Hannibal's elephants

According to a Greek historian called Polybius, when Hannibal finally reached the plains of Italy only a quarter of his army had survived the march:

> He had lost many of his men through enemy attacks while crossing rivers and ... in crossing the Alps.... His surviving forces numbered 12,000 African and 8,000 Spanish foot-soldiers, and not more than 6,000 on horseback.... The whole march ... had taken him five months.

Hannibal hoped to make up for his losses by gaining the support of the Italian cities, but most of them stayed loyal to Rome. Short of men and supplies, Hannibal nevertheless defeated the Romans and their allies in two great battles – near Lake Trasimene (217 BC) and, in the following year, at Cannae. Luckily for the Romans, the invading army was not big enough to press home its victories by attacking Rome itself. Attempts to provide reinforcements failed – including an overland march from Spain by Hannibal's brother, Hasdrubal, which ended in his defeat and death in northern Italy in 207 BC.

Hannibal remained undefeated in Italy until 203 BC, when he had to ship his army back to Africa to defend his homeland against Roman invasion. The Roman general Scipio had first conquered the Carthaginian colonies in Spain before attacking Carthage itself. The decisive battle, fought at Zama in 202 BC, was won by Scipio's well-trained army. Hannibal later fled to the East and after years in hiding he poisoned himself to escape capture.

Meanwhile, Carthage had to pay a vast sum of money to Rome and give up its colonies – including Spain, which became a Roman province. The Carthaginian army was disbanded and its warships set on fire. Rome was now master of the western Mediterranean. Even so, some Romans feared that Carthage might recover its power. One such was Marcus Cato, a leading member of the senate, who always finished his speeches with the words, 'Carth-

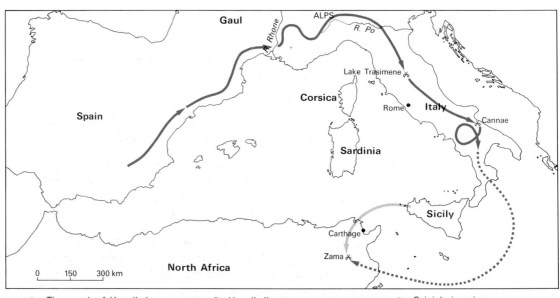

The Second Carthaginian War

→ The march of Hannibal   ┅► Hannibal's return   ⟶ Scipio's invasion

age must be destroyed.' This finally happened in 146 BC, following a bitter three-year siege of the city. Carthage was burned to the ground and its people killed or made slaves. North Africa became yet another Roman province.

Sources and questions

1. This document comes from a detailed history written by a Greek called Polybius, who lived from about 200 to 117 BC. Polybius spent more than ten years in Rome.

> The troops the Carthaginians employ are foreign and paid to fight, whereas those of the Romans are natives of the soil.... Consequently even if they happen to lose at first, the Romans overcome defeat by final success, while it is the opposite with the Carthaginians. For the Romans, fighting as they are for their country and their children ... continue to throw their whole hearts into the struggle until they get the better of their enemies. It follows that though the Romans are ... much less skilled in naval matters, they are generally successful at sea owing to the bravery of their men; for although skill in seamanship is important in naval battles, it is chiefly the courage of the marines [troops on board] that tips the scales in favour of victory. Not only do Italians in general have greater bodily strength and personal courage than Carthaginians and Africans ... they also do much to encourage a spirit of bravery in the young men.

> *Source: Polybius*, Histories, *Book VI, ii*

(a) Why do you think the Carthaginians employed foreign troops?
(b) Can you think of any additional reasons for the Roman success on top of those Polybius gives in this passage?
(c) Why were the Romans 'much less skilled in naval matters' than the Carthaginians?
(d) Is Polybius biased in favour of Rome and against Carthage? Give reasons for your answer.

2. Re-read the quotation from Polybius on page 136. Why would Hannibal's army have been attacked when crossing rivers? What difficulties would he have had at such times?

3. Imagine that Pyrrhus and Hannibal had lived at the same time and had met each other. Make up a short play in the form of a conversation between them in which they compare their experiences fighting against Rome.

4. Imagine you were a soldier on a Roman warship fighting against Carthage. Write a letter to your family or a friend describing a victorious sea battle in which you have just taken part. Give as much detailed description as you can.

'BREAD AND GAMES'

Greek sculptures, like this one of a discus thrower, were admired and copied by the Romans. The athlete on page 94 is also a Roman copy of a Greek original statue

Victory over Carthage gave Rome a taste for further conquest. In the space of only seventy years after the defeat of Hannibal, Macedonia, Greece and Asia Minor (now Turkey) came under Roman rule (see map). The conquered areas became provinces, each under a Roman governor. The senate chose governors from among those who had previously been magistrates in Rome, and changed them every year.

Many governors took advantage of their position to make personal fortunes – often by getting the people of the province to pay more in taxes than was required by Rome and then pocketing the difference. But in general the Romans ruled fairly and allowed their subjects to keep their old laws, customs and religion. In less civilised provinces, like Spain, people were often eager to copy Roman ways. The well-to-do learned Latin, wore Roman clothes and took Roman names. Sometimes the influence was in the other direction. The Greeks, for example, were more advanced than the Romans. Greek sculpture, painting and literature were admired and copied by educated Romans, many of whom also learned the Greek language.

The rich get richer

In the early years of the republic, few Romans were very rich or very poor. But foreign wars upset the old pattern of life. Those in command of the armies came home with piles of money and valuables taken from conquered cities. One Roman was said to have brought back from Macedonia 250 wagon-loads of statues and paintings. At the same time merchants' warehouses bulged with high-priced goods shipped from Africa, Greece and Turkey.

Ordinary peasant farmers were not so fortunate. All over Italy, men returned from fighting in the army to find their families in debt and their farms neglected. Those who could no longer make a decent living out of their land sold out to wealthy senators and businessmen, who grouped small plots together to make large farms. These were worked by slaves – mostly prisoners-of-war, sold in public slave markets all over Italy.

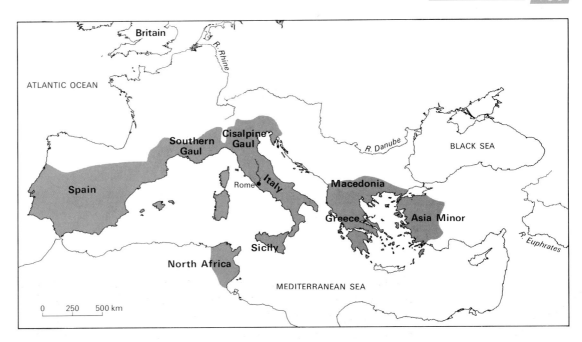

The Roman Empire in 121 BC

Slaves did not serve in the army. This made them especially useful to the owners of large estates because, unlike free peasants, they did not leave their work to go to war. Even so, there were risks involved in gathering large numbers of slaves together. Sometimes they rebelled – as in Sicily in 134 BC where tens of thousands of runaway slaves were only defeated by the Roman army after three years of bitter fighting. To try to prevent slaves escaping, their masters put them in chains. They treated them harshly in other ways, often keeping them short of food and forcing them to sleep in smelly underground barracks.

As slave-worked estates replaced small family farms, thousands of peasants were made homeless. Some of them drifted to Rome but few found work as there were no large industries in those days. They merely swelled the numbers of idle citizens crowding the slums in the low-lying parts of the city. An historian called Appian, who was born in Egypt in the first century AD, described the plight of the peasants:

> the rich, taking possession of . . . strips of land nearby and the plots of their poor neighbours . . . came to cultivate vast areas instead of single farms, using slaves they had bought as farm labourers and herdsmen. . . . So certain powerful men became extremely rich and the class of slaves multiplied throughout the country, while the Italian people declined in numbers and strength, burdened by poverty, taxes and military service.

The poor slum-dwellers of Rome were often kept from starving by hand-outs of free corn, wine and olive oil. Wealthy Romans who wanted to be elected to positions of power had to please the people in order to gain their support. One way of doing this was by providing 'bread and games' – giving away food and organising free entertainments such as fights between *gladiators* (armed professional fighters). You can read about later Roman games in Chapter 23.

Troubled times

Only the wealthiest Romans could afford to please the people and so gain their support. This meant that the magistrates, who went on to become members of the senate, were usually very rich. The senate had almost complete control of Rome's affairs. But it did not govern according to the wishes of ordinary people. Once elected, most magistrates and senators forgot about those who had voted for them and looked after their own selfish interests.

A Roman mosaic showing slaves working on an estate

The tribunes in the senate were often an exception. Although by this time tribunes came from noble families, some of them spoke up for ordinary people and put forward remedies for their discontents. In 133 BC a tribune called Tiberius Gracchus suggested that the great estates of the rich should be reduced in size and the surplus land used for resettling out-of-work peasants. But he met violent opposition from the great landowners. They stirred up riots in which Gracchus and many of his followers were killed. The importance of this for the future was summed up by a retired army officer named Velleius, writing early in the first century AD:

> This was the first time in the city of Rome when the blood of Roman citizens was shed ... without fear of punishment. After that the laws were overwhelmed by the use of force ... and disorder among the citizens, which in the past had been ended by agreement, was settled by the sword.

Ten years later, Tiberius's brother, Gaius, also became a tribune. He was a powerful speaker, able to stir the passions of the people. Gaius put forward a number of reforms to improve life for the poor, including a clever scheme to reduce the price of grain in Rome. But this met furious opposition from landowners and merchants. Gaius Gracchus's answer to the problem of unemployed peasants was to set up special 'colonies' for them, but the first of these – for 6,000 settlers in North Africa – was abandoned when Gaius, like his brother, met a violent death in a riot started by leading senators. Again fighting had broken out within the walls of Rome.

Enter the generals

A successful soldier called Marius was chosen by the people to be consul in 107 BC. He promised to finish a war which had been dragging on for some time in Numidia (North Africa). The generals chosen by the senate had been failures, yet Marius crushed the enemy and returned to Rome a hero. To allow him to deal with a fresh threat – from German tribes invading Gaul – Marius was made consul five times running (104–100 BC). This broke one of the oldest rules of the republic, that ten years must go by before a consul could be re-elected.

Marius thoroughly re-organised the Roman army. Instead of calling up ordinary citizens he took volunteers who were willing to make the army a full-time career. From now on, soldiers enlisted for at least 16 years. Marius divided each *legion* (regiment) into ten *cohorts* of up to 600 men. Cohorts were made up of six *centuries*, each containing a maximum of 100 troops. These were commanded, as before, by *centurions* – experienced soldiers usually promoted from the ranks. The foot-soliders were normally Italians, but cavalry, archers and others were mostly drawn from the provinces.

With his professional army, Marius won two great victories against the German tribes (102–101 BC). Yet the very success of Marius was storing up trouble for the future. His soldiers looked

This is what a Roman legionary looked like. The shield was made of hide rimmed with iron. The metal-tipped javelins were thrown while approaching the enemy and the short stabbing sword was used at close quarters. On the march, legionaries wore hobnailed boots and carried a heavy pack with rations, clothes and a cooking pot. They were expected to march 20 miles or more a day and build a fortified camp each evening

to him to reward them for successful campaigns by providing at least a plot of land when they retired from active service. Consequently they owed their duty to him personally. The same was true of generals after Marius: their troops were loyal to them first and Rome second. It was just a matter of time before a successful general used his army for his own ends.

Sulla, a rich and ambitious nobleman, became a consul in 88 BC and was given command of a large army for a war in the East. However, when one of the tribunes got Sulla's command cancelled Sulla persuaded his troops to march into Rome and take control of the city. His opponents were dealt with mercilessly, as Appian tells us:

> Some . . . taken unawares, were killed where they were caught, in their homes, in the streets, or in the temples. Others were hurled through mid-air and thrown at Sulla's feet. Others were dragged through the city and trampled on, none of the spectators daring to utter a word . . . because everybody was shivering with fear.

After greatly reducing the power of the tribunes, Sulla tried to strengthen the senate, but it had lost its authority over the people as well as the generals. When Sulla died (78 BC) the government of the republic was weaker than ever.

Meanwhile, disturbances all over Rome's empire threatened to bring about its collapse. There were wars in Spain and Turkey, and the Mediterranean was swarming with pirates who robbed shipping and raided coastal towns. Earlier, in 91 BC, the subject peoples of Italy had rebelled against Rome. They complained that although they provided most of the soldiers for the army, few of them had the privileges of Roman citizens. After two years of fighting they were defeated by an army under Sulla. But their demands were granted soon afterwards, when all free men in Italy were made Roman citizens.

Coin showing the head of Lucius Cornelius Sulla. Although his ruthless and violent career caused much bitterness and hatred, he survived many dangers and retired into private life in 79 BC, aged about sixty. When he died, only a few months later, his body was cremated – to prevent his enemies from mutilating it

Sources and questions

1. This account of Sulla's rule was written by Appian, more than 200 years later, using the works of earlier historians. (A *dictator* is someone with complete power whose word is law.)

   > Thus Sulla became a king, or tyrant . . . not elected but holding power by force and violence. . . . To keep up the appearances of the Republic, he allowed the election of consuls. . . . But Sulla, like a reigning sovereign, was dictator over the consuls. . . . He reduced the tribunes' power to such feebleness as practically to destroy it. . . . To the senate, which had been much reduced by the disturbances and wars, he added about 300 members. . . . To the plebeians he added more than 10,000 slaves of the men who had been killed, choosing the youngest and strongest, to whom he gave freedom and Roman citizenship. . . . In this way he made sure of having 10,000 men among the plebeians always ready to obey his commands. In order to provide the same kind of safeguard throughout Italy, he distributed to the 23 legions [about

120,000 men] that had served under him a great deal of land.

Source: Appian, Civil Wars, *Book 1, xi–xii*

(a) Write a short speech on Sulla's behalf in which he justifies to the Roman people the actions described here.

(b) Re-read the quotation from Appian on page 143 together with this passage. In what ways do they explain how Sulla managed to hold on to his power?

(c) Why do you think that Sulla wanted to weaken the tribunes but strengthen the senate overall?

(d) What effect would you expect a dictatorship of this kind to have upon the future of Rome?

2. Look at the picture of slaves working on an estate on page 140.

(a) The slaves appear to be naked. Can you think of any reasons why?

(b) Can you pick out one figure who does not appear to be a slave? What do you think this person is doing?

(c) What type of farming does the picture show?

(d) To what different uses would these animals have been put?

3. Re-read the quotation from Appian on page 139. What evidence can you find in this passage that the writer regrets the developments he is describing?

4. Why did the common people of Rome become dissatisfied with the rule of the senate?

FROM REPUBLIC TO EMPIRE

Weakened by civil war and disorder, the Roman republic was threatened, in 73 BC, by the biggest slave revolt in its history. It began in the southern city of Capua, at a 'combat school' where slaves were trained to fight in the arena. Led by a gladiator called Spartacus, a group of skilled swordsmen made a daring escape. Tens of thousands of slaves from the big farms ran away to join them. A vast slave army was soon roaming the countryside, robbing and burning the houses of landowners.

It seemed that Rome itself was in danger when the slaves twice defeated armies led by consuls. But the rebels were finally overcome in 71 BC by an army under Marcus Crassus, one of the richest men in Rome. In bitter revenge 6,000 prisoners were crucified along the Appian Way. The lines of crosses stretched over 160 kilometres, from Rome to Capua. Crassus got his reward when he was elected consul in the following year. The other consul was a popular young army commander named Gnaeus Pompey, who was soon to become the most powerful man in Rome.

Pompey and Caesar

Pompey had shown a gift for leadership on his military campaigns in Italy and Spain. He added to this reputation in 67 BC when he was given the task of clearing the pirates from the Mediterranean. With 200 warships, it took him only three months to chase them from the seas and destroy their bases. In the next year Pompey left Rome at the head of a large army to fight a war in Turkey. He was so successful that not only Turkey but also Syria and Palestine were brought firmly under Roman rule.

When Pompey came home after five years in the East he was awarded the highest honours. Some people had expected him to march into Rome with his army and make himself ruler. But he hesitated, probably deciding that the time was not ripe. In any case, he had some powerful rivals, including Crassus and a wealthy nobleman called Gaius Julius Caesar who had recently made himself popular. Caesar wanted power and would stop at nothing to get it.

Pompey 'the Great' (106–48 BC). His successes on the battlefield made him very popular and led some of his followers to compare him with Alexander the Great

Gaius Julius Caesar (100–44 BC). As a young man he got on the wrong side of Sulla and was lucky to survive. He then set out to gain popularity and support in Rome. Caesar wanted complete power. Once, when passing through a village in the Alps, he said to his companions: 'I would rather be head of this tiny village than second in command in Rome'

Caesar knew that the best way to achieve his ambition was to get control of an army and become a famous conqueror. He managed to become a consul in 59 BC and then used his position to get himself made governor of Gaul in the following year. The northern part of Gaul was outside Roman control. This gave Caesar his opportunity. In the next nine years he conquered the whole country, advancing the Roman frontier to the North Sea.

Caesar had gained a new province for Rome and shown himself to be a great general. He planned each campaign skilfully, made sure that his troops were properly trained and shared every hardship and danger with them. Not only were his soldiers devoted to him, he was also a hero in Rome. It seemed that only Pompey could stop Caesar taking over the government when he returned from Gaul (Crassus was killed on a campaign in the East in 53 BC).

Jealous of Caesar's popularity, Pompey grew more friendly with the leading nobles and senators. The senate instructed Caesar to disband his army. The order was ignored. In January 49 BC Caesar marched his army into Italy. Pompey and most of the nobles fled to Greece to raise troops. Cicero, a leading senator, wrote to a friend:

> It is civil war, though it has not sprung from division among our citizens but from the daring of one . . . citizen. He is strong in military forces, he attracts followers by hopes and promises, he desires the whole universe. Rome is delivered to him stripped of defenders. . . .

Everywhere Caesar was given a hero's welcome. After taking charge of the capital, he caught up with his enemies in the following year and defeated them at Pharsalus in Greece. Pompey escaped to Egypt where he was murdered. Caesar finished off all remaining opposition and returned to Rome, in 45 BC, as ruler of the Mediterranean world.

Murder in the senate house

Caesar's soldiers called him *Imperator* (commander-in-chief). From this we get the word *emperor*, meaning a king who rules an empire, or group of countries. Caesar did not actually take the title of king, but he was a king in all but name. He controlled the appointment of magistrates and took away most of the powers of the senate.

Rome's new master proved to be a wise ruler. He improved the government of the provinces, making methods of tax collection fairer. He tried to help unemployed Romans by setting up colonies in the provinces where they could buy land cheaply and settle down to farm it. Work was also provided by schemes to rebuild the centre of Rome and construct more roads in Italy. In these ways, Caesar halved the number of citizens receiving free bread.

Caesar made important changes in the Roman calendar. At that time its twelve months were measured by the moon, making 355 days in a year. Consequently the months gradually got in front of the seasons. Caesar ordered that in future Romans would use the *solar* (sun) calendar of $365\frac{1}{4}$ days which required a leap year every fourth year (see page 17). He renamed the seventh month Julius (now July) after his own name. Augustus, the next ruler of Rome, called the eighth month August.

Caesar planned more reforms, but he did not live to carry them out. On 15 March 44 BC, in the senate house, he was brutally murdered by a group of senators who had plotted against him. Plutarch described the scene:

> Those who had come prepared for the murder drew their daggers and closed in on Caesar in a circle. Whichever way he turned he encountered blows and weapons levelled at his face . . . for it had been agreed that they should all strike him and taste of the slaughter.

Some of Caesar's murderers, including Gaius Cassius, were jealous of his power. Others, like Marcus Brutus, believed they were doing the right thing for Rome. They hated the way Caesar was adored like a god and feared that his next step would be to make himself king.

This coin was issued by Brutus and his followers to celebrate the murder of Caesar. It shows a cap and daggers standing for liberty (felt caps like this were worn by freed slaves). The words refer to the Ides of March (the date of Caesar's murder, half way through the month)

'The Second Founder of Rome'

Caesar's murderers hoped to see a return of the republic, but they were mistaken. Control of the Roman armies passed to followers of Caesar – particularly Mark Antony, his close friend, and Octavian, his great-nephew and adopted son. At the time of the murder Octavian was only eighteen.

In a clever speech at Caesar's funeral Antony turned the people against the murderers. He later joined with Octavian to defeat them at Philippi in Macedonia (42 BC). Brutus and Cassius killed themselves to avoid capture. Antony and Octavian now divided most of the Roman Empire between them. Antony, a tough and experienced soldier, ruled the East. Octavian ruled the West, including Italy. He had none of the brilliance of Caesar, but he was firm and sensible and he learned to govern wisely.

It was just a matter of time before a power struggle broke out between Antony and Octavian. Antony had married Octavian's sister, Octavia; but not long afterwards he fell deeply in love with Cleopatra, the Queen of Egypt. A complete break between the two men occurred in 33 BC, when Antony divorced Octavia to marry Cleopatra. Octavian declared war and, in 31 BC, won a decisive battle at sea, near Actium in Greece. Cleopatra and Antony escaped to Egypt but their position was hopeless and they both committed suicide. Egypt became a new Roman province and Octavian returned to Rome as sole ruler of its vast empire.

Octavian depended on the support of the army. In fact, from now on it was necessary for every ruler of Rome to be hailed as *Imperator* by his soliders. Octavian also wanted the nobles and

Statue of Augustus dressed as a Roman senator

ordinary people to trust him. Instead of sweeping away old traditions, as Caesar had done, he pretended to bring back the republic. The senate continued to meet, magistrates were elected and laws passed. But nothing was done without Octavian's approval. He was *princeps* (first citizen), chief priest and often consul too – although he was usually known simply as *Augustus*, meaning 'His Majesty'.

Augustus kept the poor people of Rome contented by giving them free food, amusements and occasional gifts of money. He set up a police force and fire brigade and tried to keep the streets clean. So many fine temples and public buildings were put up that Augustus boasted he had found Rome a city of brick and left it a city of marble.

To keep the peace, Augustus disbanded roughly half the legions under his command and stationed most of the remainder in camps guarding the frontiers of the Empire. Distant provinces were linked with each other and with Rome by many new roads. Augustus ruled for well over 40 years, until his death in AD 14. He is often called 'the Second Founder of Rome' because he brought the civil wars to an end and established the rule of emperors which lasted for centuries.

The Roman Peace

For about 200 years, starting with the reign of Augustus, the peace in the Roman Empire was rarely broken – and then only by fighting near the frontiers. It was such a change from all the wars and disturbances of the past that this period became famous for the *Pax Romana* (Roman Peace).

At first, there was a kind of 'royal family' as each of the four emperors who followed Augustus was related to him. The last of the four, Nero (AD 54–68) loved to show off. He acted in the theatre and recited his poems in public. On one occasion he joined the gladiators in the arena and killed a lion with a club. Nero was cruel, wasteful and quick to murder anyone who stood in his way. The nobles finally turned against him and he committed suicide.

After Nero, the Empire was usually ruled by a popular army general. Some were unreliable, others strong and wise. From AD 98–180 there was an unbroken line of strong emperors. The first, Trajan, was prepared to break the peace in order to expand the Empire. He took an army across the river Danube and occupied Dacia (present-day Romania). Trajan also extended the empire in the East (see map) but these conquests were short-lived.

Hadrian, who followed Trajan as emperor in AD 117, did not attempt further conquests. According to a writer called Dio Cassius,

Hadrian travelled through one province after another . . . inspecting all the garrisons and forts . . . and he reformed and corrected in many cases ways of life that had become too luxurious. . . . This best explains why he lived mostly at peace

This Roman landmark is known as Trajan's column. It was erected in AD 113 to celebrate Trajan's conquest of Dacia (present-day Romania). All round the column are finely detailed carvings telling the story of Trajan's conquests and showing many aspects of life in the Roman army, including marching, building forts, methods of transporting equipment and treating the sick

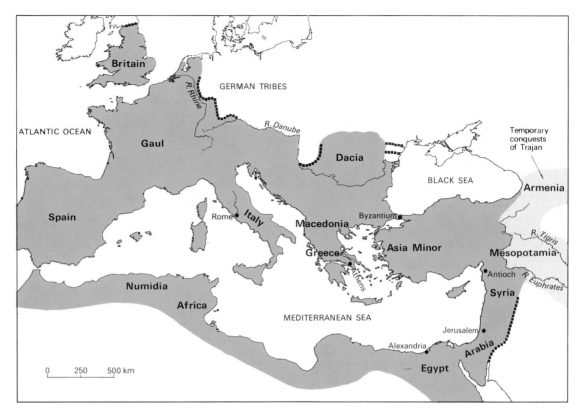

▪▪▪▪▪▪▪ Main walls and fortifications

The Roman Empire in AD 117

with foreign nations; for as they saw how well prepared he was
. . . they made no uprising.

To strengthen the defences of the empire, Hadrian built walls,
ditches and forts along the whole northern frontier. By this time
Britain had become a Roman province. We can still see remains of
the great wall Hadrian built across the north of the country. Army
camps along these frontiers grew into permanent settlements, with
their own houses, shops and baths.

Meanwhile, inside the frontiers, peace helped the growth of
trade. The roads were safe and the seas free of pirates. Peace also
helped the spread of Roman civilisation in Gaul, Spain and Britain. The better-off people of the provinces now thought of themselves as Romans. Some rose to become governors, generals or
even emperors – like Trajan who was born in Spain. Finally, in
AD 213, every freeborn subject in the Empire was made a full
Roman citizen.

DOCUMENTS: THE ROMAN ARMY

Document 1

A battle-standard in the form of a silver eagle mounted on a pole was carried in front of every Roman legion when it advanced into battle. A legion was proud of its eagle; its capture by an enemy was considered a terrible disgrace. Julius Caesar here describes the bravery of one standard-bearer during his invasion of Britain in 55 BC.

> As the Romans hesitated, mainly because of the depth of the water, the man who carried the eagle of the 10th legion, after praying to the gods that his action might bring them luck, cried in a loud voice: 'Jump down, comrades, unless you want to surrender our eagle to the enemy. I, at least, intend to do my duty to my country and my general.' With these words he leapt from the ship and advanced towards the enemy with the eagle in his hands. When the other soldiers saw this, they urged each other not to allow such a disgrace to happen and also jumped ... while the men in the ships behind followed them and advanced against the enemy.

Source: Caesar, The Conquest of Gaul, *Book IV, Chapter 25*

Document 2

The writer of the following passage, a Jew called Flavius Josephus, had been one of the leaders of a Jewish revolt against the Romans (AD 66–70). After being taken prisoner, he was spared and later became a Roman citizen and adviser to important noblemen.

This drawing is based on a carving from Trajan's column. It shows Roman soldiers who have formed what was called a 'tortoise' with their locked shields. Can you describe the kind of battle in which this formation would have been useful, and why?

> This vast empire of theirs has come to them as the prize of courage, not just good fortune. For they do not wait for war to start. ... On the contrary, as though they had been born with weapons in hand, they never have a rest from training ... each soldier daily throws all his energy into his training, as though he were in action. ...
>
> By their military exercises the Romans give their soldiers strength not only of body but also of soul; fear, too, plays its part in their training. For they have laws which punish with death not just desertion [running away] but even a slight neglect of duty.

Source: Josephus, The Jewish War, *Book III, Chapter 5*

Document 3

Flavius Vegetius, a writer born in the fourth century AD, here describes the training of the Roman army of earlier centuries.

> The Roman people owed the conquest of the world to no other cause than military training, discipline in their camps, and practice in warfare. . . .
>
> At the very beginning of their training, recruits should be taught the military step. For . . . the keeping of their ranks by all the soliders . . . cannot be achieved in any other way. . . .
>
> The soldier is to be trained in leaping also, to enable him to leap across ditches. . . . Every recruit, without exception, should in the summer months learn to swim; for it is not always possible to cross rivers on bridges. . . .
>
> They must also practise throwing their javelins at the posts from a distance in order to increase their skill in aiming and the strength of the arm. . . . The slingers should be trained to whirl the sling only once about the head when letting loose a stone. But all soliders used to be trained to throw stones of a pound weight with the bare hand.

Source: Vegetius, Military Science, *Book 1*

Document 4

This is part of a letter written in the middle of the second century AD by Marcus Fronto, a well-known teacher and writer in Rome. He is telling Lucius Verus, who ruled as joint emperor (161–69 AD), about the condition of the Roman army in Syria.

> The soldiers . . . liked to spend their time applauding actors and were more often found in the nearest tavern garden than in the ranks. Horses shaggy from neglect, but every hair plucked from their riders; a rare sight was a soldier with arm or leg hairy. . . . Few of the soldiers could vault upon their horses, the rest scrambled clumsily up by means of heel or knee. . . . not many could make their spears hurtle, most tossed them like toy lances without spirit and energy. Gambling was widespread in camp, sleep night-long, or, if a watch was kept, it was over the wine cups.

Source: Fronto, Letter to Lucius Verus, *xix*

In this carving from Trajan's column, we see Roman soldiers fighting tribesmen near the borders of the Empire. How can you tell which side is which? How are the attackers trying to break down the wall?

Questions

1. Re-write Document 1 from the point of view of an ordinary soldier of the 10th legion.
2. From the information given in these documents, what do you think were the main reasons for the military success of the Romans?
3. What skills learned by soldiers in those days are no longer important today? Explain why.
4. Is there evidence anywhere in these documents that the attitude of men towards their personal appearance was different from that of today?
5. Imagine you are Lucius Verus and you have just received Fronto's letter. Write a letter to the officers in charge of the army in Syria telling them what they must do to cure the slackness among the soldiers.
6. Do these documents suggest any reasons why the Romans were occasionally defeated in battle?

THE BUSY LIFE OF THE CAPITAL

Rome was by far the largest city of the ancient world. Hundreds of thousands of people lived there, closely packed together. Such a dense population was only made possible by the excellent water supply. This was carried from surrounding hillsides in earthenware pipes which were supported by stone arches called *aqueducts* across river valleys. A Greek writer, Strabo, who lived at the time of Augustus, greatly admired the work of Roman engineers:

> The Romans . . . are much better than the Greeks in the building of such things as roads, aqueducts and sewers to wash out the filth of the city into the river Tiber. . . . The sewers, with arches made of close-fitting stones, are large enough in some places for wagons loaded with hay to pass through them. And so much water is brought into the city through the aqueducts that . . . almost every house has cisterns, service pipes and gushing fountains.

Strabo had in mind the homes of the better-off citizens. The poor people of Rome had to get their water from public taps in the streets.

This famous Roman aqueduct (water-bridge) was built in the first century AD near Nimes in France. It carries the pipeline 55 metres above a valley

Workaday Rome

Like all big cities, Rome was full of contrasts. From the Palatine Hill, where the emperor lived in a marble palace, it was only a short walk to the noisy slum district of Subura. Here the narrow streets were piled with rubbish and crowded with tradesmen, pedlars, drunkards, thieves and beggars. No one could feel safe there when the streets were dark. At night time, those who avoided the drunks the thieves still risked injury from all sorts of rubbish thrown out of the windows, as Juvenal, a writer born in the first century AD, tells us:

> There's death in every open window as you pass along at night.... What a height it is to the lofty roofs, from which a tile comes crack upon your head, and how often broken or leaky pots are thrown from windows ... Hope, then, ... that they may be content just to empty wash basins over you.

Almost every kind of tradesman could be found in the capital. There were gold- and silver-smiths, jewellers, cutlers, clothmakers, potters, leather workers, glassmakers, stonemasons, carpenters and dozens more. Many of them made luxury goods for the rich, using materials brought from overseas. Precious metals came mainly from Spain and Africa; glassware, papyrus and perfumes were shipped from Egypt, while far-away India and China provided silk, spices, emeralds and pearls. It is true to say that the world supplied Rome, while Rome supplied the rest of Italy.

Goods were sold from either market stalls or ordinary shops, which were opened and closed with wooden shutters. Craftsmen usually worked in their own shops, assisted by slaves and apprentices. In some streets all the shops were of the same kind, for example, 'the street of shoemakers'. These were useful landmarks in directing strangers about the city, because streets rarely had names and houses were not numbered.

Here we see a Roman blacksmith at work. His assistant is keeping the forge hot with a pair of bellows. Notice that he is shielded from the heat by a screen. On the right the smith's tools are displayed, together with what looks like one of his products, a spearhead

Meeting places

In the mornings the main centre of activity was the Forum, at the

foot of the Palatine and Capitol Hills. This was the meeting place of lawyers, politicians and businessmen. They came to attend the Senate House, visit the temples or call in at the offices of bankers and merchants. The Forum was crammed with people of every race and occupation, all pushing and shoving.

Marriages, funerals and religious processions crowded the streets in other parts of the city. These often caused hold-ups, according to Juvenal.

> We in our hurry are blocked by a sea of people in front, while the multitude behind shoves us in the back. One strikes me with his elbow, another with a hard pole, one knocks a wooden beam against my head, another a wine jar. My legs are plastered with mud; I am trodden on all sides by large feet, and the hobnails of a soldier stick into my toe.

The streets were so busy that wheeled traffic had to be forbidden until nightfall, except for carts carrying building materials. It was often hard for people to sleep through the noise of wagons rattling down narrow lanes and the shouts of the drivers.

Most people left work during the afternoon and set out for one of the public baths. Roman baths were recreation centres where people from many walks of life could bathe, exercise and gossip with friends. As well as hot, cold and warm baths there were usually massage rooms. In these bathers could have their bodies oiled and massaged by specially trained slaves. Afterwards they could relax in lounges, libraries or restaurants.

Roman baths usually included a gymnasium and an ordinary swimming pool – the only place where mixed bathing was allowed. A writer called Lucius Seneca, who was for a time tutor to the emperor Nero, found the noise disturbing.

> I live over a bath house.... I can hear the grunts of men exercising hard by lifting heavy lead weights ... and whenever they release their pent-up breath, I hear their hissing.... I hear the slapping of hands on shoulders when someone is lying down having a cheap massage.... On top of that, there's the man who likes the sound of his own voice in the bath or the fellow who plunges into the swimming pool with an enormous splash.

While most people went to the baths, some young men preferred riding, wrestling, ball games or athletic sports on the Field of Mars, a large open space near the banks of the Tiber. Swimming in the river was also very popular, especially in the summer.

Public entertainments

Nowadays most people have about 120–130 days off work every year (including weekends). In ancient Rome roughly the same amount of time was given to public holidays and religious festivals. On these days public entertainments were held. They were provided free, usually by the emperor.

The biggest event was chariot racing at the Circus Maximus.

Remains of the Baths of Caracalla in Rome. Built early in the third century AD, they covered an area of about 11 hectares

This was nothing like a circus as we know it. It was a great racecourse, with places for up to 150,000 spectators. In each race four horse-drawn chariots covered seven laps of the course, a distance of about 8 kilometres. The charioteers needed great skill to take the sharp bends at each end of the arena. They wore crash helmets and padded clothing, yet there were many fatal accidents. Those who survived and were successful became rich and famous, even though they were slaves.

Most ordinary Romans found the chariot racing very exciting and there was heavy betting among the spectators. Pliny the Younger, a rich and educated nobleman who lived from AD 62 to about 110, thought differently. In a letter to a friend, he said:

> The circus races ... do not interest me in the slightest ....
> When you've seen one you've seen them all. I cannot
> understand why so many thousands of men should have such a
> childish passion for watching galloping horses and drivers
> standing in chariots, over and over again. It wouldn't be so bad
> if they were attracted by the speed of the horses or the drivers'
> skill, but all they see is the colour of the tunic. If you swapped
> over the colours during a race I'm quite sure they wouldn't
> notice the difference.

Probably Pliny would have preferred to go to a play. Actors performed in large, open air theatres like those in Greece (see page 112). The Romans also copied the Greeks' costumes, scenery and plots. The most popular plays were comedies, but the audiences also very much enjoyed scenes of cruelty. In one well-known play an evil robber and murderer called Laureolus ends up being

tortured to death. To add to the excitement, the emperor Domitian allowed a condemned criminal to replace the actor on stage and suffer a real death!

Such brutality could be witnessed all day long in the *amphitheatre* (an oval-shaped arena with seats rising all round). Rome's great amphitheatre was the Colosseum, opened in AD 80, where up to 50,000 spectators watched all kinds of cruel entertainments. Gladiators fought each other or wild beasts such as lions, panthers and bears. The senator Cicero had this to say about the 'games' put on by Pompey in 55 BC.

> What civilised person can enjoy the sight of a feeble man being mauled by a powerful beast, or a noble beast being pierced by a hunting spear? . . . On the last day it was the turn of the elephants. As usual, the crowd was greatly impressed but showed no pleasure. . . . They seem to be almost like human beings.

A favourite contest in the amphitheatre was between a fast-moving gladiator with a net and trident (three-pronged spear) and a heavily-armed opponent with a sword and shield. We see such a fight pictured below. Sometimes the arena was flooded for a sea battle between rival warships. This provided plenty of killings and drownings to amuse the spectators. Although it is difficult for us to understand, the Romans seem to have got a great deal of pleasure from watching suffering and death.

This decorated vase was made in the Roman province of Britain in about AD 200. The gladiator on the right has been disarmed and is holding up his finger to ask the crowd for mercy. If they gave the 'thumbs pressed' sign he would be spared, but the 'thumbs turned' sign meant death. The thumb probably stood for the sword; to 'turn' it was to kill and to 'press' was to put it back in its sheath. People today use such signs differently when they show 'thumbs up' or 'thumbs down' to mean good or bad

Sources and questions

1. At noon in the Roman amphitheatre condemned criminals were brought out to kill each other. Lucius Seneca described the scene as follows in a letter to a friend.

   I happened to call in at a midday show, expecting some sport, fun and relaxation – or at least something different from the usual bloodshed. It was just the opposite. The previous fights were merciful by comparison; now they really get down to business and it is pure murder. The men have no armour to protect them and with the whole of their bodies exposed to each other's blows, they never fail to hit the target.... The spectators demand that the man who has just killed his opponent should face the next man who will kill him in turn.... It is said, 'But that one was a highway robber, he killed a man!' ... Even so, does he deserve to die like this?.... The crowd cries, 'Kill him, flog him, burn him! Why does he meet the sword so timidly? ... Why is he so unwilling to die?'

   Source: Seneca, Letters, *VII, 3–5*

   (a) Compare this passage with the quotation from Pliny the Younger on page 156. How are the two situations different?
   (b) What do Pliny and Seneca think of the other spectators?
   (c) Can anything be learned from these two passages about the men who wrote them?
   (d) From the time of Augustus, such shows were usually put on by the emperor. How might an emperor's view of this spectacle be different from that of Seneca?

2. Look at the picture of the two gladiators on page 157.
   (a) What has happened to the right-hand gladiator's weapon?
   (b) What other piece of equipment did this gladiator have (on his left arm)? How was this meant to be used?
   (c) If you had to be one of the gladiators in this type of fight, which would you choose, and why?
   (d) Why do you think this kind of contest was popular with the spectators in the amphitheatre?

3. 'You have to be rich,' said Juvenal, 'to be able to afford a good night's sleep in Rome.'
   (a) Can you explain what Juvenal meant by this?
   (b) From what you have learned of Juvenal's views in this chapter, how reliable do you think he is as a source of information? Give reasons for your opinion.

4. The original sources quoted in this chapter present rather an unattractive picture of ancient Rome. Imagine you were living in the city in the first or second century AD. Write a letter to a friend in the country pointing out some of the attractions and advantages of living in Rome.

ROMAN CUSTOMS AND EDUCATION

The Romans gradually gave up distinguishing between patricians and plebeians (see Chapter 19). But great differences in wealth and power remained. At the top of Roman society were magistrates and others holding important positions in government, landowners and successful businessmen of all kinds, including merchants, bankers and tax collectors. Below were the ordinary craftsmen and shopkeepers, the 'city mob' (mostly idlers living on free bread) and large numbers of slaves.

We know a great deal about the lives of wealthy and educated Romans, from their letters and diaries as well as the remains of their homes. But we have much less information about the way of life of poorer people. While reading the next two chapters, it is therefore important to remember that those living in ease and comfort were only a small number in the total population.

Family life

Romans belonged not only to families but also to larger groups which were like Scottish clans. This can be seen in their names. It was usual to have three. The first was personal, like a Christian name. There were a dozen or so common ones for men, including Gaius, Lucius, Marcus and Publius. Popular women's names included Cornelia, Julia and Flavia. Next came the clan name, followed by the name of the family (the branch of the clan).

Poor people struggled hard to feed and clothe their children. Some kept down the size of their families by leaving new born babies outside until they died of exposure. In a letter from Egypt in 1 BC a soldier wrote to his wife:

> If you give birth to a boy, keep it. If it is a girl, expose it. Try not to worry. As soon as we are paid I will send the money to you.

A Roman father had complete control over everyone and everything in the household. Children were brought up to obey his orders instantly. Even when sons of the family were grown up and had children of their own they still had to obey their father. This

In this scene from a marriage ceremony we see the couple holding hands

discipline and sense of duty was one reason why Romans made such good soldiers.

Young Romans were rarely allowed to marry 'for love'. Instead, fathers chose husbands and wives for their children. A friend of the family might be asked to help, as we can see from this letter written by Pliny the Younger:

Dear Junius Mauricus, You asked me in your letter to look out for a husband for your brother's daughter.... I think young Minicius Acilianus is just the man.... He is handsome and noble-looking, with an honest expression and a healthy complexion – every inch a senator. Perhaps I shouldn't say this but ... his father also happens to be very well off.

Roman girls often got married as young as twelve or thirteen. Many husbands were not much older. After the wedding ceremony the groom pretended to snatch his bride from the arms of her mother. Then followed a procession to the newly-weds' home.

The bride was carried over the threshold. This was to avoid stumbling which the Romans considered very unlucky. The wife wore a ring on the third finger of her left hand, just as married women do today.

Once they were married, Roman women enjoyed respect and some freedom. The Greeks rarely allowed their wives to meet strangers. They shut them indoors and spent little time with them. But a Roman wife was her husband's close companion and helper. She would often go out with him, to dinner parties, the baths or public entertainments. Whenever he was away, she took over the running of the household.

Dress and fashion

Most Romans dressed fairly simply. Indoors, men wore a short-sleeved tunic – a kind of knee-length shirt, gathered at the waist by a belt. Tunics were usually made of wool, although rich men often preferred linen or silk embroidered with gold thread. Out of doors, men changed from sandals to leather shoes and put on a *toga*. This was a large piece of white woollen cloth, rather like a blanket, with one edge straight and the other curved. It was wound round the body, over the shoulders and under the arms.

Only Roman citizens were allowed to wear a toga. This was

Statues and carvings on tombs provide plenty of evidence of Roman clothing and hairstyles. On the left we see a man in a toga holding busts of his ancestors; right an elaborate hairstyle

important in earlier times, before the Italians and others were granted citizenship. People were proud to be seen in their togas, even though they were awkward to wear and had to be taken off for any kind of hard work or exercise. Senators distinguished themselves from ordinary citizens by wearing a toga with a stripe. Cloaks of various kinds were put over the top in chilly weather, but hats were rarely worn, except in very hot sun.

Women wore plain togas in the early years of the Roman republic, but these were gradually replaced by coloured cloaks. Underneath they wore a linen vest and breast band (brassière) covered by a long-sleeved cotton or silk tunic, reaching to the ankles. Women liked to wear lots of jewellery – rings, bracelets, necklaces, brooches and earrings – and complicated hairstyles. They sometimes grew their hair very long and piled it in coils on top of their heads. Wigs, false hair-pieces and hair dyes were commonly used. So were perfumes, cosmetics and other aids to beauty such as eyebrow tweezers and nail files.

Roman schooling

In the early years of the Roman republic there were few schools because most children were taught by their fathers. Apart from learning the 'Twelve Tables' of the law by heart, they did little more than basic reading, writing and counting. But after the conquest of Greece, in the second century BC, Greek methods of education became very popular. In the towns private schools were set up, many of them with Greek teachers.

Children of well-to-do parents were first taught at home by a private tutor (often a Greek slave). Then, at the age of about

A Roman school. The pupils are reading from volumes or scrolls

seven, boys went to an elementary school. Fees were charged, for there were no state schools like we have today. Girls usually continued their education at home, because learning to manage a household was an important part of it.

Most elementary schools were small, with perhaps 30 or 40 pupils and a teacher in one large room. They might be in the schoolmaster's home or in a rented room nearby. Classes normally began before dawn and ended around noon. So pupils carried lamps on their way to school. Their tutors went with them and sat at the back of the room while the teaching was going on.

Discipline was very strict. Some teachers flogged pupils, with a cane or strap, not only for disobedience but also for making the slightest mistake. At this stage most of the time was spent on reading, writing and counting. Capital letters were learned first (almost the same as the ones we use today). Then the children learned a joined-up style of writing. Sums were difficult with Roman numerals. As in Greece, younger pupils counted on the beads of an *abacus*.

When they were about twelve boys went to a 'grammar school', if their parents could afford the fees. Here they learned Greek and studied the works of well known Greek and Roman writers. Pupils had to write essays and compose their own poems. They were also taught some mathematics and a little history, but the main aim was to train them in *oratory* (the art of public speaking). Most of the important men in Roman life were lawyers and politicians, all of them skilful speakers. One such was Tacitus who, in about AD 100, had this to say about the value of oratory:

> The more a man could influence others by his powers of speech, the quicker he would get into an important position ... the more he would be favoured by great men, gain the respect of the senate and fame with the common people. These were the men ... who even when out of office had power, because they could win over both the senate and the people by their advice.

To develop their powers of oratory, pupils learned and recited long passages of poetry and famous speeches from the senate. After the age of sixteen or so, those from the wealthiest families went abroad to continue their studies in Athens, Alexandria or one of the other great centres of learning.

Books and writing

As in Greece, children learned to write with a stylus on wooden boards covered with wax. Adults also used wax boards for notes and short letters. Two or more boards could be tied together by passing a cord through holes in the edges (see picture on page 111). Paper was still unknown in Europe. The nearest things to it, papyrus and parchment, were both expensive.

Papyrus was first made in ancient Egypt (see page 46). Parchment came later. It was produced from the skins of animals, usually sheep and goats. Although heavier and stronger than

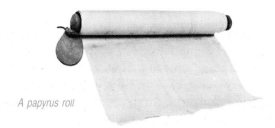

A papyrus roll

papyrus, it was too costly for most uses. Pointed reeds or goose feathers were used for writing on these surfaces. Ink was made by mixing various ingredients, including soot, water and resin – a gum obtained from plants.

Books were not made as they are today. Sheets of papyrus, 20–25 centimetres wide, were glued together to form a roll which might be as long as 10–12 metres. This was called a *volume*, from the Latin word *volvo*, meaning 'I roll'. The volume was glued to a stick of wood or ivory, rolled on to it and fastened with cord or leather thongs. As it was read, the volume was unrolled. Parchment was used in a similar way at first, but by the third century AD it began to be cut into sheets which were bound in a cover, like a modern book.

All volumes had to be copied by hand. Some book-sellers had dozens of copy-slaves working in a separate room behind the shop. The original text was read aloud to them so that a number of copies could be produced at the same time. Rich families built up large collections of volumes, many written by Greeks, but most people used a public library. By the fourth century AD there were twenty-eight libraries in Rome.

Sources and questions

1 Marcus Porcius Cato (234–149 BC) was a famous politician and writer. This description of the education of his son was written by a Greek, Plutarch, more than two centuries after Cato's death.

> As soon as Cato had a son, only some urgent business of state prevented him from being present when his wife bathed the baby and dressed him.... The mother nursed the baby herself and often nursed the children of the slaves as well so that, by bringing them up together, they might be friends. As soon as the boy showed signs of understanding, Cato himself took charge of him and taught him to read, even though he had a clever slave called Chilo who was a teacher.... Cato himself said that he did not think it was right for his son to be told off by a slave, or have his ears tweaked if he was slow in learning, and he thought it wrong for his son to have to depend on a slave for such a priceless thing as his education. So Cato

himself taught his son reading, the law and athletics, and he taught him not only to hurl the javelin, fight in armour and ride a horse, but also to box, to stand up to both heat and cold, and to swim. . . . He says he also wrote out his *History* himself in large letters so that his son could learn about his country's ancient traditions.

Source: Plutarch, Life of Cato the Elder, *Book XX, Chapters 3–6*

Also on the subject of education, a famous Roman professor, Quintilian, wrote this in the first century AD:

There should be one person at least attached to the boy who has some knowledge of speaking and who will, if any incorrect expression is used by the nurse or teacher in his presence, at once correct the error and prevent it from becoming a habit.

Source: Quintilian, Institutes of Oratory, *Book I, i*

(a) From the evidence in the first extract, what kind of life did Cato expect his son to lead?

(b) What seems to be the attitude of Cato and his wife to the slaves in their household?

(c) How would Plutarch have known so much about a man who died long before he was born? How reliable do you think this passage is?

(d) Can you explain why Quintilian was especially concerned about the way a child learned to speak?

(e) How far does the quotation from Quintilian help to explain Cato's attitude towards his son?

2. Look at the picture of the teacher and pupils on page 162.
(a) What sort of lesson seems to be going on?
(b) Roughly how old do you think these pupils are meant to be? Give reasons for your answer.
(c) Can you work out from this picture the way in which the writing was set out in a volume or scroll?
(d) What do you think the figure on the far right is doing? What is he carrying in his hand?

3. Find *three* important differences between education today and in Roman times.

4. What reasons might a Roman parent have had for allowing a girl child to die at birth? Why do you think those in power allowed it to happen?

HOMES AND HOME LIFE

Much of what we know about Roman houses comes from findings at Pompeii, near Naples, and Ostia, the port at the mouth of the Tiber. In the centuries since the end of the Empire most Roman towns have been pulled down and built over. The ruins of a few, like Ostia, have been safely buried in thick layers of river mud. But the best preserved is Pompeii. In AD 79 the volcano Vesuvius erupted, burying the town and many of its inhabitants under showers of ash, pumice-stone and lava.

An eye-witness of the disaster was Pliny the Younger. He was staying with his uncle, the commander of the Roman fleet which was in port in nearby Misenum. Here is part of a letter he wrote to his friend Tacitus:

On 24 August, in the early afternoon, my mother pointed out to uncle a cloud of unusual size and appearance. . . . At that distance, we could not make out which mountain it came from but later found out that it was Vesuvius. The cloud was rising in a shape rather like a pine tree because it shot up to a great

Part of Pompeii today. Before the archaeologists got to work, all this was covered with a layer of ash and volcanic mud. Some of the buildings have been reconstructed and have had roofs put on

Remains of apartment houses in Ostia. These have shops or warehouses on the ground floor. In Rome, blocks of flats were normally larger – some as high as five or six storeys

height on a sort of trunk, then spread out at the top into branches. . . . Sometimes it looked white, sometimes blotched and dirty, according to the amount of soil and ashes it carried.

Nearly 1,700 years passed before archaeologists began to dig out Pompeii. Gradually houses, squares and public buildings were uncovered. Among the bones of the dead and the rubble of fallen roofs lay furniture, statues, cups, plates and even remains of food on tables. These findings have greatly increased our knowledge of life in Roman times, especially of the homes people lived in.

The apartments of the poor

In the larger towns, like Rome and Ostia, only wealthy families could afford separate houses of their own. Poorer families usually rented one or two rooms in apartment houses – blocks of flats with long flights of stairs. Many of these people had no beds to sleep on. They had to make do with mats on the floor. Their only furniture was a table and benches or stools.

Flat-dwellers fetched their water from the nearest public fountain. They also depended on public lavatories, although many families kept a pot under the table and emptied it out of the window after dark. Windows in these houses had no glass. They were opened and closed with wooden shutters. When the weather was chilly people had to choose between a cold draught (if they opened the shutters) or darkness (if they closed them). The commonest form of lighting was an olive-oil lamp, but this was expensive. Most people preferred to go to bed early and get up before sunrise, to make full use of daylight hours.

There were no fireplaces or chimneys in apartment houses. For cooking and heating an open fire was lit in a brazier (a metal container, still used today by street workmen). This was very dangerous. If one of the tenants carelessly knocked over their fire the whole building could burn down in a few minutes.

The houses and villas of the rich

The town houses of wealthy families were roomy and comfortable. They were built of brick or stone, often on one floor only, and they faced inwards, away from the noise of the streets. As an extra protection against noise the front of the house, on either side of the entrance hall, was often sealed off from the living rooms and rented out as shops (see plan below).

The entrance hall opened into a central living room called the *atrium*. This had a hole in the ceiling to let in daylight and let out smoke from the fire. Below it was the *impluvium*, a shallow tank cut in the floor to collect rainwater. In earlier times the whole family worked, ate the slept in the atrium. Sometimes small bedrooms and storerooms opened off it, and there was usually a back garden.

Wealth gained during the foreign wars of the republic allowed many families to make large extensions to their houses. Bedrooms, studies and other rooms were built on to the atrium, which became just a reception room or lounge. The richest families converted the back garden into a whole new section of the house. This was the *peristyle*, a courtyard with a covered walk or verandah running along the sides. In the centre were flower beds, a pool or fountain and often a sundial.

Around the peristyle were additional rooms, usually including a kitchen, dining room, summer lounge, bathroom and lavatory.

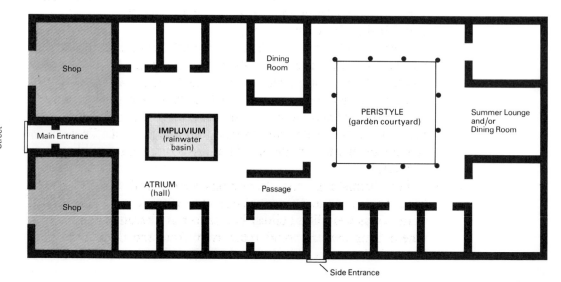

Plan of a single storey town house. The unmarked rooms would have included living rooms, bedrooms, a study and kitchen

The peristyle or back garden from a restored house in Pompeii

Many of these houses had a kind of central heating system. This was called a *hypocaust* (hot underneath) because hot air from a furnace passed through hollow tiles below the floor – and sometimes inside the walls as well.

Romans did not fill up their rooms with furniture as we do. But as houses grew larger furnishings became more luxurious. Bare stools, chairs and tables were inlaid with ivory or silver. Ornamental lamp-stands and small statues of bronze or marble were brought from Greece or the eastern provinces. Pictures were painted on the walls and mosaic floors were laid. These were designs or pictures made up of hundreds of coloured stones set in concrete.

Fine furnishings and decorations were found not only in the town houses of the rich but also in their *villas* (country mansions). Some villas were like holiday homes, set in pleasant surroundings, where their owners could relax away from the noise and stuffy heat of the town. Pliny the Younger had a villa like this at

A sundial. It is a slab of marble, divided into sections, on which an iron marker casts a shadow. The Roman day was divided into twelve equal hours which were longer in summer and shorter in winter. The end of the sixth hour was always noon. Most Romans were content to get a rough idea of the time from the position of the sun

Laurentum, on the coast just south of Ostia. He described it in a letter to a friend:

> It is seventeen miles from Rome, so it is possible to spend the night there after a full day's work in the city.... The villa is large enough for my needs but not expensive to keep up.... At the front and sides it seems to look out on to three seas, and at the back has a view ... to the woods and mountains in the distance.

Villas could also be farmhouses – the centres of large profit-making estates (see page 208). Pliny had property of this kind in northern Italy and, as we see in another of his letters, he was on the look-out to buy more.

> The estate next to mine is for sale ... and I am tempted to buy it.... Both could be put under ... the same foreman, and it would only be necessary to keep up and furnish one house.... The land is fertile, there is plenty of water, and the ... fields, vineyards and woods produce enough to make a steady income.

Household slaves

Large town houses and country villas needed a lot of looking after. This was work for slaves, both male and female, who were purchased at public auctions. A family had to be really poor not to own at least one household slave. The rich had dozens of them. Slaves without much skill or intelligence were mostly sent to work on farms. Those with some education or training – which made them much more expensive to buy – became household servants and also secretaries, teachers, librarians and so forth.

Slaves were the property of their owners – they were possessions. Many who toiled on farms or in mines and quarries were over-worked, under-fed and branded with red hot irons to try to stop them running away. Those accused of theft or dishonesty could expect to be whipped, put in chains or even executed by their masters. But although such cruelty was fairly common, most owners realised they could get more out of their slaves if they treated them well.

Pliny the Younger felt strongly that slaves should be treated like human beings. In a letter to a friend, he was not ashamed to admit having tender feelings for his servants:

I have been very upset by illness among my slaves and by the deaths of some of the younger men.... I am well aware that some people look upon misfortunes of this kind as simply losing money, and think themselves fine men ... but men they certainly are not. A true man is affected by sorrow and has feelings.

Pliny tells us that he set free some of his slaves, as a reward for good service. When this happened, the freedman or woman did not have quite the same rights as other people, but their children became full citizens.

Food and eating habits

Ordinary families lived mainly on bread, made from wheat or barley. Olive oil was used instead of butter, and cheese was usually made out of goats' milk. Vegetables such as broad beans, lettuces and cabbages were fairly plentiful, but potatoes and tomatoes were not yet known in Europe. The commonest fruits were apples, pears, cherries, plums and grapes. As well as beef, mutton and pork, Romans liked the costly meat of flamingoes, peacocks and storks. Above all, they loved good quality fish. Wine was drunk by rich and poor alike, for there was no tea or coffee.

Most Romans had a light breakfast at dawn. There was always a great hurry to get to work, so a drink of wine or water and a little bread and cheese or fruit was about all they had time for. The first proper meal was at midday. It might consist of cold meat, vegetables, bread and wine, with fresh fruit to follow.

The main meal of the day was dinner, about four hours later. Poor families would make do with only a little meat and fill up on bread, vegetable stew or porridge. Wealthy families had several courses of meat or fish, with vegetables and fruit. The wine was usually warmed and diluted with about three times as much water.

This carving shows a Roman butcher's shop, with a woman on the left waiting for her order to be prepared. She is holding a shopping list, written on a wax tablet. Notice the butcher's scales on the right

Slaves prepared and served the food. The stoves they used had hollows in the top filled with charcoal which was fanned into a fire beneath the cooking pots.

At one time the family sat on chairs round a table in the atrium. Later they had a separate dining room and copied Greek customs of eating. They lay on couches and helped themselves to the dishes on a low table in the middle. Spoons and knives were used but forks were unknown. Most of the eating was done with the fingers, so slaves carried napkins and finger bowls.

Sometimes friends or relations were invited to a dinner party. Unlike an ordinary family meal, this might go on far into the night and there would be a lot more drinking. A writer called Martial, who lived in Rome in the first century AD, described a dinner for himself and six friends:

> Now then, the menu. Well, there are marrows . . . plus lettuce, leeks, some mint and chicory from the garden. Then we'll have sliced eggs and mackerel served with parsley, and sow-belly done in the brine of salted tuna fish. That's for starters. For a main course, a piece of lamb . . . meat balls . . . beans and tender sprouts. On top of that there'll be a chicken and the remains of the ham we had the other day. When we've eaten our fill, we can have ripe apples and a wine that's matured a year or two.

Between courses, entertainments were often arranged for the guests. Slaves read poetry aloud, and there were sometimes musicians and jugglers, even acrobats or dancing girls.

DOCUMENTS: SLAVERY IN THE ROMAN WORLD

Document 1

Marcus Cato was a soldier, writer and member of the senate who lived from 234 to 149 BC. This account is taken from a book about his life written by the Greek, Plutarch, more than 200 years after his death.

> Cato purchased a great many slaves out of the prisoners taken in war, but mainly brought up young ones, who, like puppies and colts, could still be reared and trained.... When at home, a slave had to be either at work or asleep. Indeed, Cato greatly preferred the sleepy ones, finding them easier to control than those who were wakeful.... When he grew richer and gave feasts for his friends, as soon as dinner was over he used to go with a leather strap and flog those who had made the slightest mistake in preparing or serving it. Also, he always made sure of stirring up trouble among his slaves because he suspected and feared unity and agreement between them. Those who were thought to have committed on offence deserving of death he had judged by all the slaves together, and put them to death if found guilty.

Source: Plutarch, Life of Cato the Elder, *Chapter 21*

This carving on a tombstone shows a slave being sold in an auction. What sorts of slaves would have fetched the highest prices?

Document 2

In this passage from a book called *On Landed Estates*, the author, Marcus Varro (116–27 BC), offers advice to the owners of large farms on how to get the best out of their slaves.

> Slaves ought to have men over them who know how to read and write and have some little education, who are dependable and older . . . for they will be more respectful to these than to men who are younger. . . . The foremen are to be made more enthusiastic by rewards, and care must be taken that they have a bit of property of their own, and mates from among their fellow slaves to bear them children; for in this way they are made more reliable and more attached to the place. . . . Slaves are made to take more interest in their work by being given extra food or clothing, time off, or permission to graze some cattle of their own on the farm . . . so that if they are given a particularly hard task, or punished in some way, they will remain loyal to their master and think well of him.

Source: Varro, On Landed Estates, *Book 1, Chapter 17*

Document 3

Lucius Seneca, writing in the middle of the first century AD, also offers advice on the treatment of slaves.

> Kindly remember that he whom you call your slave is also human, is smiled upon by the same skies, and, like yourself, breathes, lives and dies. . . . This is my advice in short: Treat those below you as you would be treated by those above you. And whenever you think of how much power you have over a slave, remember that your master has just as much power over you. . . . You should therefore . . . show yourself to your slave as a pleasant person and not proudly superior. Slaves ought to respect you rather than fear you.

Source: Seneca, Letters, *XLV, ii*

Here we see a Roman mother giving birth to a baby. As well as the midwife, on the right, she is being helped by a slave girl. What sort of relationship do you think this slave had with her owner?

Document 4

Pliny the Younger wrote a letter to his friend Acilius about the misfortunes of a slave owner called Larcius Macedo.

Here is the terrible story, deserving much more than a letter, of how Larcius Macedo, a senator . . . has fallen a victim to his own slaves. To be sure, he was a cruel and domineering master, too ready to forget that his father had once been a slave, or perhaps only too well aware of it. He was having a bath in his villa at Formiae when he was suddenly surrounded by his slaves. One seized him by the throat, another struck him in the face, while others beat him on the chest, stomach and – shocking to say – in his private parts. When they thought he was dead, they threw him on to the hot stone floor of the bathroom . . . At length, he was carried outside. . . . Some of his faithful slaves took him in their arms . . . weeping and wailing. Roused by their cries and by the fresh air outside, Macedo opened his eyes and moved his limbs. . . . When they saw this, the guilty slaves fled in all directions, but most of them were recaptured and a search is going on for the rest. Macedo was kept alive with some difficulty for a few days, but at least he died with the satisfaction of having revenged himself, for he lived to see the murderers executed. There you see the dangers, outrages and insults to which we are exposed. No master can feel safe. . . .

Source: Pliny, Letters, *III, 14*

Questions

1. Why do you think Cato allowed his slaves who were suspected of wrongdoing to be judged by the other slaves?
2. Imagine that Cato and Seneca had lived at the same time. Write or act out a conversation between them in which they criticise each other's attitudes towards slaves.
3. Compare the advice given to slave owners by Varro and Seneca. Which do you think the owners would have been most likely to follow, and why?
4. From the evidence in Document 4, do you think the sort of thing Pliny is describing happened often? Give reasons for your views.
5. Whose side do you think Pliny is on, Macedo or the slaves who attacked him? Give reasons to back up your answer.
6. Using the evidence in these documents, describe in as much detail as you can what life must have been like for slaves in this period.

RELIGION AND THE RISE OF CHRISTIANITY

Like the Greeks, the early Romans believed there were spirit gods all around them – in the home, the earth, sea and sky, the rivers, forests and fields. These gods were thought to influence every human action, for good or evil. Therefore the people tried to please them. They built altars and temples and they offered sacrifices. Most Roman religion was a straightforward bargain. The people honoured their gods and the gods, in return, were supposed to bring them good luck.

Roman gods

The gods of the household were called Lares and Penates. The first were supposed to protect the home and bring the family good fortune; the second made sure the store cupboard was never empty. There were also the Manes, the departed spirits of ancestors. Their happiness in the after-world was thought to depend on the respect given them by their living relations. On a shelf in the atrium there was usually a shrine or altar with little statues representing the household gods and the family's ancestors. Offerings of flowers, fruit and wine were made to them every day.

The Romans also had gods who watched over the town and country as a whole. Under the influence of the Greeks, these became equal to the gods of Olympus (see Chapter 13). For example, the Roman gods Jupiter, Juno and Minerva were the same as the Greek gods Zeus, Hera and Athena. Instead of Hestia, the Roman goddess of the hearth the home was called Vesta. At her temple, in the Forum, there burned an everlasting fire, looked after by priestesses called Vestal Virgins.

Some of the most important gods had their own priests, called *flamens*. On festival days these priests made offerings to their gods. Animals were sacrificed and their livers cut out. These were carefully inspected, for the priests claimed they could discover signs (omens) showing the will of the gods. Signs were also seen in things like thunder, lightning and the flight of birds.

Romans were very superstitious. They would never attempt to do anything important at a time when the omens were not favour-

Remains of the temple of Vesta in the Roman forum. The Vestal Virgins, who looked after the temple and its sacred fire, were chosen from young girls aged between six and ten. They had to remain virgins for at least thirty years; any who failed to do so were buried alive

able. And there were a great many superstitions about the way priests should behave, as the following passage shows. It was written in the second century AD by Aulus Gellius, a lawyer who enjoyed collecting writings about Rome's past.

The carvings on this stone coffin show a Roman funeral procession

> The priest of Jupiter must not pass under a trellis of vines. The feet of the couch on which he sleeps must be smeared with a thin coating of clay, and he must not sleep away from his bed for three nights in succession. . . . The cuttings of his nails and hair must be buried in the earth under a fruitful tree. . . .

From the time of Augustus onwards the emperor himself often became a god. Sacred altars were set up and citizens worshipped the emperor's statue. The emperor Caligula (AD 37–41) took his godliness very seriously, as the historian Suetonius tells us:

> Caligula had statues of the gods . . . brought from Greece, in order to remove their heads and replace them with his own. . . . He also set up a temple to himself as a god. . . . In this temple stood a golden life-size statue and it was dressed each day in clothes such as he himself wore. Very rich people gained the honour of being chief priest.

By this time large numbers of people had lost faith in the old gods. In Italy and the western provinces they began to turn to Eastern beliefs, which did more to comfort doubts and fears. Some promised an after-life, like the Egyptian gods Isis and Osiris, or Mithras, the Persian sun god. Soldiers were especially attracted to Mithras, for he was believed to give courage and eternal life.

Meanwhile, many educated people began to disbelieve *all* gods. They agreed with certain Greek thinkers who claimed there was no after-life and advised men to try to achieve happiness on earth. In the midst of all these different ideas, belief in the Christian god of love and forgiveness began to spread from the eastern Mediterranean.

Early Christians and the persecutions

Christ was born during the reign of Augustus, in Judea, a province of Palestine. The date was not AD 1, as we might expect, but a little earlier, probably 4 BC. So our present method of counting the years is not quite correct.

We can read about the life and teachings of Jesus in the New Testament. He was about thirty when he left Nazareth and began to travel through Palestine preaching to the people. Great crowds gathered to hear him, attracted by his religion of love and his promise of heaven for the faithful. They went away believing Jesus was the *Messiah* or Saviour, whose coming had been foretold by the prophets.

The chief priests and other Jewish leaders refused to accept the word of Jesus. They expected a great and glorious Messiah, not a carpenter's son who favoured the poor and unfortunate. Jealous of his popularity, they warned Pontius Pilate, the governor, that Jesus was a danger to the peace and good order of the Roman government. Jesus was arrested, tried and condemned to death for treason. The year was probably AD 29.

The *disciples* (followers) of Jesus now took up the task of preaching the Christian message. The book of the Acts of the Apostles tells how Christianity was spread, first through Syria and then to Asia Minor, Greece and Rome itself. The conversion of the Gentiles (non-Jewish people) was led by St Paul, a businessman from Tarsus in Asia Minor. At first Paul was opposed to Christianity, but one day, on the road to Damascus, he had a vision of

Mosaic showing victims sacrificed to wild animals. Some Christians were killed in this way

Christ. From then on he devoted his life to preaching the new faith and organising groups of Christians into the first churches.

Christians made themselves unpopular when they criticised slavery and the cruel sports of the amphitheatre. But the thing that really got them into trouble was their refusal to worship any of the Roman gods. They began to be blamed for all kinds of disasters and misfortunes. When a great fire destroyed a large part of Rome in AD 64, Nero turned the anger of the people on the Christians. The historian Tacitus, who was a child at the time of the fire, tells us:

> No matter how hard he tried. . . . Nero could not stop people thinking that he had ordered the fire to be started. So to put an end to the gossip and the suspicions, he blamed . . . the Christians. . . . Their executions were made into a mockery: they were covered in animal skins and torn to death by dogs, or they were nailed to crosses and, when the evening came, set on fire to provide light. Nero had offered his gardens for this spectacle. . . .

This was the real start of the persecutions, which lasted, off and on, for 250 years. Many thousands of Christians were crucified, burnt or thrown to wild animals. Christians were forced to meet in secret and bury their dead in *catacombs* (underground caves). But this made people even more suspicious of them, for it was feared that they were plotting against the government.

The acceptance of Christianity

Despite the persecutions, the Christian Church went on growing. Its strongest support came from the poor, who were given new hope by Christ's promise of heaven for those who lived by his teachings. But rich people also took up the new faith. They admired Christians for the goodness of their lives and the courage they showed in dying for their beliefs.

As Christianity spread throughout the Empire, regular councils were held to discuss doctrine (the teaching of the Church) and methods of organisation. In addition to ordinary priests, bishops were appointed in all the main cities. We are told that the first bishop of Rome was St Peter, and that he was executed, along with St Paul, at the time of Nero. Later bishops of Rome were regarded as leaders of the Church. They got the name of Pope from the word *papa*, meaning father.

The last full-scale persecution of Christians was started in AD 303 by the emperor Diocletian. But he was fighting a losing battle, for Christianity was by then widespread. The turning point came when the emperor Constantine ordered that all religions, including Christianity, should have complete freedom of worship (AD 313). He was eventually baptised a Christian on his deathbed.

The future of Christianity was assured. But further obstacles had to be overcome. There were still many non-believers, especially in the backward country areas. They were called pagans, from

In this sculpture Christ is shown as the Good Shepherd

the Latin *paganus*, meaning a peasant or villager. In AD 361 the emperor Julian tried to revive the old pagan religions. But he was killed two years later, fighting the Persians. Pagan worship was finally forbidden in AD 392 by the emperor Theodosius and the old temples were closed.

Sources and questions

1. When Pliny the Younger was about fifty years old, the emperor Trajan made him governor of the Roman province of Bithynia (in modern Turkey). It was early in the second century AD. We know from his letters that Pliny often wrote to the emperor for guidance. In this letter he seeks advice about the treatment of Christians.

> I usually refer to you, sir, all matters which I am not sure about. As I have never taken part in any trials of Christians I do not know how far offences are punished.... I am not sure, for example, whether a person who repents should be pardoned for giving up Christianity or punished for having been a Christian....
>
> Meanwhile, I shall tell you what I have been doing when Christians have been reported to me. I have asked them if they are Christians and, if they admit it, questioned them again twice, threatening them with punishment. Those who continue to believe, I execute, because such stubbornness and obstinacy should be punished....
>
> An anonymous [unsigned] document was published containing many names. Those who denied that they were or had been Christians I set free, but only after they had prayed to the gods, offered wine and incense to your statue, and cursed Christ – for I understand that no true Christian can be made to do any of these things.... To get to the truth, I tortured two slave-women, who were called deaconesses, but I found nothing else but a wicked and exaggerated superstition.

Trajan wrote back:

> You have done the right thing, my dear Pliny.... It is not possible to lay down a fixed rule. The Christians are not to be hunted out; if they are charged and found guilty, they must be punished, but not if they deny being Christian and prove it by worshipping our gods. Then they must be pardoned, even if they behaved suspiciously in the past. Do not pay any attention to anonymous accusations. This would be a dangerous policy to follow.

Source: Pliny the Younger, Letters, *Book 10, Letters 96 & 97*

Statue of the emperor Nero. He persecuted many Christians

(a) Do you think Trajan really believed that Pliny had done 'the right thing'? How might the emperor have acted differently if he had been in Pliny's position?

(b) What do you think is Pliny's opinion of Christians and their religion? Give reasons to back up your answer.

(c) What do these letters tell you about Roman ideas of justice and fairness?

(d) Imagine that Pliny's letter had been sent to an emperor such as Nero who deliberately persecuted Christians. Write the emperor's reply.

2. Look at the picture of a funeral procession on page 177.
   (a) What sort of family would have had a funeral like this and why?
   (b) Can you describe three kinds of instruments played by the musicians on the right?
   (c) At funerals of this kind it was usual to hire mourners – women who had the job of wailing and crying with grief. Can you find any in the picture?
   (d) Can you find the widow of the dead man in the picture?
   (e) What does this procession tell you about the beliefs and attitudes of the Romans?

3. What were the main differences between Roman gods and the god of the Christians? Why do you think that Christianity triumphed over the other beliefs?

4. Imagine you were a Roman citizen living in the first century AD who has decided to give up worshipping the old gods and become a Christian. Write a letter to a close friend in which you explain the reasons for your conversion.

DECLINE AND FALL

After two centuries of peace and prosperity under strong government, the Roman Empire began to weaken from about AD 200. One of the main causes of the decline was frequent attacks along the Empire's northern frontiers by people known as barbarians. A line of strong emperors might have held back the invaders. But this did not happen. The rot began to set in when one of the most admired of all Roman emperors, Marcus Aurelius, died (AD 180) and was followed by his nineteen-year-old son, Commodus. After twelve years full of plots and executions, Commodus was strangled and civil war returned.

There was no fixed method of choosing an emperor. This encouraged ambitious and selfish men to fight for power. Time after time successful generals, backed by their armies, killed the reigning emperor, only to suffer the same fate themselves. In the space of 73 years (211–84) there were twenty-three emperors and twenty of them were murdered.

During these years the duties of government were often neglected. The senate lost its power almost completely while the soldiers supporting the emperor gained great influence. Respect for the law declined. Robbers and pirates increased in number and threatened trade routes by land and sea. Meanwhile famine and disease swept through some of the provinces of the Empire. To make matters worse, the population was falling – at a time when extra taxes were needed to strengthen defences along the frontiers.

Division of the Empire

The decline was halted for a few years by the emperor Diocletian (284–305). He was vain and conceited but an able and respected ruler. A fourth-century historian called Aurelius Victor said this about him:

> Valerius Diocletian, commander of the palace guards, was chosen emperor because of his wisdom. A mighty man he was . . . he was the first to wear a cloak embroidered in gold. . . . Indeed, he was the first after Caligula and Domitian to allow

This bronze statue of the emperor Marcus Aurelius, made in the second century, stands on the Capitol Hill in Rome. Although he did not seek power, preferring the life of a scholar, he took the duties of emperor very seriously and ruled justly. He personally took charge of his armies fighting to defend the northern frontiers of the Empire

Remains of the palace the emperor Diocletian built for his retirement at Split (in present-day Yugoslavia)

himself to be called 'lord' in public and to be worshipped as a god.... This showed a proud and extravagant nature.... But Diocletian's faults were outweighed by his good qualities.

To defend the Empire, Diocletian greatly increased the size of the Roman army. He was able to afford this because he reformed the methods of collecting taxes so that it was much more difficult for people to avoid paying up. Diocletian even tried to control rising prices by fixing maximum prices for goods throughout the Empire. During the troubles of the previous 100 years large areas of farmland had been abandoned, resulting in food shortages. Diocletian tried to put a stop to this by forbidding farmers and their sons from doing any other kind of work. The same rules were applied to certain essential trades.

Diocletian decided it was no longer possible for one men to govern the whole Empire. Therefore he ruled the East, from his palace at Nicomedia in Turkey, while a soldier called Maximian looked after the West. In 305 Diocletian retired. But immediately there were struggles between rivals for the throne. Order was restored by Constantine (307–37) who was proclaimed emperor by his soldiers at York in Britain. Realising Rome was too far away from the threatened frontiers, Constantine transferred the capital to Byzantium, which he renamed Constantinople (330).

Although Constantine did not intend to split the Empire, from then on Italy and the western provinces were seriously weakened. When the emperor Theodosius died (395) the Roman Empire finally broke into two separate pieces, each with its own emperor. The East, ruled from Constantinople, remained strong and well defended. It contained the most highly civilised countries, including Greece, Turkey, Syria and Egypt. But the Western Empire, centred on Rome or some other Italian city such as Ravenna, grew steadily weaker. In less than 100 years it collapsed.

The barbarian invasions

The word 'barbarian' usually makes us think of a brutal and uncivilised person. But in the days of the Roman Empire all foreigners living beyond its northern frontier were called barbarians, however civilised they may have been. These people were not as refined or educated as most Roman citizens, but they were far from being wild savages. The Roman historian Tacitus, who travelled among the barbarians, had this to say about them at the end of the first century AD:

> In spite of their vast numbers, they all look the same: fierce blue eyes, reddish hair, tall build. . . . It is well known that none of the German tribes lives in cities . . . they live [in villages] separately and scattered. . . . All wear a short cloak, fastened with a clasp or, failing that, a thorn. . . . The richest men are distinguished by the wearing of underclothes. . . . They also wear the skins of wild beasts. . . . The women dress like the men, except that some wear underclothes of linen embroidered with purple. . . . Their diet is simple: wild fruit, fresh game, curdled milk. . . . No race offers more generous hospitality and entertainment; to close the door against any human being is a crime.

There were many different tribes, such as the Goths, Vandals, Franks, Angles and Saxons. Together they were known as Ger-

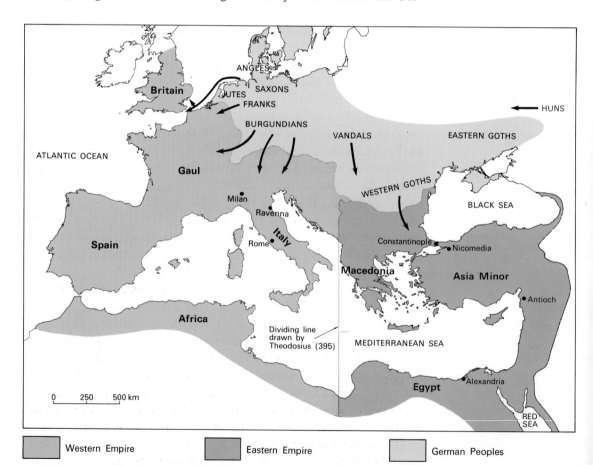

The Roman Empire Divided, AD 395

Western Empire   Eastern Empire   German Peoples

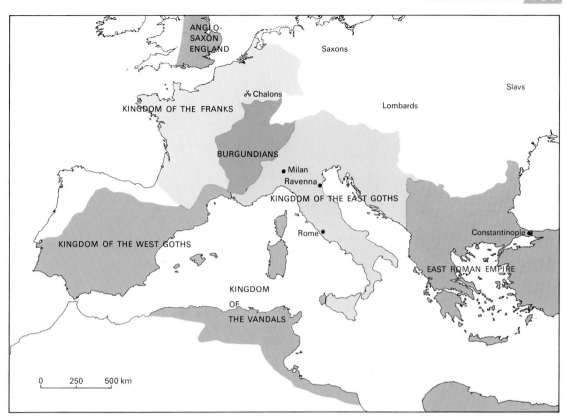

The Barbarian West in the fifth century

mans, although many other races are descended from them, including the English, Dutch and Scandinavian peoples.

For centuries barbarian tribes had been trying to get inside the Roman frontiers. They wanted to settle further south, in a milder climate, and trade with the Roman provinces. There was not enough land for everyone, so the legions drove them back each time they tried to invade the Empire. But by the end of the second century the Romans were having increasing difficulty in defending all the frontiers. Rome was forced to come to terms with some of the German leaders. Their people were allowed to settle in under-populated areas within the Empire and some of their warriors joined the Roman army.

A dramatic change came towards the end of the fourth century, when a new and terrible enemy appeared. It was the fierce Huns, wandering herdsmen from Asia, who were moving west to find fresh grasslands for their cattle and horses. They were dark-haired, short and stocky, with slanting eyes and flat noses. Their unexpected arrival resulted in great stirrings among the peoples of Europe.

In 376, a large number of Goths were allowed to cross the Danube frontier to shelter from the Huns. Before long, thousands more were swarming into the Empire without permission. The Romans were powerless to stop them. Their policy of hiring barbarians to fight with the legions meant they had handed over some of the defence of the Empire to the people who were invading them! Once the frontier was broken it could not be restored.

The Goths marched westwards, overrunning Greece and then Italy. In 410 their chieftain, Alaric, led them into Rome itself. For

This mosaic from Carthage in North Africa was made in about AD 500 or soon afterwards. The horseman's German-style clothing suggests that he belonged to the tribe of Vandals who conquered this part of the Roman Empire in the fifth century

two days they ransacked the once mighty city – the first time it had been captured since the invasion of the Gauls, 800 years before. Meanwhile, early in 406 the Rhine froze hard. A great horde of Vandals swarmed across the river into the Empire and soon overran Spain.

Spain later became the home of the western Goths, while the Vandals conquered a large part of Roman North Africa. Vandal armies were often cruel and destructive. They were greatly feared, especially by wealthy landowners who were forced off their estates. This is what a Christian bishop in North Africa, named Synesius, wrote about the Vandal invasion:

> We have planted our crops only for the enemy to burn.
> Everything we possess has gone – the flocks of sheep, the herds of camels and horses. I am writing this behind walls, under siege.

The whole of the Western Empire of the Romans was gradually divided into barbarian kingdoms. Even Britain was invaded across the North Sea by Angles, Saxons and Jutes.

The dreaded Huns, meanwhile, had conquered eastern Europe. In 450 a great army of Huns, under their fierce leader Attila, poured across the Rhine into Gaul. The Goths joined with the remains of the Roman army to fight the common enemy, at Châlons. After a long and terrible battle the Huns were defeated (451). They eventually settled on the plains of Hungary.

Rome was ransacked again in 455, this time by Vandals. For two whole weeks they plundered sacred buildings, including the emperor's palace. Tonnes of valuables were taken down to the river and loaded on to their waiting ships. The Western Empire was now almost at an end. In 476 its last emperor, Romulus Augustulus, was removed by a Gothic leader, Odoacer, who proclaimed himself king of Italy.

The Roman Empire was not completely dead. The eastern part, later called Byzantium, resisted all invasions for another thousand years. But from the sixth century onwards the emperors that ruled at Constantinople did not speak Latin and no longer had any connection with Rome.

What the Romans gave Europe

The German invaders spoiled many towns and allowed the roads to decay. But in other ways they were greatly affected by Roman civilisation. Some tribes had been in close contact with the Empire for centuries. They were aware of its achievements.

Rome continued to be the headquarters of Christianity in the West. Many barbarians were already Christians before they entered the Empire. Roman law and language also lived on. The Romans taught millions of people to have respect for order and justice. The laws of many European nations today are based on those of Rome. In the same way, modern languages like French, Spanish and Italian are based on Latin. English is closer to the languages of the German tribes, but it still has many Latin-based words.

The Romans were less artistic and less inventive than many other ancient peoples. But they were much more practical. They had the finest army, and they built the best roads, bridges and aqueducts. Under them trade and industry flourished. Above all,

View of the Roman forum (market place) as it looks today

the Romans knew how to govern a vast empire, with many different races, religions and customs. As conquerors, these stubborn, disciplined and often bloodthirsty people were more just than any before them.

Sources and questions

1. In his book on the barbarians of Germany, Tacitus describes their attitude to war.

   > Many young men of noble birth who come from settled communities which have long been at peace deliberately join tribes which are at war. Peace is unwelcome to these people, and they find it easier to prove themselves when facing danger. Besides, a great band of warriors can only be kept going by war and violence; they depend on the generosity of their chief for their war horses and deadly weapons. Feasting and a homely but generous hospitality take the place of pay.

   Source: Tacitus, Germany, *Chapter XVI*

   (a) Why do you think Tacitus mentions only young men of noble birth?
   (b) To get men to fight with him, what things would a chief have to provide, in addition to food, weapons and horses?
   (c) How did the Romans try to give these people opportunities to fight, without destroying the Empire? Why was this a dangerous policy?
   (d) If you did not know the author of this passage, how could you tell he was a Roman?

2. Look at the picture of the man on horseback on page 186.
   (a) What sort of man would have been pictured in a mosaic? Assuming he is a Vandal, how might he have achieved his social rank or position?
   (b) What do you think would have pleased him about the way in which he has been portrayed here?
   (c) Does the picture tell you anything about the landscape and climate of this region?
   (d) Can you see any ways in which the horseman has been influenced by Roman civilisation?

3. Re-read Tacitus's description of the Germans on page 184. In what ways do they appear to be different from the people of Italy at that time?

4. Imagine you are one of the Germans who travelled south and settled within the Roman Empire. Write down, in as much detail as you can,
   (a) the ways in which your new life is better, and
   (b) the things you miss about your homeland.

ROMAN BRITAIN

A NEW PROVINCE FOR ROME

One morning in the summer of 55 BC a fleet of about eighty ships was seen approaching the coast of Britain, at the point where Dover now stands. Made of oak, with sails of leather or skins, these vessels came from Gaul, where they were commonly used for trading. But this time there were no merchants on board. The ships carried two legions of Roman soldiers; more than 10,000 of the world's best equipped and most highly trained fighting men. They were commanded by the great Julius Caesar, conqueror of Gaul.

Caesar's army probably crossed the Channel in merchant ships of the kind shown in this mosaic

The people of the Mediterranean lands had known about Britain for at least 500 years before Caesar's time. Carthaginian merchants visited its shores and carried away valuable cargoes of tin. But not until Caesar came was there any real connection between Britain and the Roman Empire. In the previous five years Caesar had advanced the frontier of the Empire as far north as the Channel. Now he set out to explore Britain. He claimed that its people had been helping the Gauls in their wars against Rome. But he had other reasons for visiting the country. He knew that he would gain even greater popularity in Rome if he could conquer this mysterious country, which Romans called 'the islands at the end of the earth'.

Julius Caesar – a visitor from Gaul

Caesar wrote very full descriptions of his campaigns, so for the first time we have a written account of events in British history. From his book called *The Conquest of Gaul*, we know that his first visit to Britain only lasted about three weeks. He was probably content to find out as much as he could about the island and its people, in the hope of attempting a more serious invasion the following year.

The Britons gave Caesar's army a hostile reception. Men armed with javelins lined up on the cliffs, backed by cavalry and warriors in chariots. Nevertheless, after fierce fighting they were forced to retreat by the more disciplined Romans. Caesar advanced a short distance inland but soon decided to return to Gaul after storms damaged a number of his ships.

The following summer (54 BC) Caesar went back to Britain. This time he was prepared for a full-scale invasion, with five legions and 2,000 cavalry in several hundred ships. According to Caesar, the Britons, 'frightened by the sight of so many ships. . . . had retreated from the shore'. He described the Roman advance as follows:

> A night march of about twelve miles brought Caesar within sight of the enemy, who . . . tried to bar his way by attacking from a position on higher ground. Forced back by his cavalry, they hid in the woods. . . . But the soldiers of the 7th legion, locking their shields together over their heads . . . drove them out of the woods at the cost of only a few men wounded.

Before Caesar could press home his advantage, he heard that another sudden storm had damaged many of his ships. Ten precious days were lost while repairs were carried out. When Caesar again marched inland, he found that

> larger British forces had now been assembled from all sides, and by common consent they had given the overall command and conduct of the campaign to Cassivellaunus.

Cassivellaunus was the leader of the Catuvellauni, the most powerful tribe, who lived north of the river Thames. After several days

This ditch, at Wheathampstead in Hertfordshire, is thought by many historians to have been part of the stronghold of Cassivellaunus mentioned by Caesar

of hard fighting, however, Caesar was able to cross the Thames and enter their territory.

Cassivellaunus, realising that the Romans could not be defeated in open battle, withdrew about 4,000 charioteers and tried to upset the invading army with surprise attacks from hidden positions. When this failed he retired to a stronghold among the woods; it was surrounded by marshes and protected by an earth wall and ditch. The Romans immediately stormed the stronghold. Caesar tells us that

> After a short time the enemy proved unable to resist the violent attack of the legions, and rushed out of the fortress on another side . . . many of those trying to escape were captured or killed. . . . Cassivellaunus, alarmed by so many defeats and by the devastation of his country . . . sent messengers to Caesar to agree terms of surrender.

Before the messengers arrived, Caesar had already decided to abandon the invasion, 'for fear any sudden rising should break out in Gaul'. He led his army back to the coast and returned to the Continent. It is difficult to say whether Caesar hoped to conquer Britain in 54 BC, or whether he intended to return at a later date. As it happened, events in Gaul kept him fully occupied for the next few years, after which he marched in triumph to Rome (49 BC).

Who were the Britons?

The people Caesar had fought were closely related to the Gauls. Both the Britons and the Gauls were descended from the powerful Celtic race, which had settled in large areas of north-western Europe several hundred years before. Celts normally had fair or red hair and blue eyes. They were generally taller and more

Maiden Camp, an ancient British stronghold in Dorset

strongly built than the Mediterranean peoples. They were also less civilised, of course, although they were not the savages they are often imagined to be.

Celts settled mostly in the south-east of England, on light soils. They built wooden farm houses, grew corn and reared cattle and sheep. For defence in tribal wars they built forts on the tops of hills, surrounded by huge banks and ditches. Remains of these hill-forts can still be seen in some areas. The most famous is Maiden Camp in Dorset, which is more than half a mile long.

In the upland areas of the north and west the people were less advanced. But they must have learned many things from the Celts, including possibly their language. The Celts were the first people in Britain to make pottery on a wheel and to ride horses and use chariots. They also introduced the use of iron. This is much more plentiful than copper and tin, which the earlier Britons used for making bronze. Iron is harder than bronze and therefore better for making tools and weapons. Iron bars of different sizes were at one time used as money, but coins (some of them gold) were common by the time of the Roman invasion.

Only about twenty years before Caesar landed, a wave of new settlers had arrived in Britain. They were the Belgae, a mixed race of Celts and Germans, who were attracted to the fertile lands around the mouth of the river Thames. The Belgae were more advanced than the Celts. They made many clearings in the forests and tried to farm the heavier soils with their metal-tipped ploughs.

The Claudian invasion

After Caesar's departure, nearly a hundred years went by before a Roman army was again seen in Britain. Civil wars in Rome put a stop to foreign adventures for some time. Then, when these were over, Augustus spent more than forty years restoring peace and order. Not until the reign of the emperor Claudius (AD 41–54) was an invasion of Britain attempted. Claudius was eager to begin his reign in a blaze of glory. It was thought that the cost of the campaign would be more than repaid by the extra taxes and increased trade that would result. Britain was known to be rich in metals and it was a good land for growing wheat and raising cattle.

In AD 43 Claudius sent an invasion force of 40,000 men, commanded by Aulus Plautius, an experienced general. It was much stronger in cavalry than Caesar's army had been, and so better suited to British warfare. The Catuvellauni tribe, which now controlled most of the south-east corner of Britain, had also learned from past experience and tried to avoid open battle. Their tactics were later described by the historian Dio Cassius:

> The Britons . . . would not come to close quarters with the Romans but hid in the marshes and forests, hoping to wear them out through pointless effort, so that, just as in the days of Julius Caesar, they should sail back with nothing achieved. As a result Plautius had a great deal of trouble in searching them out.

When the Romans at last forced the Britons into a full-scale battle near the river Medway, it took them nearly two days to overcome their brave resistance. The leader of the Catuvellauni, Caratacus, lived to fight another day. Realising the hilly regions of the west might be more difficult to conquer, he fled to Wales. There he gathered a group of supporters and prepared to resist the Roman advance.

Bronze head of the emperor Claudius

After crossing the Thames, Plautius called a halt and sent for Claudius to come and receive in person the surrender of several British tribal chiefs. This took place at Colchester, which had become an important centre of the Catuvellauni. It was not really a town, just a collection of scattered huts surrounded by earth banks for defence. Claudius only stayed sixteen days in Britain.

The Roman conquest of Britain, to AD 47

Area conquered by Aulus Plautius (43-47 A.D.)   Area invaded by Caesar (54 B.C.)

Bolt from a Roman catapult embedded in the spine of a Briton found at Maiden Camp. It had entered the body from the front

Before returning to Rome to celebrate victory he made Plautius the governor and left him instructions for the conquest of the rest of the country.

The tribes that had been defeated were the most advanced in Britain. But if Plautius expected less resistance from those further inland he was soon disappointed. Some tribes held out in their hill-forts and the Romans suffered heavy casualties storming them. At Maiden Camp (captured in AD 44) archaeologists have unearthed large numbers of skeletons from this period which show the marks of a bitter struggle. Many were beheaded or had smashed skulls.

After more than three years of hard fighting, Roman armies had occupied Britain as far north and west as the rivers Humber and Severn. As they advanced they built a network of roads. The Britons only had tracks or footpaths, which were unsuitable for marching large numbers of soldiers. Therefore the Roman legions had to spend much of their time quarrying stone and building roads and bridges. Extra labourers were obtained from conquered tribes.

Most of the main roads in Roman Britain were built soon after the invaders arrived. They followed direct routes, often cutting through belts of uninhabited forest. One of the first was Watling Street, which ran from the Kent coast, through Canterbury and London, to Chester. Altogether 5,000 miles of roads were built by the Romans in Britain. They had firm foundations of stone and rubble, a smooth surface of paving stones, and drainage ditches alongside. The best of them were as good as the roads of the Mediterranean provinces.

Sources and questions

1. Dio Cassius, writing nearly 200 years after these events took place, describes the emperor Claudius's part in the invasion of Britain (AD 43).

> Instead of advancing further, Plautius decided to guard what he had already won, and sent for Claudius. . . . When the message reached him, Claudius . . . set out for the front. He sailed down the river to Ostia, and from there he was taken to Marseilles. Then, advancing partly by land and partly along the rivers, he reached the ocean and crossed over to Britain, where he joined the legions that were waiting for him near the Thames. Taking over the command of these, he crossed the river, defeated the barbarians who had gathered on his arrival and captured Colchester. . . . He brought over to his side a number of tribes, some by agreement, others by force. . . . He took away the weapons of those he had conquered and handed them over to Plautius, telling him also to take over the remaining areas. Claudius himself now hurried back to Rome, sending ahead the news of his victory.

> *Source: Dio Cassius*, Roman History, *Book 60, Chapter 22*

   (a) From this description, use an atlas to work out a possible route for Claudius from Rome to Britain and make a sketch map. Explain your choice of route across France.
   (b) Why would Claudius have thought it worth travelling over 1,000 miles to Britain for a stay of just over a fortnight?
   (c) Do you think Dio is exaggerating in any part of this account? Give reasons for your answer.
   (d) When Claudius finally met up with Plautius, can you imagine what the two men would have said to each other? Dramatise or write a short script of their conversation.

2. Look at the picture of Maiden Camp on page 192.
   (a) The camp is nearly a kilometre in length; why do you think the flat area on top is so large?
   (b) What makes it a good position to defend?
   (c) How would you have planned an attack on the camp?
   (d) What are the disadvantages of this kind of stronghold, from the defenders' point of view?

3. Can you find any evidence in this chapter to explain how the Romans, despite being heavily outnumbered, were able to defeat the taller and more strongly built Celts?

4. According to Caesar, Cassivellaunus was 'alarmed . . . by the devastation of his country'. In what ways would the invading army have caused 'devastation'? How would it have affected the lives of ordinary people?

MAKING THE PROVINCE SECURE

The Romans soon discovered that Britain divides roughly into two natural regions. The first, a lowland area extending from the south-east coast to the Midlands, had already been occupied by AD 47 (see map on page 194). The second region, the north and west, contained many upland areas. It proved much more difficult to conquer, even though it was thinly populated.

Caratacus and Boudicca

When the Romans advanced into the hills of South Wales they met fierce resistance from a tribe called the Silures. These were organised and led by Caratacus, who had escaped after the Battle of the Medway. He divided his men into small groups, scattered among the hills. From well-concealed hideouts they made surprise raids on the Romans, retreating before the enemy had a chance to recover.

After nearly two years of fighting Caratacus was defeated, captured and sent to Rome in chains (AD 51). However the emperor Claudius was so impressed by his spirit and courage that he pardoned Caratacus and allowed him to live freely in the capital. The next few years in Britain were fairly peaceful. In the Roman-occupied areas roadbuilding continued, the first towns were established and forts were built as bases for the legions.

The Romans continued their advance into Wales in AD 59, when an experienced soldier, Suetonius Paulinus, became Governor. Marching through the mountains, he had reached the Isle of Anglesey when news came of a serious uprising led by the Iceni, a tribe from what is now Norfolk. Their queen, Boudicca (often called Boadicea) and her family had been abused by some Roman soldiers – as the historian Tacitus tells us:

> Boudicca was whipped and [her] daughters raped; all the chief men of the Iceni tribe had their lands taken away, and the King's relatives were treated as slaves. Moved by this outrage and the fear of worse to come . . . they took up arms.

Boudicca's forces attacked the Roman town of Colchester and

This layer of ash found by archaeologists below London was probably caused by Boudicca's attack

burned it to the ground (AD 60). Its citizens were slaughtered. The nearest Roman legion was more than 100 miles away, so Boudicca, riding at the head of her army in a chariot, made for London – the site of another Roman settlement. Within a few days both London and nearby Verulamium (St Albans) had been reduced to ashes.

Suetonius's main army now arrived from Wales, after marching along Watling Street. They were greatly outnumbered, but their superior weapons and discipline again proved the deciding factor. Boudicca foolishly allowed her forces to advance between two areas of woodland, where they crowded together and got in each other's way. Choosing the right moment to charge, the Romans massacred them. Boudicca poisoned herself to avoid capture, but thousands of her supporters were rounded up and killed by an enemy eager for revenge.

Agricola conquers the North

The Romans regained control of south-east Britain and rebuilt the three ruined towns. They had resumed their advance into the upland areas when, in AD 78, Gnaeus Julius Agricola was made governor. He was already familiar with Britain, having served in the country first as a young officer and then, some years later, as commander of a legion. We know a lot about Agricola's governorship because the historian Tacitus, who married his daughter, wrote a book about him. As far as we know, Tacitus never saw Britain for himself, but he was able to get information directly from Agricola.

Agricola crushed all remaining opposition in England and then marched into Caledonia (Scotland), building roads and forts on the way. He reached the Highlands of the far north without serious opposition, but then decided that it was not worth trying to bring this difficult and dangerous land under Roman rule. He contented himself with a victory in battle in AD 84 over some Highland tribes at *Mons Graupius* (Grampian Mountain) which was probably not far from present-day Inverness. According to Tacitus,

> The Britons were at a disadvantage with their small shields and large, unwieldy swords which had no sharp point and were therefore unsuitable for hand-to-hand fighting. Our soldiers rained blow after blow on the Britons. . . . They overran the enemy on the plain and then pushed on uphill. . . . The pursuit was only ended by nightfall and the exhaustion of our troops. About 10,000 Britons lay dead, while on our side we lost 360 men. . . .

Site of a legionary fort in Scotland – at Ardoch in Perthshire – showing defensive ditches and rampart (earth wall)

The plight of the defeated Highlanders is movingly described by Tacitus:

> The Britons wandered all over the countryside, men and women together wailing, carrying off their wounded and calling out to the survivors.... Sometimes the sight of their dear ones broke their hearts, more often it drove them to fury.... The next day ... there was a grim silence everywhere, the hills were deserted, only here and there was smoke seen rising from chimneys in the distance....

A few months later Agricola was recalled to Rome by the emperor Domitian. He had almost completed the Roman conquest of Britain and won high honours. Yet he was more than just a general on the battlefield. He took a keen interest in the British people and, according to Tacitus, encouraged the spread of education and Roman ways of life (see page 207).

Hadrian's Wall

As the Highland tribes recovered from the defeat of *Mons Graupius*, they began to attack the forts built by Agricola. The Roman garrisons, greatly outnumbered, were forced to abandon the forts, one by one. In about AD 117 the tribes from Scotland made a full-scale raid into northern England and caused widespread destruction. The Romans' hold on that part of the province was threatened.

The emperor Hadrian travelled to Britain in AD 122 to see for himself. Like Agricola, he came to the conclusion that the Highlands could not be conquered without a huge army and great

This carving, from Trajan's column in Rome, shows legionaries in the second century AD building a fort out of turf – in much the same way as the Romans in Britain would have done at this time

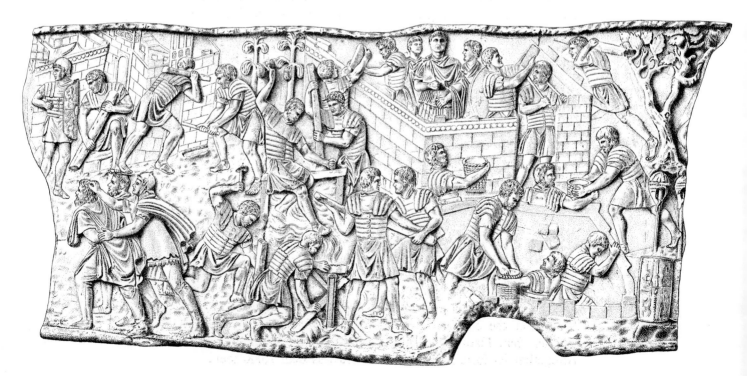

expense. So he decided to cut the country in two with a permanent walled frontier, running from coast to coast. Hadrian's wall ran from Bowness-on-Solway in the west to Wallsend-on-Tyne in the east – a distance of 80 Roman miles (120 kilometres). It defended an area roughly equal to present-day England and Wales.

Soldiers from the legions had the tough task of constructing the wall, and local Britons were forced to help them. The foundations were laid in trenches. Then the outsides of the wall, about 3 metres apart, were built from carefully trimmed stones and the space between them was packed with a mixture of broken stones and mortar. Turf was used in some places, where stones were difficult to get. The finished wall was over 6 metres high, including battlements and a sentry walk along the top.

About 14,000 soldiers were needed to patrol and defend the frontier – a third of the total Roman army in Britain. They were housed in forts, castles and turrets built at regular intervals along the wall. Roughly 5 miles apart were sixteen forts. They had barracks large enough to hold a cohort of soldiers (500 or more) as well as stables, a hospital, granaries (grain stores) and workshops for stonemasons, carpenters and blacksmiths.

Filling the gaps between the forts were milecastles, so called because they were roughly a mile apart. (A Roman mile was just under 1,500 metres – a little shorter than the modern measurement). Such castles could hold up to 100 men. In between each pair of milecastles were two watchtowers, or turrets, about 500 metres apart. These were much smaller and contained sentries who took turns to keep watch. Soldiers in both the milecastles and turrets were ready to pass on smoke signals (or light fires if it was dark) at the first sign of an attack.

The construction of Hadrian's wall was probably finished soon after AD 130 – allowing for the completion of the buildings and also a defensive ditch, 3 metres deep, running along the north side of the wall. For the next 250 years it protected the Roman province against attack from the tribes of Caledonia. On the rare occasions when invaders got through, they found it almost impossible to return with stolen cattle or crops. Indeed, they ran the risk of being trapped behind the wall, at the mercy of the Romans.

Bronze head of the emperor Hadrian (AD 117–38), made during his lifetime. Hadrian was the first reigning emperor to visit Britain since Claudius, nearly 80 years before

The Antonine Wall

We know from coins and other archaeological evidence that the Romans were not content just to defend Hadrian's Wall. The legions continued to march into Caledonia, and in about AD 140 they began to build a second frontier across the narrow neck of land between the estuaries of the Forth and Clyde. It was a 60-kilometre wall of turf, known to historians as the Antonine Wall after the emperor Antoninus Pius (138–61). It was much simpler than Hadrian's Wall and had no milecastles or turrets. Altogether its forts probably contained less than 7,000 men.

A stretch of Hadrian's Wall, near Housesteads fort

The new frontier only seems to have lasted for about forty years. Around AD 180, tribes from Caledonia swept across the Antonine Wall and it appears to have been abandoned. The Romans retreated to Hadrian's Wall, but not even that could hold back a further invasion some twenty years later. Parts of the great wall were demolished and the legionary fortress at York overrun. A Greek-speaking historian from this period called Herodian records an appeal for help addressed to the emperor, Septimius Severus:

> The governor of Britain wrote to say that the barbarians of the province had risen and were overrunning the country, carrying off plunder and causing great destruction.... This was welcome news for Severus, by nature a lover of glory, who wanted to win some victories in Britain.... So he announced that he would make an expedition there.

Severus arrived in Britain in 208. During the next two years he defeated the northern tribes and pushed them back into the Highlands. He also inspected closely the repairs to the damaged sections of Hadrian's Wall. These were so extensive that for a long time historians believed that Severus had actually built the wall. The emperor was old and crippled; on most of his travels he had to be carried on a *litter* (a kind of couch with handles). In 211 he died, at York, but his expedition had done enough to make the civilised part of Britain safe and secure. The British frontier now had almost a hundred years of peace.

Sources and questions

1. Tacitus describes some of the achievements of his father-in-law as governor of Britain.

   > Agricola understood the feelings of the province [Britain], and he had learned from the experience of others that little is gained by conquest if it is followed by injustice.... He made the payments of corn and taxes easier to put up with by ensuring that the burden was shared fairly, and put a stop to profit-making schemes [of tax collectors] which were more bitterly resented than the actual taxes.... Meanwhile, he allowed the enemy no rest, making sudden raids and plundering their lands. Then, when he had done enough to inspire fear, he showed mercy and held out to them the attractions of peace. As a result many tribes which had remained independent gave up their opposition, and ... they were taken over with less difficulty than any part of Britain had previously been.

   Source: Tacitus, Agricola, *Chapters 19–20*

   (a) How far can we rely on what Tacitus says about Agricola? Give reasons to back up your answer.
   (b) What earlier happenings in Roman Britain could have taught Agricola that 'little is gained by conquest if it is followed by injustice'?
   (c) What does Tacitus mean when he says that Agricola held out to the Britons 'the attractions of peace'? Were there any disadvantages in peace on Agricola's terms?
   (d) Agricola claimed to have treated the Britons well. How, then, could he have justified ordering his soldiers to take plunder (crops, cattle and other goods) from the Britons?

2. Look at the picture of legionaries building a fort on page 200.
   (a) Can you pick out the figure of the emperor Trajan? How has the artist helped us to identify him?
   (b) What do you think the wicker baskets are for?
   (c) What do you think is happening in the bottom left hand corner of the picture?
   (d) Is there any sign that the soldiers had to be alert to possible danger?
   (e) Can you describe any other activities in the picture?

3. What do the three quotations from Tacitus (above and on pages 199 and 200) tell you about Agricola's character?

4. Imagine you are Agricola, governor of Roman Britain. Write a letter to the emperor Domitian (who came to power in AD 81) in which you set out your reasons for not trying to conquer the whole of northern Britain.

LIFE IN ROMAN BRITAIN

Tombstone of a Roman surveyor, showing the instrument he used for measuring right-angles

At the time of the Roman invasion the nearest thing to a town in Britain was a collection of huts protected by banks and ditches. Without delay, the Romans set about building towns, which were essential to their way of life. It was through towns that they governed their empire and also spread their influence among the 'barbarians' they had conquered.

Britain's first towns

As far as possible, the Romans aimed to develop existing settlements, no matter how small. So former Celtic strongholds became market towns and centres of government for each tribal area. This is how towns such as Cirencester, Canterbury and Leicester came into being. Where there had been hill-forts a new settlement was usually established on lower ground. For example, Maiden Camp was replaced by nearby Dorchester.

Tribal leaders and other important Britons were usually made Roman citizens and encouraged to take up Roman customs, including the wearing of the toga. They were expected to play a part in local government. Each tribal centre had magistrates, elected by the people, and a town council, which was like a miniature Roman senate. As well as keeping law and order, magistrates were expected to provide games and other entertainments.

In a few areas the Romans established a special kind of town called a *colonia*. This was a settlement or 'colony' of mainly retired Roman soldiers from the legions. Each received a plot of farming land in the surrounding countryside. The first *colonia*, at Colchester, was still under construction in AD 60 when it was destroyed in Boudicca's rebellion. But it was soon rebuilt. Further 'colonies' were established at Lincoln, Gloucester and York – which became an important military centre after the building of Hadrian's Wall.

London may also have been a colonia in later years, although we do not know for sure. In many ways London was different from the other towns of Roman Britain. It was probably the place where the governor of the province was stationed and the coins minted. Roads led to London from all directions, like spokes of a wheel. It was the centre of trade and the chief port of the pro-

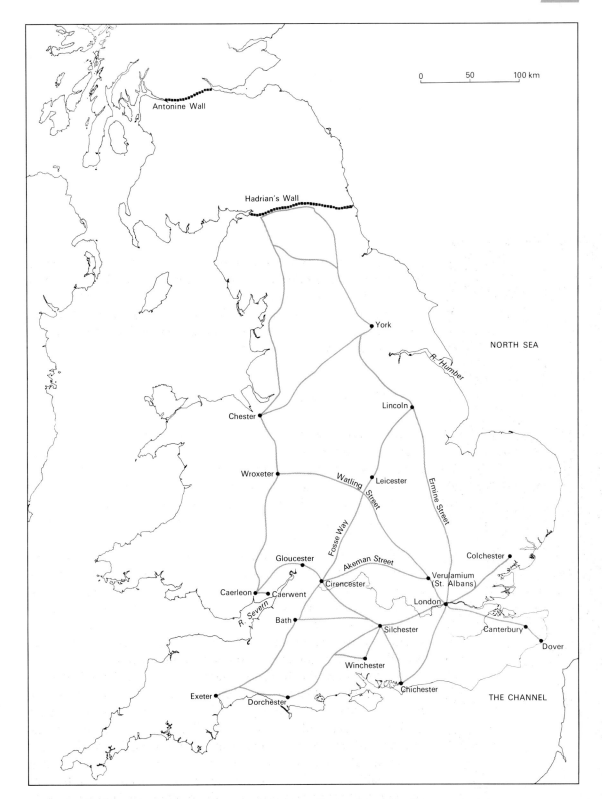

The main roads and towns of Roman Britain. The modern names of many British towns give a guide to the position of former Roman settlements. For example, the Latin word for a camp or fort is castra, and we find many towns today whose names end in -chester, -caster or -cester

vince. Most of the country's exports were shipped from London, including iron and other metals, hides, hunting dogs and wheat. In return came luxuries of the Roman world such as glass tableware, silk, spices and wines.

Nearly all the main towns were situated in the peaceful south-eastern part of Britain. Here the Roman way of life took firm root.

In the more troubled regions of the north and west the main settlements were forts. The three largest – the fortresses of York, Caerleon and Chester – had several thousand soldiers each. At first their defences were made of wood and banks of earth, but these were soon replaced by huge stone walls. Inside were streets and public buildings just as in an ordinary town.

Modern painting to show what Roman London probably looked like in the early part of the second century AD – when it had become one of the largest towns north of Italy. Notice that by this time a wooden bridge had been built over the river Thames

Britons learn Roman ways

The towns of Roman Britain were generally much smaller than those in the Mediterranean lands. Most had well under 5,000 inhabitants. But in other ways they were typically Roman. Each had a *forum* (market place) in or near the centre and a *basilica* (town hall) where public meetings and the law courts were held. There were also temples for religious worship and a public baths.

Amphitheatres were situated outside most of the main towns. Ordinary theatres might be built instead, as for example at Verulamium (St Albans) where both games and theatrical performances were held. Entertainments would not have been as lavish as those that thrilled the crowds in Rome. Instead of animals like lions and leopards, there would probably have been bull- and bear-baiting, cockfighting and fights between gladiators. Chariot races must have been rare, although there is evidence that they were held regularly at Lincoln.

The houses in British towns were usually smaller and less comfortable than those in the Mediterranean provinces. Even so, wealthy families frequently had ten, twelve or more rooms, joined together by an outside corridor or verandah. They had special quarters for the household slaves and a separate kitchen and dining room. There were even flush lavatories, baths and under-floor heating in the most luxurious houses.

Wealthy Britons copied the Romans not only in the design of their houses but also in their dress, language and other customs. We know from Tacitus that Agricola encouraged such things:

> In order that people who were scattered, uncivilised and fond of fighting would learn to enjoy the comforts of peace, Agricola personally encouraged . . . the building of temples, public squares and private houses. . . . Furthermore he provided education for the sons of the chiefs . . . with the result that instead of disliking the Latin language they now became keen to master it. In the same way, our style of dress became fashionable and the toga was seen everywhere.

In the towns, even workmen could read and write Latin. We know this from words found scratched on tiles, bricks and pieces of pottery. For example, on the site of the Roman town of Silchester a box-tile (a square hollow length of pipe) was found bearing the scribbled message, *Fecit tubulum Clementinus* (Clementinus made this box-tile). Notice that the writer had also been given a Roman name.

The remains of the theatre at Verulamium (St Albans). The stage was just in front of the pillar

Corn measure – used for judging the amount of grain collected by the Romans from native farmers

Craftsmen lived in simple wooden houses with the side facing the street usually turned into a shop. The goods on sale might be expensive imported articles. But more often they were local British products such as ironmongery, pottery or window glass, made in a workroom behind the shop. Every household, rich or poor, spun and wove most of its own cloth.

Native farms and Roman villas

The building of towns was like a trademark of Roman occupation. Even so, the great majority of the British population went on living in the countryside and farming the land in much the same way as their ancestors had done. Their timber-framed huts or farmsteads were usually one-roomed and circular in shape. Nearby were pits, lined with clay or wicker-work, where dried grain was stored. In some areas peasants made their own tools and farming implements out of iron.

In the lowlands of Britain the main crop was wheat, grown in small, square fields. Many peasants also kept pigs and a few cattle or sheep. In the upland areas, where it is often hard to grow crops, the Britons depended on their cattle and sheep. This was noted by Julius Caesar on his second visit to the country, in 54 BC: 'Most of the tribes in the interior do not grow corn but live on milk and meat, and wear skins.' Their fields had to be fenced to protect the animals from wolves, which were then common in Britain.

Many peasants, especially those living in remote hilly areas, would hardly ever have seen a Roman. The only real change in their lives resulting from the conquest would have been the Roman government's demand for taxes. At regular intervals they had to travel to a special collection point and hand over a certain amount of their produce – usually grain or hides. Some of it was sent to Rome, but a large proportion was kept to supply the army in Britain.

It is unlikely that the peasants owned the land they farmed. They were probably granted it by the tribal chiefs, who received some of their produce in return. These powerful Britons also kept large estates for themselves, and it was here that the influence of the Romans could be seen most clearly. Celtic farm houses of wood, reeds and clay were rebuilt in the style of Roman villas, with solid stone foundations and walls of flint and mortar.

Depending on the wealth of its owner, a villa could be anything from a simple farm cottage to a great mansion with dozens of rooms and a large staff of servants. In Britain, villas were not 'holiday houses' like those found in parts of Italy (see page 169–70). They were centres of profit-making farming estates. As well as the main living quarters, there were barns and other outbuildings to house farm labourers and livestock and to store tools and farm produce. A rich owner might have hot-air central heating, private baths, mosaic floors and decorated walls.

Most villas grew in size and comfort throughout the period of

Fine mosaic found in a large villa at Fishbourne in Sussex

Roman occupation. The remains of hundreds of them have been discovered in Britain – mainly in the south-east. This area contained most of the good farming land and the bulk of the population. It is also likely that in the northern regions such open settlements would have been thought unsafe because of frequent raids by hostile tribes.

Not all country dwellers farmed the land. Some worked in mines and stone quarries which were scattered all over Britain.

A Celtic god, Taranus, which some Romans took over from the Britons

One of the reasons for the Roman conquest had been their desire to profit from Britain's rich deposits of minerals. Most important were lead mines, which the Romans worked not only for the lead itself but for the silver which could be extracted from it. Iron was mined in large quantities, and copper, tin and coal were also valued. At least one Roman gold mine has been discovered, in South Wales.

Religious beliefs

Like most heathen peoples, the ancient Britons worshipped a great variety of nature gods. The sea, sky, mountains, rivers and trees were believed to have powerful spirits who demanded regular sacrifice and prayer. In some Celtic religions pigs, bulls, horses and snakes were also thought to have magical powers. Above all, Britons worshipped the sun (the source of light and warmth) and the moon (the measure of time).

The Romans usually allowed conquered peoples to keep their own religions. In Britain they did the same – with one important exception. The Celts had powerful priests called Druids whose practices included human sacrifice in their sacred oak groves. The victim's throat was slit and the Druids claimed to be able to foretell the future by inspecting the flow of blood and the twitching of the dying body. The Romans ordered that such ceremonies must stop. They also insisted that the Druids could no longer act as judges and make laws. These commands were ignored, so in AD 60 Suetonius Paulinus decided to wipe out the Druids by attacking their stronghold on the Isle of Anglesey.

As the Roman soldiers came ashore, wild priestesses ran about holding flaming torches and the terrified priests screamed curses at the invaders. But Suetonius showed no mercy, as Tacitus tells us:

> The troops . . . charged behind their standards, cut down all who met them, and cast the enemy into his own flames. The next step was to . . . demolish their sacred oak groves, for [the Druids] considered it their holy duty to . . . make human sacrifices to their gods.

At this stage a messenger arrived bringing news of Boudicca's rebellion in East Anglia. It was just too late to save the Druids. Nothing more was heard of them in Britain.

By the time of Claudius's invasion, emperor worship had become an 'official' religion of the Roman Empire – in addition to the old gods like Jupiter and Juno (see page 176). A great temple to Claudius was built at Colchester immediately after the Roman conquest. Stone was brought from far and wide and no expense spared in making it. But the Britons showed little interest. They generally preferred their own gods.

Little is known about the arrival of Christianity in Britain. The faith was probably introduced during the second century, but it was slow in taking root. We are told that the first Briton to be put to death for being a Christian was Albanus (usually known as

Alban), a citizen of Verulamium. He was beheaded on top of a hill, probably in 209. In later times a church was built there, and this is the spot where St Albans abbey now stands. Not many traces of Christian worship have been found among Roman remains in Britain. This suggests that Christians were few in number.

Roman mosaic showing Christian symbols. The Greek letters khi (X) and rho (P) are the first two letters of the Greek word for Christ

DOCUMENTS: ROMAN VIEWS OF THE BRITONS

Document 1

Julius Caesar wrote the following account during his second visit to Britain, in 54 BC.

Britain's interior is inhabited by people who claim to be the first to have lived there, its coastal district by Belgic immigrants who came to plunder and make war . . . and later settled down to farm the land. The population is exceedingly large; homesteads very similar to those of the Gauls are met with at every turn and the cattle are numerous. For money they use bronze or gold coins or iron bars of fixed weights. . . . By far the most civilised inhabitants are those living in Kent . . . whose way of life is not much different from that of the Gauls. . . . All the Britons dye their bodies with woad, which gives a blue tint, and shave the whole of their bodies except the head and the upper lip.

Source: Julius Caesar, The Conquest of Gaul, *Book V, Chapters 12 & 14*

Coins like these were being used in Britain about 20–30 years before Claudius's invasion in AD 43. They were minted by a powerful tribal leader called Cunobelinus who ruled most of south-east Britain. What do these coins tell us about the Britons at that time?

Document 2

This account of the Britons, written by Tacitus about 150 years after Caesar's visit, was probably based upon the eye-witness reports of his father-in-law, Agricola. The Silures lived in what is now South Wales.

It is not known whether the first inhabitants of Britain were native to the soil or immigrants. . . . But differences in physical appearance give some clues. The reddish hair and large limbs of the Caledonians indicate that they came from Germany, the swarthy faces of the Silures suggest that Spaniards came over in ancient times and occupied the land, and the people who live nearest to Gaul are like the Gauls. . . .

Originally the people were subject to kings; now they are . . . under the influence of rival chiefs. Indeed, nothing has helped us more in wars against their strongest tribes than their failure to band together. Rarely will two or three peoples unite against a common danger; so they fight separately and all are conquered. . . .

The Britons themselves cheerfully accept taxes. . . . and other charges imposed upon them by the Empire, so long as they are properly treated. But they bitterly resent being wronged; they are willing to be obedient but not to be slaves.

Source: Tacitus, Agricola, *Chapters 11–13*

Document 3

This comes from Dio Cassius's *Roman History*, written early in the third century. It is one of the few surviving sources which tells of events in Britain during the later years of the Roman occupation. Although he was born in Turkey and wrote in Greek, Dio was the son of a Roman senator and himself reached the position of consul and governor of a Roman province. Here he describes the unconquered tribes living to the north of Hadrian's Wall.

> Their country is full of rugged and waterless mountains and barren, marshy plains. They have no walls, cities or cultivated fields, but live on their flocks, wild game and certain fruits. Though they have plenty of good fish they do not eat them. They live in tents and have no clothes or shoes. . . . They are very fond of plundering, so they choose their boldest men as rulers. . . . They can put up with hunger and cold and any kind of hardship, for they plunge into the marshes and live there for many days with only their heads above the water. And in the woods they live on bark, roots and . . . a certain kind of food, a piece of which the size of a bean will keep them from feeling either hunger or thirst.

Source: Dio Cassius, Roman History, *Book 77, Chapter 12*

Document 4

Another Greek-speaking historian called Herodian wrote this brief description of the North Britons in the middle of the third century.

> Most of Britain is marshland. . . . Its barbarian people usually swim in these swamps or run along in them, submerged up to the waist. Of course, they are almost naked and do not mind the mud because they are not used to wearing clothes, and they adorn their waists and necks with iron, valuing this metal as an ornament and a sign of wealth in the way that other barbarians value gold. They also tattoo their bodies with various patterns and pictures of all sorts of animals. This explains why they do not wear clothes: they do not want to cover the pictures on their bodies. They are very fierce and dangerous fighters, protected only by a narrow shield and a spear, with a sword slung from their naked bodies.

Source: Herodian, History, *Book III, Chapter 14, 6–8*

Part of Hadrian's Wall, photographed in winter when in this region snow and freezing temperatures are very common. How far does this picture fit in with the descriptions of the tribes living beyond the Wall in Documents 3 and 4?

Questions

1. We are told that the Britons dyed their bodies with woad (Document 1) and that they tattooed themselves with patterns and pictures of animals (Document 4). What do you think would have been the point of such behaviour?

2. Are there any signs in Tacitus's description of the Britons that he had previously read Caesar's account?

3. What does Document 2 tell you about Tacitus's attitude towards the Britons?

4. Documents 3 and 4 are probably based upon travellers' tales, as it is very unlikely that either Dio Cassius or Herodian ever visited Britain. Which parts of these two accounts do you think could have been true and which parts seem far-fetched? Give reasons for your opinions.

5. What evidence is there for believing that the people Caesar saw were better off than those described by Dio Cassius and Herodian? How might such differences be explained?

6. Imagine you are a Roman soldier from Italy whose legion is about to be sent to northern Britain. What would your thoughts and feelings be if you read Documents 3 and 4?

THE LEGIONS GO HOME

Towards the end of the third century Britain began to be threatened by sea-raids from Saxons, Franks and other 'barbarian' peoples from the Continent. Many of the raiders started out as pirates, attacking shipping. Then they began to land on the coast and carry away crops, livestock and anything else of value they could lay hands on.

The 'Saxon shore'

To protect their province against sea-raids, the Romans were forced to build coastal defences. According to a monk called Gildas, who wrote a history of Britain in the middle of the sixth century,

> The Romans . . . placed towers overlooking the sea at intervals on the south coast, where their ships lay: for they were afraid of the wild barbarian beasts attacking on that front.

From archaeological evidence, it seems that these 'towers' were like forts. They housed both soldiers and sailors and could be used as bases for sea patrols which reported the movements of enemy ships. Such forts were built not just in the south but also up the east coast of England, at least as far as the Wash. Because of the sea-raids, this whole coastal region became known as the 'Saxon shore'.

Britain's shore defences seem to have been fairly successful until the middle of the fourth century. Much the same was true of Hadrian's Wall, where the Roman legions continued to hold back the fierce northern tribes. Rich families felt safe and secure enough in these years to go on adding to the luxury of their homes. Mosaics were laid in the larger villas, walls and ceilings were painted and often under-floor central heating was installed too.

The peace was shattered in AD 367, when Roman Britain was attacked by enemies on all sides. Large numbers of Saxons banded together and landed in the south-east, while at the same time the northern frontier was attacked by both land and sea. The Picts

This gold buckle was part of a large hoard of Roman gold, jewellery and silver found in 1979 near Thetford in Norfolk. Experts say it was made on the Continent in the late fourth century, which suggests that luxury goods were still being imported in the last years of Roman Britain

(now the chief tribe of Scotland) swarmed on Hadrian's Wall and broke through, while the north-west coast was invaded by Scots – a Celtic tribe from Ireland who later settled in the country that bears their name.

Caught in a three-pronged attack, the Roman legions suffered a crushing defeat. The Count of the Saxon Shore, head of coastal defences, was killed, along with many of his forces. Dozens of villas were destroyed and thousands of slaves set free. The invaders, armed with swords and battle-axes, took valuables, weapons, tools and as much food as they could carry. Those who had come by sea slaughtered cattle to restock their ships with meat and then sailed away with their plunder.

Roman Britain never fully recovered from these disasters, although a determined effort seems to have been made to rebuild its defences, including Hadrian's Wall. This time the Romans did not attempt to restore either the milecastles along the wall or the smaller turrets in between. All the troops were based in the repaired forts, together with their families.

The end of Roman Britain

Rome itself was now in danger. Barbarian invasions along the northern frontiers of the Empire were straining its defences to breaking point (see page 184). More and more soldiers had to be withdrawn from the outer provinces, including Britain, to defend the heart of the Empire. As a result, the tribes from Scotland could no longer be held back. In about AD 383 Hadrian's Wall was again overrun. This time there seems to have been no attempt to rebuild it. In any case there were not enough soldiers left to man the forts properly.

As the Empire grew weaker, it became impossible for the Roman government to protect a province as far away as Britain. Archaeological evidence from this period shows a rapid decline of the towns. They depended upon trade, yet the growing menace of the barbarians endangered trade routes by land and sea. Buildings that had been ransacked and burned were not restored. In the once rich country villas, damaged mosaics were roughly patched, outbuildings abandoned and tradesmen's tools left to rust.

Finally, in AD 410, the Roman emperor Honorius told the Britons that they would have to defend themselves as best they

Ivory carving of the emperor Honorius, who ruled the West Roman Empire from 395 to 423. It was he who withdrew the remaining legions guarding Britain and instructed the Britons to look after their own defence. Honorius unfortunately failed to live up to the Latin inscription on the standard he is holding: 'In the name of Christ may you always be victorius'

could. This was the year in which the Goths under Alaric ransacked the city of Rome (see page 185) and it was probably the time when the last Roman legion left Britain. No Roman coin dating from a later period has been found in the British Isles. The Romans may have hoped to return to Britain if they could defeat their enemies. There is evidence that at least some of the leading Britons wanted them to come back. In about 446 they wrote to Aëtius, the Roman commander in Gaul. Part of the letter went as follows, according to Gildas.

> The barbarians drive us into the sea; the sea throws us back on the barbarians; and so two kinds of death await us: we are either drowned or slaughtered.

No help came. By this time the province of Britain was completely lost to Rome. The heathen Angles, Saxons and other tribes from the Continent began to invade the country and settle on its fertile soil. Villas and towns became deserted as Britons fled westwards into the hills to escape the invaders. Many of those who stayed to fight were killed or enslaved. The story of the Anglo-Saxon invasions is told in the second book in this series: *The Middle Ages*.

What the Romans left behind

A large part of Britain had been a province of the Roman Empire for roughly 350 years. However the effects of the Roman occupation varied greatly between the north and the south and between rich and poor people. Peasant farmers, especially those in the 'military' areas of the north and west, had very little contact with the Romans. Some sold corn, meat and hides at markets which grew up around the forts. This may have enabled them to purchase a little Roman pottery or metal-ware. But otherwise their way of life hardly changed.

In the more peaceful south-east, on the other hand, many people lived like the Romans in Italy – especially if they were wealthy. Towns and trade grew and people learned Latin, wore Roman clothes, had Roman furniture and decorations in their homes, and often worshipped Roman gods as well. But it was this *Romanised* area that suffered the full force of the Anglo-Saxon invasions. The new settlers made no attempt to carry on Roman customs. They lived a simple village life, allowing the deserted towns to crumble, the roads to decay and Roman knowledge to be forgotten. Even the Christian religion began to disappear.

A few traces of the Roman occupation nevertheless remained. Even today, the routes of many main roads are almost the same as those laid down by the legions. It was in the Roman period that London first developed as an important centre of trade and the natural capital of Britain. Furthermore, the fact that the Romans had been in the country may in some way explain why the Angles and Saxons who came to Britain soon became more advanced than those who stayed behind in northern Europe.

The Fosse Way today. It shows how the Romans tried to make their roads as straight as possible

Sources and questions

1. The two documents below give contradictory accounts of the end of Roman Britain. The first is from the monk Gildas, whose history, called *The Ruin of Britain*, was written in the sixth century. The second was written by a Welsh monk called Nennius, whose *History of the Britons* probably dates from the early ninth century.

The Romans . . . informed our country that . . . the British should stand alone, get used to warfare, fight bravely, and defend with all their powers their land, property, wives, children, and, more important, their life and freedom. Their enemies were no stronger than they. . . .

They [the Romans] gave the frightened people stirring advice, and left them manuals on weapon training. . . . Then they said goodbye, meaning never to return.

Source: Gildas, The Ruin of Britain, *edited and translated by Michael Winterbottom, Phillimore, 1978*

The Romans had ruled the British for 409 years. But the British overthrew the rule of the Romans, and paid them no taxes, and did not accept their kings to reign over them; and the Romans did not dare to come to Britain to rule any more, for the British had killed their generals.

Source: Nennius, British History and the Welsh Annals, *edited and translated by John Morris, Phillimore, 1980*

From what you know of Roman Britain, which of these two accounts is likely to be nearer the truth? (This time, try to write your answer in the form of an essay, giving as many reasons as you can for your opinion.)

2. Look at the picture of the fort on page 216.
   (a) Find Portchester on a map (it is near Portsmouth). Why do you think the Romans – and later the Normans – thought it a good position for building defences?
   (b) What sorts of buildings do you think would have been inside the walls in Roman times?
   (c) Why would the Saxons have wanted to build a church inside a fort? What does this tell you about life in Anglo-Saxon England?
   (d) The rounded towers attached to the outer wall are called *bastions*. What do you think was the point of building them?

3. Find out if you live near one of the many places in Britain where remains of a Roman settlement are on public display, and make a visit if you can. It would be a good idea to take some photographs (or buy postcards) to illustrate your work on Roman Britain.

4. *Either* (a) Imagine you are a Saxon raider on your first expedition to plunder the Britons. Describe the landing, your impressions of the country and a successful raid on a nearby down or villa.
   Or (b) Imagine you are a soldier's wife stationed on Hadrian's Wall some time in the 370s. You are keeping a diary. What does it say during a typical week?

INDEX

Page numbers in **bold** type denote illustrations

ACKNOWLEDGEMENTS

We are grateful to the following for permission to reproduce photographs and other copyright material:
Aerofilms, pages **192**, **216**; Ancient Art & Architecture Collection, pages **13**, **30–31**, **40**, **100–101**, **103**, **106**, **116**, **125**, **148–149**, **160**, **167**, **182–183**, **183**; Archivi Alinari, pages **99**, **122**, **154**, **177**; Barnabys Picture Library, pages **62**, **91**; Bildarchiv Preussischer Kulturbesitz, page **100**; Britain on View (BTA/ETB), page **207**; British Museum, London, pages **17**, **29**, **46**, **46–47**, **50**, **79** *right*, **84**, **92**, **105**, **108**, **114**, **123**, **130** *above*, **136**, **143**, **147**, **170**, **181**, **193**, **201**, **211**, **212**, **215**; Mrs June Butler, page **49**; Bob Campbell, page **11**; J. Allan Cash, pages **48**, **66**, **134**; M. Cass, page **189**; F. Clark Howell, page **16–17**; Colchester & Essex Museum, page **157** *below*; British Crown Copyright/MOD Reproduced with the permission of the Controller of Her Britannic Majesty's Stationery Office, page **219**; Professor M.H. Day, page **8**; Department of the Environment, page **202**; Deutsches Archaologisches Institut, Athens, page **146**; Edinburgh Photographic Library, page **214** (Simon Fraser); Ekdotike Athenon S.A, page **119**; English Heritage, page **21**, **22**, **23**, **202**; from: Michael Crawford, *The Roman Republic*, Fontana, page **130** *below*; Werner Forman Archive, pages **67** (Private Collection), **68–69** and **70** (The Robert H. Lowie Museum of Anthropology, University of California, Berkeley), **71** *above* (Museum of American Indian, New York), **71** *below*, **73** (Ohio State Museum); Courtesy of the Freer Gallery of Art, Smithsonian Institution, Washington D.C., page **63** *below*; Photographie Giraudon, pages **35**, **148**; The Griffith Institute, Ashmolean Museum, Oxford, page **43**; Grosvenor Museum, Chester, page **142**, **208**; Guildhall Museum, London, page **198**; Sonia Halliday Photographs, pages **18–19**, **32**, **82**, **97**, **118–119**, **169**; C. Hallward, page **86**; Robert Harding Picture Library, pages **38** right, **39**; André Held, page **112–113**; Hirmer Verlag München, page **27**; Michael Holford, pages **109**, **186**; The Hulton-Deutsch Collection, pages **34**, **166**; Miss Kathleen Kenyon, page **15**; A.F Kersting, pages **42**, **107**, **187**; from: Peter Connolly, *Greece & Rome at War*, Macdonald, 1981, page **118**; Magnum Photos Ltd, pages **162**, **180**; The Mansell Collection, pages **94**, **152**, **161** *right*, **171**, **174**; Ray T Matheny, El Mirador Project, page **75**; The Metropolitan Museum of Art, Fletcher Fund, page **108–109**; Museo Campano, Capua, page **173** *above*; Museum of Fine Arts, Boston, page **83**; Museum of London, page **206**; National Archaeological Museum, Athen, page **93**; National Geographic Society, pages **77** *left* (George Mobley), **77** *right* (George E. Stuart), **78** (George Mobley); Natural History Museum, London, pages **9**, **10** *left* (Professor Leakey), **10** *right*; New China Pictures Co, Beijing, China, page **63** *above*; The Oriental Institute of the University of Chicago, page **101**; from: Cornell & Matthews, *Atlas of the Roman World*, Phaidon, page **200**; Philipons Ltd, page **210**; The Art Museum, Princeton University. Museum purchase gift of the Hans & Dorothy Widenmann Fund, pages **80**, **113**, **115**; Arthur Probsthain, page **54**; The Royal Commission on the Ancient & Historical Monuments of Scotland, page **199**; Oscar Sario, pages **111**, **164**; from: Victor von Hagen, *Search for the Maya*, Saxon House, page **79** *left*; Scala, pages **129**, **138**; reproduced by permission of the Trustees of the Science Museum, London, page **204**; Society for the Anglo-Chinese Understanding, page **64**; Staatliche Museen Preubischer Kulturbesitz, Berlin, page **110**; *Sunday Times Magazine*, page **209**; The Telegraph Colour Library, pages **55**, **87**, **128**, **156**, **157** *above*, **161** *left*, **176–177**; Graham Tingay, page **191**; Roger Wood, pages **41**, **140**, **145**, **178**.
We are unable to trace the copyright holders of the following and would be grateful for any information that will enable us to do so, pages **26**, **36**, **38** *left*, **44**, **51**, **52–53**, **57**, **59**, **151**, **153**, **195**, **217**.